INTRODUCTION

My object in living is to unite
My avocation and my vocation
As my two eyes make one in sight
$\qquad$ —Robert Frost

Until I began to assemble this book, I had always thought of myself as a low-key and reasonably clubbable fellow—open and well met, the kind of person who is more likely to fit in than to stomp off. But the paper record argues otherwise. In reviewing the file of my published work, it became clear that over these past several decades I have moved steadily from one scrape to the next, either advancing our cause as I saw it, or pushing back against those who opposed our cause as they saw it. Alongside my cherished allies in the conservative movement—many of whom are celebrated in these pages—I have been part of what amounts to a permanent insurgency. There is no rest, it seems, for the ideologically tendentious.

Some of the skirmishes have been high-stakes affairs, even epochal. I became a committed anti-Communist in the '60s and enlisted as a Cold Warrior for service both public and private over the span of three decades. Several pieces in this book, and especially those featuring Ronald Reagan, reflect that commitment.

I have long wrestled with the rhetorical challenge of how to convey to young people the sheer ugliness of the Soviet Union. I settled on the oddity that first attracted my own notice. For political prisoners of the Soviet Union, banishment to a cell far distant from the homeland was a fate far too comfortable. Rather, those poor souls were sent to the living hell of internal exile. That is to say that the Soviet Union was *itself* a penal colony. And just how formidable, young people then ask, was the Soviet empire? Was it really an existential threat to the West? I feel obliged to inform everybody under the age of 40 that, *pace* the fashionable academics, the Soviet Union did not "fall of its own weight," any more than the Romans or the Spanish or the Japanese did in their own terminal throes. Empires need a good push and the Soviets fell because Ronald Reagan leaned on them every day of every week for eight years with the full weight of the American enterprise—military pressure, to be sure, but economic, political, psychological and, yes, moral pressure, as well.

Another battle-without-end has been the struggle to preserve and regenerate the free economy. I take pride in noting that on both of the critical fronts in the economic war—taxation and regulation—I could always be found, alert and trigger-happy, at my post on the defense perimeter. The free economy, which is the action plan for the American Dream, is always in peril and relies on each succeeding generation for its repristination. A few victories for the freedom movement, and more than a few defeats, are chronicled in this volume.

By a wide margin, the bulk of this book is devoted to skirmishes involving and frequently instigated by William F. Buckley Jr., who was at first my intimidating boss and then my professional colleague and then my treasured friend. (Ask yourself. Were you ever lucky enough to have a boss with that kind of emotional range?) WFB, as he shall be known in these precincts, was both a serial fight-picker and a tireless combatant. He liked to mix it up and he had more battle stripes than space on his sleeve to accommodate them. One skirmish seemed to flare up just as its predecessor was flickering out: we junior officers came to think of life with Bill as a permanent campaign.

It was of critical importance to me and to those many others who rallied to his standard that he was, hands down, the best platoon leader ever. He had the heart of a lion-in-the-wild. He had the patch-up skills of a combat medic. I was about to add that he was a happy warrior but that overstretched term by now covers everything from the harmless logorrhea of Hubert Humphrey to the manic mendacity of Debbie Wasserman Schultz. WFB's was that juiced up, let's roll, real American strain of *joie de vivre*. He never had to conscript us. We raced to volunteer.

I omit from these pages almost all of the small-beer battles WFB and I waged over the years. While they seemed monumentally important at the time, I confess at this remove, perhaps with a touch of PTSD, that I can't remember even the larger details. As the historian A.J.P. Taylor once described his own stand against the *zeitgeist*, WFB and I frequently stood squarely for "extreme views, weakly held." What I have chosen to reproduce here, instead, are pieces that excited large bags of reader mail (not all of it congratulatory, and not all of it written with a single selection from the Crayola box), pieces that WFB singled out for special notice, and pieces that moved the needle on public perception and, sometime thereafter, on public policy. One of the latter is "Neo-Nazi Olympics." That piece attracted the attention of a small and eclectic group: the author James Michener, the Olympic decathlete Rafer Johnson, the FDR-whisperer Thomas (Tommy the Cork) Corcoran, and a neighbor of mine from the Virginia suburbs, a kid-Senator named Orrin Hatch. We formed a little committee, began to rub people the wrong way and—presto!—a few weeks later Jimmy Carter chose to pull out of the Moscow Olympics. It was a victory for human freedom and we had something to do with it. Another example is "An Almost Golden Age." For those of you still curious as to who or what it was that broke the oligarchic grip of the broadcast networks over American television, here's an *NR* bombshell disguised as a kid's sparkler. Cutting the umbilical cord between local stations and the networks—moving from Ma Bell's landline to the cornucopia of satellite distribution—was the equivalent of an emancipation proclamation for America's captive television audience. As another example, the column slugged "Justice" helped free an old friend, the honorable Franklyn (Lyn) Nofziger, from the coils of the so-called criminal, so-called justice system. The power of the press, at least when it's pushing events in a salutary direction, can be a beautiful thing.

Lest you think I'm putting a thumb on the scale in weighing my professional accomplishments (and with the apostrophic observation that, under contemporary standards, journalists seem permitted to use both thumbs), I include a piece called "It's Kemp." I filed this piece just before Bush 41 picked his vice president for the 1988 race. As you will see, I suggested that nuggets of news, carefully culled and then filtered through insight born of encyclopedic political experience, led me to believe that Jack Kemp would be the guy. What I didn't suggest—because I had promised not to—was that an unimpeachable source had told me that Kemp would in fact be the guy. My source was so unimpeachable that he was related to Kemp *by blood*. His story was so rock-hard that I merchandised my scoop *urbe et orbe*. Indeed, I was yakking on the radio in New Orleans about how I had bested the national press corps *at the exact moment* that Bush 41 announced his selection of J. Danforth Quayle. Never mind. For the next few years, maybe ten, whenever there would be chitchat about a conspicuous job opening—about the next chairman of the Fed or the CEO of General Electric or the lead tenor at the Met—WFB would flash that stuff-eating grin at me and exult, "It's Kemp!"

Over the course of my long association with *National Review*, now 54 years and counting, I have with almost metronomic regularity agreed with management on issues of public moment. As a presidential encomium might put it, *NR* editors have been right so often, they must be sick of being so brilliant. On a few occasions, *NR* editors have backed a position on which I took the lead. Much more frequently, I have found their positions, and the arguments marshalled to support them, to be fully persuasive. There are exceptions, of course, and they are in this kind of *omnium gatherum* better acknowledged than ignored.

In the post-WFB years, there have been two major tactical disagreements. The first concerned the Tea Party and its spontaneously-combusted adherents. I did my sworn reportorial duty, strolling among them at rallies, chatting them up, following them later by email. At the end of a deep think, I judged the vast majority of Tea Partiers to be both politically hygienic and ideologically invigorating and I welcomed them to our movement. The editors of *NR* have explained their own position elsewhere, but it's fair to say that their enthusiasm was much better contained. My views can be found in "The Conservative Moment."

The other disagreement was over Donald J. Trump. None of *NR*'s senior writers backed him during the campaign, and several of them remain dyspeptically critical in the early going of his presidency. I explain my own modulated endorsement in "What Trump and Trumpism Really Mean." (WFB, like Trump, was on the "charismatic" side, over against the "bureaucratic" side, of what Max Weber identified as the central tension in the modern world. I can thus say without fear of contradiction that WFB *might* have supported Trump. He did, after all, support John Gardner for vice president in 1968, an endorsement that prompted the classic, incredulous, hunched-shoulder bark from GOP nominee Richard Nixon: "Buckley said that?")

The most heated disagreement I had with *NR* management, the most consequential by far, was over the Iraq war. And when I say "management" here, I mean to include all three of the Buckley, John O'Sullivan and Rich Lowry archaeological layers of management. And when *all* of the magazine's editorial principals, joined in turn by *all* of their senior associates, expressed full-volume support for the invasion of Iraq—yes, if you're asking, it did occur to me that I might be crazy. You can find my side of that anguished story in "*NR* Goes to War."

It was one thing, of course, to disagree with John O'Sullivan or Rich Lowry. They were comprehensively informed on matters of geopolitical import, impressively so, but it was generally believed that they put their pants on one leg at a time. It was quite another thing to disagree with The Founder Himself, with whom I had a serious disagreement no more than once in a blue-blue moon. Those rare face-offs made me acutely uncomfortable. I knew not only that WFB's position had been arrived at fastidiously—for him, a "casual observation" would have been oxymoronic—but that he would defend his position fiercely. He was a born debater (as also, quite possibly, a congenital debater). It was an awkward passage for both of us but considerably more so for me as the junior officer. It was thus with lung-clearing exhalation that, 18 months later, I received a draft of his syndicated column walking back his support for the Iraq invasion. Across the top he had scribbled, "This one's for you, Pal." Peace, praise the Lord, had returned to the fever swamps.

I never had cause to change my opinion that the 2003 invasion of Iraq had been butt-stupid. But, soon enough, I had reason to tote up the cost of expressing that opinion. In 2002, I had been running the largest television production company in Washington, D.C. We produced series for both domestic and foreign networks, documentaries, commercials, corporate films. Our company was highly profitable and over a period of years we took home a shelf-full of journalistic awards, including an Emmy and the industry's most prestigious award, the George Foster Peabody medal. As an unreconstructed conservative, I had long tangled with the Left, more or less holding them at bay as they took runs at my work and my company. But when Beltway supporters of the Iraq invasion—the war party, in the parlance of that overheated day—came after me, I found myself engaged in a two-front war, which, as students of war could have predicted, soon proved to be one front too many. By the end of 2003, I was running the smallest production company in Washington. Contracts were not renewed. Clients walked out the door. Foreign broadcasters were scared off. Grants from front-running foundations dried up. It was a very long year, in the course of which I became accustomed to being called "unpatriotic," and worse, by erstwhile allies. By early 2004, my company was all but out of business and my seven-figure salary had dwindled to a no-figure salary. Free speech, as it turned out, wasn't all that free.

In the spring of 2004, Jane and I decided to take a break from the ongoing turmoil. We drove up to our summer home in Maine. It turned out to be a break, all right. We stayed for four years. And it was all good. With the bloody politics of D.C. fading in the rearview mirror, and with a loving God smiling broadly, we had a great run in Maine—in business, in the public life of that beautiful state, in friendships quickly and durably made—and we departed only when a larger opportunity beckoned in Florida. (Take a look at "Let Slip the Dogs of (Tax) War." Some nice people have said that speech sparked the debate that produced Maine's first tax cut in living memory.)

In the Philanthropic Wars section, you will find accounts of the early days of the Foundation Management Institute (FMI), which I founded to remind the nonprofit management class that, just as capitalism depends on capitalists, philanthropy depends on philanthropists. (Some members of the management class seemed to have forgotten that datum.) The centerpiece here is "The *Robertson v. Princeton* Case: Too Important to Be Left to the Lawyers," which recounts the tale of a watershed legal battle between an honorable donor family and an arrogant grant recipient. It was something more than a skirmish. During the case one of the plaintiffs died, the presiding judge retired and more than a few careers were stalled or redirected. The lawsuit, which lasted almost ten years from front to back, and sucked more than $50 million in legal fees from the contending parties, prompted two inevitable questions. If I had known at the outset what I knew at the end, would I have signed up for the assignment? Of course not. But was it worth doing? Of course it was, a point that I hope the piece makes unmistakably clear.

I pause here to record my debt to the chairman of FMI, Pete du Pont. He was perfect in that role, for two reasons. First, he was a shining example of old money that had not gone crazy, guilt-stricken Left. (There aren't all that many other examples, to be honest.) His formal name, Pierre S. Du Pont IV, had taken a century to polish to full luster. And second, and much more important, he didn't blink in the face of establishmentarian criticism. When I traveled to Wilmington to propose an alliance with the Robertson family—taking Pete to lunch at the city's best hotel, which by an odd chance was named the Hotel du Pont—he took it all in, asked a few lawyerly questions, smiled, and said only, "This might be a bit awkward—I've just been asked to chair my college reunion at Princeton—but let's do it."

I have worked for three presidents, campaigned for seven candidates and known more than a dozen other men and women who sought the office. Of only two people have I ever said to myself, "that candidate should be president." One was Ronald Reagan and the other was Pete du Pont.

The longest section of this volume is slugged "People: Appreciations, Intros and Obits." It could have been much longer. What has sustained our national experiment in freedom all these years are those stiff-backed citizens who, when freedom is impinged, decline to sit down and shut up; indeed, they have sustained us from our break with tyranny more than two centuries ago through the ongoing scrum with the socialists of all parties (as Hayek once put it). We are a scrappy lot, we Americans. It's been my privilege to work with some of you. And to remember you here.

The all-but-final section of this volume, For the Good of the Order, includes some battles joined and won, some battles joined and lost, and some unsatisfactory people identified and quite properly spanked. One of the signal victories, recorded in full in the "Reagan (with a Nod to Barry Goldwater)" section, was the effort to privatize international satellite communications. It was more than a skirmish, too. It was more like a land war in Asia. Reagan gave me and two colleagues the task in 1983 and we got it done, finally, in 2002. Yes, I'll be frequent-flying for the rest of time. And I can now confirm from personal experience that while the French may not be of much use in a shooting war, when it comes to bureaucratic war, they are simply *magnifique*.

In the final section, Road Adventures, I collect a few oddments—episodes that were unforgettable for me, heuristic, possibly, for you. (If, for instance, you've ever wondered how to win your own Stanley Cup ring, look no further than "Eschatology on Ice.")

Throughout this volume, much as I have been tempted to revise and extend my remarks, what you see here is what you would have seen on the day of original publication. Be gentle, reader. Some of these pieces were written before you were born.

I hope you enjoy this journey. I did. I wouldn't have missed a bit of it, but next time I might be more attentive to Ibsen's admonition that one should never go out to fight for freedom in one's best trousers.

Neal B. Freeman
Amelia Island, Florida
April 2017

TABLE OF CONTENTS

People: Appreciations, Intros and Obits

For the Good of the Order

Road Adventures

WM. F. BUCKLEY JR., THE MAGAZINE AND THE MOVEMENT

National Review
December 19, 2005

MEETING BILL BUCKLEY

W hat did I think on meeting Bill Buckley? My first impression, to be candid, was that he must be the guy standing next to Patsy Buckley, the luminiferous Mrs. Buckley, six feet of young womanhood so astonishing as to make your lungs walk off the job. For the balance of that first evening and for some decades thereafter I fixed her with what your tabloid press might call a stalker's stare. My second impression was that Bill Buckley was speaking a language with which I was familiar but somewhat insecurely so. Things seemed to approach other things only *asymptotically*. Grammatical barbarians, loosed on the streets, were apparently committing a wave of *litotes*. Certain things could be properly compared to other things only after checking with someone named *Mutatis Mutandis*.

My further impression was that Willmoore had been right. (Willmoore Kendall had pounded me into ideological shape at Yale a generation after he had done the same favor for Buckley.) It was Willmoore's opinion, rendered with the finality of Mosaic proscription, that among Buckley's many talents one was pre-eminent. He was the world's finest conversationalist. That's a heavy reputation to lug to any dinner table but Buckley flipped it around like a poker chip. He knew about art and boats and cities and history and Scripture and music. I was then working at Doubleday and he seemed to know more about the books I was working on than I did. He was plainly supercalifragilistic (okay, not a Buckley word but a gratifying eight syllables nonetheless) and I soon slipped into full-engagement mode. I don't know how late I stayed but it quickly became *NR* lore that Bill had offered the kid a job as the only way to get him out of the house.

I consulted two people on Bill's offer. The first was Jim McFadden, who had become *NR*'s indispensable business-side executive after leaving a job in mainstream publishing. Mac's words stick with me: "Bill says

he's going to change the world. I think he might do it and I'd like to help."
I know, that sounds like rhetorical bump-and-tickle, just a wee bit of four-beer talk. All I can tell you is that the young Buckley was capable of making words like those sound plausible, almost modulated. The second consultant was my father. He had invested heavily in my white-shoe education and had been left unmoved by the ecumenical spirit of the day. He summed up the career move with a question: "You're going to leave one of the world's great publishing houses for an Irish Catholic rag?" Yes, sir!

What did the job entail, being Bill Buckley's right-hand man? Some of this, some of that, all of it in the Buckley style aimed at high purpose and pursued in high spirit. I was the political reporter and the Washington correspondent. (Now that Mark Felt has talked it can be revealed that, yes, I was Cato.) I ran the mayoralty campaign office and started his TV show. (It's true. Bill never forgave me for calling it *Firing Line*.) The most fun was selling his newspaper column city to city: For several seasons he was the hot cross bun of the syndicate business. But it was years before I realized that the most important part of the job may have been what I then regarded as a tiresome chore: handling Bill's correspondence. In those early days, at the dawn of the conservative era, he emboldened and guided and connected them all—from Ronnie and Barry to Phyllis and Brent to Clare and Roger to Dan and Kieran to almost 300 others. The first generation of the conservative movement can be identified neatly. They were the people who corresponded with Bill Buckley, a committee of correspondence that he built into a national political force. And along the way—it must have been either *inter alia* or *pari passu* or *in medias res*—he changed the world. Nice going, boss.

National Review
October 19, 2015

FINALLY, THE RECOUNT

Looking back at WFB's 1965 mayoral campaign

O ur text today is a pair of classic Buckley quips from the great 1965 vintage. People who remember nothing else about William F. Buckley Jr.'s brief foray into elective politics recall his reply when asked what he would do if elected mayor of New York: He would "demand a recount." And they remember, as well, his response when asked how he felt as he emerged from a meeting with the editorial board of the *New York Times*: He felt as if he had "just passed through the Berlin Wall."

Somewhere in my attic is a photograph of Bill's introductory press conference. He is grinning wolfishly and I am wincing in pain. He has just been asked what he would do as his first act of office and we both know what was coming next. He had come up with the "recount" crack a few weeks earlier and I had urged him not to use it in public. It was a Buckley-grade witticism, to be sure, but it was not likely to be good for unit morale. But Bill was a writer and not a politician, which is to say that he was constitutionally incapable of letting a great line go unused. He thus proceeded to roll it across the press room with perfect timing and to predictable effect. Merriment bounced off all four walls.

As we all have come to learn, painfully or otherwise, japes have consequences. Before even the first news cycle had expired, a press narrative had begun to take shape: that Bill's campaign was something of a lark, some elaborate form of self-entertainment. In the dismissive parlance of the day, Bill's was "not a serious campaign," whatever that might be. Our fundraising receipts, never torrential, slowed to a dribble, and the volunteer effort flagged. The Buckley for Mayor campaign was off and limping.

What turned it around, I would like to report, was the incandescent performance of our candidate, ingenious stratagems devised by management, and a flawless, five-borough ground game executed by our vaunted field operation. It would be more accurate to say, however, that what turned the campaign around was a scheduling quirk.

In the early days, before we had learned a thing or two about crowd management, we felt free to expose Bill to large groups of self-selected citizens. Most of these exchanges were high-minded, even civic-virtuous in tone. But when an ideological match touched dry tinder, a raging rhetorical fire could break out. One meeting with a group of excitable feminists, for instance, became a high-decibel, low-information event, and I had no ready answer when Bill asked me later, "Remind me why we did that, would you?"

On another occasion, Bill and I found ourselves the only whites in a large room packed with angry black voters. They were angered by what they perceived to be Bill's unthinking support for a racist police force, the NYPD. Needless to say, the game was on.

Back and forth they went. Bill and his audience talked about crime. Black crime. Black-on-white crime. Black-on-black crime. And they talked about leadership: community leadership and moral leadership. It was a long, hot 90 minutes and Bill sweated through his preppy, blue button-down, the stains spreading down his flanks. Discount this judgment for sycophancy if you like, but he was magnificent. By the end of the meeting, something had changed.

There remained not a single person in that room who thought Bill's views on race and crime were unthinking. He was deeply informed and maintained an intellectual clarity throughout the raucous colloquy. His audience listened to him and gave him their respect, if not their support.

For his part, Bill became a changed candidate. As a polemicist for a little magazine, he had been poking liberal shibboleths through the bars of a cage. As a candidate on the big stage, he was poking those shibboleths from inside the cage. There was no place to hide now. He was fighting for his public life.

There were two other changes that day. The first occurred within and around our security detail. Now, I can't say with any confidence whether it happened that day or a month earlier or a month later, but I can say with absolute certainty that in the summer of 1965 the NYPD fell in love with Bill Buckley. I don't mean just the Irish and Italians, either, but the black, Hispanic, and Asian cops, too. Bill was stating their case with eloquence and verve and doing so at a time when few other public figures would stand with them. (Not unlike today, in 1965 there were reputable people and reputable publications who claimed to believe that one of the principal causes of urban crime was police misconduct. Not unlike today, those claims were evidence-free and ideologically powered.)

The cops' support for Buckley for Mayor, which soon spread to the firemen, and to some of the building trades, had two effects, one long-term and the other proximate. To my eye, which is by now experienced if still unscholarly, the long-term effect of the NYPD–WFB alliance ran in an almost unbroken psephological line through the blue-collar support for Johnson and Nixon during the Vietnam War, thence to the Reagan Democrats of the early Eighties and, ultimately, to the "values voters" of today—the people who vote not with their class or race or gender but with their patriotic hearts. A significant development, that.

The proximate effect of NYPD support seemed more important. As some of you will remember about the Sixties, and the rest of you will have read, the public square could be a dangerous place. Political figures who stirred dissent beyond the edge of consensus could, and not infrequently did, excite gunfire. John Kennedy, Martin Luther King, Robert Kennedy, and others less well known were all gunned down at or near public events. *Bang, you're down.*

When Bill Buckley died peacefully at his Connecticut home in 2008, the news of his passing was met by an outpouring of admiration and unfeigned affection. By that time, manifestly, he had become America's favorite conservative, beloved by his many followers and respected by his few public foes. Times change, happily. When he ran for mayor in 1965, Bill was not yet Mr. Nice Guy. He was, rather, a right-wing insurgent marching against the citadel of self-satisfied liberalism . . . and the denizens of the citadel were not amused. To put the matter carefully, Bill was a controversial figure.

There is an apostrophic point that must be made here. It should be remembered that Bill Buckley was conservative long before conservatism was cool. In 1965, he was not seen to be the charming, white-shoe Yalie that retrospective analyses have portrayed. He was, in the contemporaneous view, a black-shoe cop-lover, fronting for dark forces that the elite media professed to fear: He was the "tip of the spear" of a reactionary Right. So let us pause here to salute those who joined our cause in the early days, when the historical outcome could not be known and the risk to professional reputation was palpable. Let us pause to salute Jim Buckley, who played flawlessly the role he was born to play—older and wiser brother of the candidate; Don Pemberton (our indispensable man in Brooklyn); Art Andersen (who kept our books almost balanced); Aggie Schmidt (Bill's tireless amanuensis); Phil Nicolaides and Geoff Kelly (our admaking Mad Men); Kieran O'Doherty (the Conservative-party stalwart who worked himself to the very cliff of cardiac incident); Marvin Liebman (who produced our rallies and carbonated our staff meetings); and the sturdiest warrior of them all, William Rusher (he of the Princeton and Harvard pedigree who gave his aging mother palpitations by departing a Wall Street law firm for a little magazine with only a tenuous grip on respectability). These were the winter soldiers of our revolution. Times change, happily. Only a few years later, by which time Bill had become the toast of the town and his wife, Pat, began to adorn the Best Dressed lists, it had become de rigueur to embrace the advice Nixon had famously abjured and do the easy and popular thing, which was to make your way briskly into the fabulous social circle of Bill and Pat Buckley.

It shouldn't have come as a surprise for us to review the thickening file of threats made against Bill. It shouldn't have, but it did, anyway. The reports were hair-curling. The stone canyons of New York City seemed to be crawling with bloody-minded crazies, many of them on a mission from one higher power or another. (I note for the record that I was more rattled by these reports than was our imperturbable candidate. To borrow Ben Bradlee's description of one of his notably intrepid reporters, Bill clanked when he walked.)

What lifted our spirits (and lowered staff blood pressure) was a follow-on briefing by an emissary from the NYPD. The cops were all in, thoroughly prepared to take fast, discreet, professional action in whatever contingencies might arise. Nobody was likely to mess with a single hair on the head of their man Buckley. File closed. As was his habit, the best summary line came from Bill Rusher, who sat in on one of the threat meetings. Said Rusher of the crazies, "I'm beginning to feel sorry for these poor bastards." By Labor Day, everything was copacetic. We had come to feel that the safest place in all of New York City, safer even than Grand Central Station at straight-up noon, was to be standing next to Bill Buckley at a campaign event.

There was another change. It took place, asymptotically as Bill might have described it, among our regular press corps, some of whose members were grumpy about their assignments to our campaign. (Campaign coverage in those days was assumed to be a ticket to a regular gig at City Hall, with the winning candidate pulling in his own beat reporters. There may have been a conflict of interest in there somewhere.)

Early on, the press was of one mind, with their impressions of the principal candidates frozen in presupposition. John Lindsay? He was tall (*agreed*), he was liberal (*do tell*), he was mahvelous (*until he opened his mouth*), and he was destined to win (*yeah, probably*). Abe Beame? He was a colorless bureaucrat and a machine Democrat (*no argument there*). Short in stature and shorter still on charisma (*or there*), he had a fighting chance, at least if the unions got in gear (*conceivably, I supposed*). Bill Buckley? He was a Creature from the Hard-Right Lagoon, his chances pegged between slim and none and doubtless closer to the latter (*WFB concurring, alas*). Presuppositions are a durable barrier against improved understanding. They died hard.

But while our regular press gaggle may have come for the gotcha patrol—that cold-stare vigil for the verbal slips that could be inflated into categorical slurs against women, gays, blacks, Jews, Latinos, Asians, fat people, short people, or variously challenged people, not to mention commonsense-impaired people—they stayed for the *bons mots* that Bill sprinkled around promiscuously, as if they were bead necklaces tossed from a Mardi Gras float. Bill was good copy. And it didn't hurt that he was running against Beame, five-feet-five-inches of banality, and Lindsay, six-feet-three-inches of vapidity. (Beame and Lindsay seemed to be quotable only when quoting Bill, usually in high, theatrical dudgeon.) The press couldn't help themselves. They liked Bill. Some of them even became his pals. (It was during the campaign that Bill became lifelong friends with the great Murray Kempton, who, while he wrote for a downmarket lefty rag, seemed to reserve special affection for the candidate who persisted in talking over the heads of his proletarian readership.)

There was something else. The press noted and was impressed by Bill's courage. His courage, that is, in both its physical and moral forms. It was Bill and only Bill who waded into those last-man-standing bouts in halls stuffed with red-faced citizens. While Beame and Lindsay were surrounded by platoons of handlers, who busied themselves clearing voter-free paths for the great men, Bill was lucky if he had me and an off-duty cop in tow. The press noticed.

Again, I can't tell you which hour of which day it happened, but the press narrative began, finally, to shift. At first a few reporters, and then more, and then at last the full mewling herd began to concede that maybe, just maybe, Bill's was a serious campaign. One reporter, the legendary McCandlish Phillips of the *New York Times*, began to toy with another idea: Perhaps Bill's was the *only* serious campaign.

Then there was that meeting at the *Times*, the one behind the Berlin Wall. This was 1965, remember, in a land far away. The *Times* may have been only one of seven New York daily newspapers (not counting the *Wall Street Journal*, which was considered a trade publication in those days), but its stature was belied by the blandly taxonomic term *primus inter pares*. The *Times* didn't just open and close Broadway shows and puff up and snuff out political aspirants. It set the agenda for municipal discussion—and then coined the vocabulary in which it would be conducted. In terms of mass mind-control, there is nothing in contemporary culture with which to compare the dominance of the Sixties-era *New York Times*.

When Bill Buckley strode into that editorial-board meeting, he found himself surrounded not just by the editorial writers who would craft the paper's endorsement and the executives who would put their chops on it, but by reporters and editors from the principal beats—transportation, education, housing, health care, and the rest. Bill was surrounded, if you will, by contemporary liberalism's A-Team. The next two hours would prove to be a real education. For them.

This is unsubstantiated surmise on my part, but that meeting may have been the first time in their lives that most of the *Times*men had faced an articulate and informed conservative in close encounter.

In support of that surmise, I offer only this shred of evidence. In 1965, the platform of choice for opinionmongers was neither a cable-news slot nor a radio talk show. It was the syndicated newspaper column. In the mid Sixties, there were hundreds of nationally syndicated features, three of which—three!—could be fairly described as conservative. There was David Lawrence, the grand old man of *U.S. News & World Report*, who was by that stage of his career more old than grand. There was James Jackson Kilpatrick, the clarion voice of southern traditionalism. And there was William F. Buckley Jr., the leader of an emerging national conservatism. Bill Buckley was the new new thing.

Bill did not, of course, win the endorsement of the *New York Times*. But he won the argument. And everybody in the room knew it.

I am still contacted from time to time by people who have stumbled upon, and then become fascinated by, the Buckley campaign of 1965: historians, political scientists, city planners, journos, pols. They sense that something special happened, something heuristic. One conversation with an eager-beaver thesis writer, according to my notes, went this way:

> EBTW: Mr. Freeman, can you confirm that the Buckley campaign issued 22 policy proposals?
> NBF: No, I can't confirm that, but it sounds ballparkish.
> EBTW: Can you confirm that 20 of those proposals were subsequently adopted by New York mayors—many by Giuliani, some by Koch, and the remaining few by Bloomberg?
> NBF: No, but you may well be correct.
> EBTW: You don't sound surprised.
> NBF: No, not at all.

Well, that's the essence of our story, isn't it? Why were we not surprised by the serial successes of the Buckley campaign? We were not surprised, I would submit, because we recognized that what Bill Buckley was preaching in 1965, and what he would practice for the rest of his life, was the politics of reality: the certain knowledge that, over the course of time and under the weight of experience, ideological abstraction will yield ultimately to either the obdurate facts of public finance or the timeless imperatives of the human spirit. One or the other. What Bill Buckley taught us was that there is not only a conservative way to raise the young and care for the old. There is a conservative way to collect the garbage and shovel the snow.

It's been 50 years now since Bill Buckley demanded a recount. Perhaps we owe him one. So let's pop the big one: Who really won that race back in 1965? The best answer to that question may be another question: Is anybody publishing an anniversary collection of the speeches and papers of John Lindsay or Abe Beame? Anybody? Anybody?

Shortly after Election Day, Bill invited me to a postprandial meeting at the New York Yacht Club. Something was up. Bill held all of his important meetings off-site, as the walls of *NR*'s warren-office had ears and the interruptions were incessant.

I had picked up a rumor that Bill would be moving to Switzerland to take on what we had long referred to as the Big Book. For several years past, Bill had been urged by both mentors (Willmoore Kendall and others) and protégés (me and others) to write a serious work of political philosophy, a Big Book that would make Bill's bones as a heavyweight intellectual. Journalism was fine, we thought, but scholarship was better: A Big Book was exactly what was needed to undergird Bill's burgeoning career as he reached age 40. We even had a title teed up, "The Revolt against the Masses," with the book intended as a rebuttal to and extension of Ortega y Gasset's classic work, *The Revolt of the Masses*. I was intrigued. Perhaps what I needed as a restorative was a bit of head-clearing, long-form work.

Bill and I had a drink and began to swap campaign stories, at one point laughing so hard that a club employee was dispatched to restore house decorum. Good luck with that. It was a time for laughing.

As a second drink arrived, Bill turned to business. He reported with enthusiasm that a publisher had offered a handsome advance for a book on the campaign. Bill wanted to do it, both to inscribe the record indelibly and, I suspected, to relitigate some of the campaign spats. He said that I would be "indispensable" to the project and outlined a generous financial arrangement, ski passes very much included.

I don't know whether my heart sank, but my shoulders sagged. The last thing I wanted to do was to wallow in campaign minutiae for another four or five months. I had raccoon eyes and needed to get my teeth fixed and get my license renewed and begin the citywide search for the dry cleaner who was holding my clothes in some undisclosed location. If Bill had offered me the 70 virgins of martyrdom, I would have countered at 35. I needed a break.

I loved Bill and I hated saying no to him, but this was a mission for which I could find no motivation. So after two years of dawn-to-dinner collaboration, we agreed to go our separate ways, he to do the campaign book and I to develop a television project. The meeting did not end well.

But the story did, almost serendipitously so. While he may have set off to write a quickie campaign book, what Bill came back with was *The Unmaking of a Mayor*. Here we are a half century later and people who would understand American urbanology or the history of New York City or the beginnings of the modern conservative movement still feel obliged to read and ponder and come to terms with it. Over the course of his hyperproductive career, Bill wrote 54 books—all of them readable, many of them consequential, one of them a classic. *Unmaking* became, quite inadvertently, Bill's Big Book and cemented his reputation as a public intellectual of the first rank.

The television project worked out, too. The series debuted in the spring of 1966 as *Firing Line*, hosted by William F. Buckley Jr., and it ran for more than 30 years.

Postscript: In my personal calculation, Bill's signal contribution to A.D. 1965 was to introduce me to his new office manager, Miss Jane Metze of Harriman, N.Y. She was highly attractive and a constant distraction, a distraction, in fact, to which I have chosen to ascribe all responsibility for the rookie mistakes recounted in Bill's book.

There were rivals for the attention of Miss Metze. Being a charitable sort, I will leave the married celebrity unnamed. Of the others, the most formidable was the journalist John Phillips, a big, rawboned fellow with hands that could palm basketballs. John was a diligent reporter and a fine writer, and his copy made for good reading. Until one morning, that is, when, lingering over a campaign breakfast of coffee (black) and pizza (cold), I came upon a reference to Miss Metze as a "honey blonde with an oozy voice." Really, John!

When John showed up at headquarters that morning, I accosted him, pushing the newspaper into his chest and saying in a voice louder than necessary, "This is beneath even you, John. Using the *New York* frigging *Times* as a dating service!" My sworn testimony is that the legendary John Phillips, who wrote under the fancypants byline "McCandlish Phillips" . . . *blushed*.

On an impulse never regretted, Miss Metze and I were married on a cold day in March 1966. Bill was still in Switzerland, dashing down mountains and dashing off books. Just before the service was to begin I received a telegram. It was signed by General Pulaski and it read, "I won't be attending your wedding if you won't attend my goddamn parade."

Wall Street Journal
February 27, 2016

BILL BUCKLEY'S LESSONS FOR TODAY'S CONSERVATIVES

Watching the current field of presidential contenders, I often find myself thinking: How would they have done on *Firing Line*? How would Bernie Sanders perform if, instead of chatting with congenial hosts on MSNBC, he had to submit to searching queries about the nature of socialism from William F. Buckley Jr.? How well would Donald Trump be able to keep his intimidation games going while sitting opposite a serenely amused *Firing Line* host?

Firing Line made its television debut 50 years ago, a few months after the conservative founder of *National Review* magazine had stirred considerable attention but few voters by running for mayor of New York City. Under the brilliant management of his brother Jim and myself, Bill had finished a distant third.

He had begun the race as the editor of a small magazine—a man as well-known, roughly speaking, as the editor of *The New Republic*—but he finished it by granting valedictory interviews to the big American networks, the BBC and other overseas media outlets.

As soon as the Board of Elections had certified his defeat—asked during the campaign what he would do if he won, he had famously replied: "Demand a recount"—Bill took a victory lap and asked me to tag along.

Morning, noon and night, he was feted by the grandees of publishing, broadcasting and many organizations in need of charismatic leadership. Almost every meal or meeting would end with an offer for Bill to work full-time or part-time or—OK, what about almost-no-time?

After cursory deliberation—Bill was almost always an impulse buyer, rarely the comparison shopper—he accepted three offers. He rejiggered syndication arrangements for his newspaper column, setting it on a path to explosive growth. He signed a contract with Viking for a book that would be published a year later and become a best-seller, *The Unmaking of a Mayor*. And he signed a development deal with RKO General to host his own public-affairs television program.

The company CEO welcomed us to his huge, *Mad Men*-style office, floor-to-ceiling shelves crammed not with books, of course, but with plaques, statuettes and testimonies to industry eminence. He eased into a monologue on the many splendid qualities of William F. Buckley Jr., after which, assuming Bill to have been comprehensively schmoozed, he pressed a button on his desktop.

The producer assigned to the new project appeared from a side door. He certainly looked the part, sleek and well-tailored. He began by reciting a long list of production credits, all—all—of which were lost on Bill. Popular culture was not Bill's strong suit. He once leaned over to me at a news conference and whispered, "Who is this Mickey Mantle they speak of?" But Bill was the polite sort, so he nodded agreeably as the recitation rolled on.

Mr. Producer wrapped his presentation by stating that, given his vast experience in talent management, he was confident he could mold Bill into a national television personality. Oops. The last man who had tried to mold William F. Buckley Jr. had been William F. Buckley Sr. Bill was not a man for molding.

He cleared his throat and drawled in the way that would soon become familiar to millions of Americans, "Well, this is a bit awkward . . . inasmuch as I have retained my own producer." The CEO, incredulous, asked, "And who might that be?" Bill arched an eyebrow and replied, "Uhhh, Neal has agreed to produce the show." I shot my cuffs and tried to look as if my flabber had not been gasted.

The soul of insouciance, Bill then flew off to Switzerland to work on his campaign book, leaving the details of production and distribution to his newly minted "producer." I did not for a moment mistake my new assignment as a vote of confidence. Bill was a man of the printed word. In those days, he never watched television and tended to regard it as more of a persistent rumor than a cultural reality. When he returned to New York in the spring, he was surprised—and a bit put out—to learn that we would be going on the air in a few weeks. He was especially grumpy about the name *Firing Line*, which he deemed far too "combative."

The series debuted in April 1966 on New York's WOR-TV—an also-ran at a time when the big three networks overwhelmingly dominated the airwaves.

Those of you who remember *Firing Line* as a clubby forum for literary lions wouldn't recognize those early shows. John Kenneth Galbraith and Christopher Hitchens were nowhere to be seen. The guest list was much more likely to include a race hustler, a war resister, a campus crazy or a gender bender. The ideological clashes were raw, frontal and intentional.

"Combative" turned out to be the right message of the show's title. WOR promoted it as "The Fight of the Week," and the question implicit in every guest invitation was, "Think you can last eight rounds with Kid Buckley?" To which the answer, week by week, in the judgment of both viewers and critics, was . . . "apparently not." Bill was young, handsome, tack-sharp and, yes, highly combative.

The program soon built an audience in the New York area and we began to sell it across the country. Within only a few months it was clear that *Firing Line* was becoming a hit and that Bill was becoming a star. Despite the early success, Bill continued to think of TV as a short-term gig. If he had known then that, three decades hence, he would be locked in competition with Johnny Carson for the title Longest-serving Series Host in Television History—well, he might have quit on the spot. In the end, *Firing Line* was the longest-running public-affairs TV show with a single host; it ran for 33 years and 1,504 episodes.

With the series well-established and widely syndicated, I felt free to leave and resume my corporate career. To replace me, I recommended a young man named Warren Steibel. Unlike his predecessor, Warren was an experienced professional. He managed the transition to PBS in 1971 and settled Bill into his role as the more intellectually elegant, American version of that British bumpkin, Alistair Cooke. Warren produced the programs many fans remember—with Galbraith and Hitchens, Norman Mailer and Milton Friedman, the electric Jeff Greenfield and the great Tom Wolfe.

In later years, Bill didn't like to be reminded of the early, rough-and-tumble *Firing Line*. In his book on the show's 25th anniversary, he barely mentions it. But he was proud at the time and proud later of his accomplishment. He had competed and won on commercial television's own terms.

What did *Firing Line* add to the culture of its day? It became, first, a national megaphone for conservative values. It wasn't one of dozens of right-leaning talk shows. It was one of one.

Second, it became a foundation stone for the emerging political movement of which Bill Buckley was the principal architect. It was a laboratory where fresh conservative ideas were proposed, rejected, battle-tested, reformulated and—for those that survived—polished for general circulation. Third, and not at all incidentally, it became a promotional vehicle of lifesaving value to *National Review*.

No history of *Firing Line*, however abbreviated, would be complete without remarking on the sheer theatricality of that performance.

There was, first, the power of language. Bill deployed his overstuffed vocabulary to instruct and illuminate, but almost as often to stun or intimidate. When he would ask a guest, for instance, if his position was "mere velleity" or, for another instance, if the guest's position approached statistical reality "asymptotically," the guest's eyes would widen—maybe appearing on *Firing Line* had been a bad career choice. (I'd tell you what those words mean, but Bill would have preferred that you look them up.)

There was also the body language. Given a rough-hewn bench, or even a slab of concrete, Bill could drape his long frame across it in a pose of cocktail-lounge cool. The guest would be sitting bolt upright, strapped into the middle seat on a commuter flight.

Then there was the voice. Bill Buckley spent much of his life in search of the perfect word for the right moment. When he found it, which he did more often than anybody else, he would cherish it, squeezing every nuance from it in a syrupy accent that was part English public school and part a mysterious one of Bill's devising.

Finally, there was the dramatic arc of the show itself, particularly those in the early days. Bill would script the opening, talking directly to camera as he framed the topic. Of the first three sentences, at least one would be so long and winding as to be undiagrammable by Cleanth Brooks. Bill would then introduce the guest, juxtaposing a $64 adjective to a $64 noun with an effect so befuddling that you could almost hear the guest ask himself, "What did he just call me?"

Bill would then pose what we in the control room came to call The Question. He would press upon the guest a debater's choice between Alternative A, which was Very Bad Indeed, and Alternative B, which was Utterly Unacceptable. Almost invariably, and fatally, the guest would lunge for Alternative A.

The terms of engagement had been set. The witness had been read his rights and, with his lawyer unavoidably absent, the interrogation would begin. Over the balance of the show, Bill would nudge the guest gently but firmly down the slippery slope to forensic demise. It was an intellectual execution administered by a most genial hangman.

Hard to imagine today, but there was once a charming and commanding conservative presence at the center of American culture. It is an indictment of the media that to the degree that conservative views are aired these days, they are largely restricted to roped off areas on cable television or talk radio. Remember, the bulk of the *Firing Line* run was on PBS.

Then again, it's not clear that today's media, with its rewards for a coarser, quicker kind of combat, would have any tolerance for someone of Bill's erudition and willingness to tease out an argument slowly. And while he certainly also had the tools for the rough stuff, he probably would have been disinclined to use them as now required.

But modern conservatism itself isn't without fault. The proponents of smaller government, free markets and individual freedom are too often unwilling, or unable, to make their case with anything approaching the verve and clarity that Bill Buckley brought to the subject—and brought into the homes of millions of Americans. For them, William F. Buckley Jr. personified conservatism, and it sure looked like fun. Say what you will about the Republicans running for their party's presidential nomination, none of them comes close to conveying the intellectual joy of conservatism once displayed by a guy who ran for mayor of New York.

National Review
October 24, 2016

FIRING LINE AT 50

Review of Open to Debate: How William F. Buckley Put Liberal America on the Firing Line, *by Heather Hendershot*

I t is the contention of liberal scholar Heather Hendershot that *Firing Line*, the long-running television series hosted by William F. Buckley Jr., was bracing, original, occasionally electric, frequently heuristic, and, all weighty things considered, a major contribution to civilized discourse. Allowing for typical professorial understatement, I think she may be on to something.

Professor Hendershot, who teaches media studies at MIT, has just published a magisterial account not only of a television program, but also, more ambitiously, of the political culture from which it sprang and within which it thrived. She tells this story with style and insight and good humor, some of the latter borrowed from WFB but much of it her own. The gem of her hefty book is a long introduction that limns memorably the narrative line and the leading character, all of it based on what appears to be, as the leading character might have put it, Stakhanovite research.

Hendershot screened every one of the 1,500 taped episodes and read every piece of paper in the *Firing Line* archive, claims that not even WFB himself could credibly make. And she did not return from library hell with empty hands. She has the front story, the back story, and even the story that was never meant to be told. She reveals here the identity of the man responsible for the birth of *Firing Line*. Now that she's spilled the beans, I might as well spill a few more.

Tom O'Neil was a senior member of the controlling family at RKO General, a conglomerate that combined, principally, a small entertainment company (RKO) with a large tire manufacturer (General). O'Neil was utterly charmed by WFB's turn in a New York mayoralty campaign and, with the swagger of 20th-century capitalism, directed RKO executives to give WFB his own show on the company's television station in New York City. (We ask by unanimous consent, Mr. Chairman, that Tom O'Neil be inducted posthumously into the Conservative Hall of Fame.) Buckley was always protective, even secretive, about O'Neil's role. WFB was controversial in those days—in some circles, toxically so—and public association with him could have embarrassed O'Neil with his colleagues, customers, and even, it was rumored, a few family members.

As anybody who has passed through the halls of corporate America will understand, a rocket from headquarters meets a mixed reception when it lands at the division level. In WFB's first meeting with RKO executives, it became clear that they were prepared to comply with orders from HQ; they had been utterly uncharmed by WFB's mayoralty campaign; and they didn't like being told how to make television programs by a tire manufacturer.

Their position, expressed with articulation enough in body language, became more vivid still as the operational plan was rolled out. The series would get an initial commitment of no more than 13 weeks, probably not long enough for the program to find an audience in a crowded TV market but long enough to assure HQ that respect had been paid. The crew assigned to the new project was thin and picked-up and would not have been confused by neutral observers with a team of broadcast all-stars. The budget was fixed at a level so monastic as to allow for nothing more than two chairs, a rickety coffee table, and a bare, poorly lit set. It was "let's get Mr. Wilson's barn and put on a show" time. (It was at this meeting that WFB gave me a battlefield promotion to producer: He wanted at least one ally somewhere in the building. We made a good match. I was as unqualified to produce the show as he was to host it.)

Against this background, the magnitude of WFB's achievement can be traced in high relief. *Firing Line* went on the air in April 1966 and would run uninterruptedly for the next 33 years. When the series died peacefully of natural causes in 1999, it stood as the longest-running program with a single host in the history of television, a record that stands unbroken today. (Hey, Fallon, watch what you eat. And get your butt to the gym.)

The main section of Hendershot's book is a march through the *Firing Line* decades and the several ideological movements that inflamed them: Goldwater and the rise of the new conservatism. Civil rights and Black Power. (Huey Newton, arriving on set bristling with an aura of violence, was hit by this tranquilizing dart from WFB: "It may be that one of the difficulties you have as chief spokesman for the Black Panther Party is your total incoherence.") Women's liberation. (It's true: Germaine Greer was almost as big a flirt as Clare Boothe Luce.) Vietnam. Nixon. (That is to say, the looming and then engulfing and finally lingering question of what the heck to make of Richard M. Nixon.) And, in a concluding section, Reagan and what some of us like to call his revolution.

Hendershot artfully weaves cultural and social commentary through and around the topics and guests featured in the programs. Some readers, myself included, would have preferred a bit more Buckley and a bit less Hendershot, but she gives both sides a fair shake. Most of the time. When she detects a tone of triumphalism in WFB's take on the Reagan years, to cite a conspicuous exception, she adds her own summary judgment of the decade: "For liberals, conversely, it was a most alarming time. It was a decade when women's reproductive rights were under assault. When billions were spent on a missile-defense system the mechanics of which had been far-fetched from the get-go. When the Christian Right gained tremendous visibility. . . . When the Mental Health Systems Act was repealed. When radical cuts to the Department of Housing and Urban Development [*blah-blah-blah*]. . . . When the Environmental Protection Agency was [*blah-blah-blah*] . . ." and so on and so on in the the-glass-is-bone-dry mode of overripe liberalism. In her telling, good and decent people, despite all the peace and prosperity breaking out around them, barely survived the Eighties.

In these yes-but passages, Hendershot reminds me of the long blue line of *Firing Line* guests, almost all of whom would say as they were ushered from the studio one of two things. Either, "Did I embarrass myself?" To which the approved answer, factually defensible if not wholly responsive, was, "Embarrass yourself? This show will make you famous." Or some variation of "When he brought up the welfare question, I should have cited the Farnsworth study." To which the careful answer was, "That might have been effective." What Professor Hendershot has proved once again is that it was devilishly hard to win a debate with William F. Buckley Jr. Even eight years after his death.

National Review
September 24, 1974

ODD MAN IN

Review of United Nations Journal: A Delegate's Odyssey *by William F. Buckley Jr.*

There were some Americans who slept better each night knowing that William F. Buckley Jr. would be their representative at the United Nations. For those unimpressed with the UN, Buckley's appointment as a "public member" seemed a happy coincidence of torch and tinder. Buckley's views on the UN, if not widely known, were at least widely assumed to be inflammatory. Buckley himself was taken with the pyrotechnic possibilities. Contracting a rare case of Mittyism, "I saw myself there, in the center of the great assembly at the UN . . ., holding the delegates spellbound as I read to them from Solzhenitsyn, as I described the latest account of concentration camps in Mainland China . . . The press of the world would rivet its attention on the case the American delegate was making for human rights, repristinating the jaded vision of the international bureaucrats."

Partisans of the home team were to be disappointed. Nary a wisp of smoke curled from the Talk Factory on the East River. Buckley's voice, however eloquent (or mischievous) it might have been in the private councils of the U.S. delegation, did not carry beyond the elegant glass walls. He was stilled. Yes, THEY GOT TO HIM TOO.

From this point the story within the story gets interesting, and with Buckley at center stage, irresistibly engaging. The bad guys, it seems, were really the good guys. When some bureaucratic whiz kid conceived the "public member" gig, it was recognized all around that the widow Roosevelt could not be denied the charter membership. Harry Truman, a man of little gallantry and strong butt-covering instincts, did the sensible thing: he had the public member's tongue cut out. Public members, by law, speak only when spoken to and then only under the guidance of a ventriloquist. The irony peaks when Buckley, an accomplished stylist, is handed his maiden speech by a GS-14 ghostwriter. (Close students of Buckley will assume, rightly, that he found an excuse not to deliver the boilerplate.)

Mark it down as another setback for the legions of bureaucracy. Denied that forum to express his views, Buckley looks for another. Thus this book, Buckley's revenge. Not to put too fine a point on it. *United Nations Journal* is one of his best, as remarkable in its way as the incandescent *God and Man at Yale* and better written than any of the nine volumes since. From Albert Jay Nock whence it grew, the Buckley style has reached full manhood, strong, gentle, layered, synecdochical. If the Buckley sentence could be poised seesaw-wise, with the fulcrum jutted into the very middle, it would tilt sharply to the right, with meanings and submeanings piling up toward the end of the sentence. Difficult to write, easy to read.

The content of the book might be described as a child's treasury of diplomatic incidents. Of the Soviet mission chief, our delegate remarks: "One wishes one could say about Malik that he is the last of the Stalinists, as one wishes one might say, looking up at a falling tree, that it was the last to suffer from the Dutch elm disease." (At diplomatic stroking Buckley does not excel.) Of the six perfectly respectable but totally anonymous recipients of the Human Rights prizes: ". . . it was as if, in the year that Lindbergh crossed the Atlantic, the aviation trophy had been awarded to the stunt pilot at the Dutchess County Fair. The shadow of Solzhenitsyn was over that Assembly . . ." (Unfortunately, not far enough. In searching, unsuccessfully, for a friendly delegation to extend a UN invitation to Solzhenitsyn, Buckley perceives the rude reality of American imperialism: We have no client states. We may pay for them, but they don't stay bought.)

And on being seated at lunch with the ambassador from Gambia: "I wish I had known that ahead of time, as I'd have looked up Gambia, and learned something about it. . . . I asked how was the weather in Gambia, and he replied that the weather in Gambia was always fine, and I replied of course Gambia is famous for its wonderful weather, and we beamed at each other."

The trouble he makes turns out to be conventional rather than nuclear, but it does command the attention of Ambassador Scali and occasionally of Secretary Kissinger. Scali seems just right for his post: articulate, slightly fancy dan, apparently oblivious to the fact that issues of genuine consequence are resolved almost anywhere but at the UN. Scali disappears in mid-journal for medical repairs, but not before closing several loopholes Buckley has discovered in the Truman–Eleanor Roosevelt Non-Aggression Pact. Kissinger drops into the narrative frequently, which visitations are described with great sympathy. There is a special relationship between the two men which Buckley's account illuminates.

As the weeks of his assignment roll by, Buckley confronts the paradox that greets every antistatist on his first experience with government. The bureaucracy, which redundantly has earned our distrust, is manned by the most exemplary bureaucrats. They are hard-working, intelligent, enormously well trained, attractive. Familiarity can easily breed respect, even awe for the prodigious expenditure of sincerity. These people are not so much working as serving. Which presents the servee with special problems. It is so—*rude*—to inform missionaries that they are preaching a false religion. So Buckley limits himself to those occasions when it is absolutely necessary to do so. One doubts that his self-restraint will be long remembered.

In the end Buckley's judgment of the UN is characteristically unambiguous (though not as combustible as that of his Fighting Irish predecessor, Daniel Patrick Moynihan). As Buckley puts it, not uncharitably, in the epilogue to his journal: "The United Nations is the most concentrated assault on moral reality in the history of free institutions, and it does not do to ignore that fact or, worse, to get used to it."

The American Spectator
June, 2006

NR GOES TO WAR

I t evolved into a useful mechanism, the *National Review* Board of Directors.

We knew early on that there would be no such thing as a free dinner. After the meeting and the reception, after the Beef Wellington and the soufflé, even after the good cigars of suspect provenance, the evening would still be young and dangerous. At any moment the host might ring his goblet and call on one of us to declaim on some obscure issue that then engaged him. Over time we got used to it, but you never really forgot your first turn in the barrel at Wm. F. Buckley's dinner table. In my own case, I was asked to assess the "recent events at NATO headquarters." It being the closing weeks of the NFL season those events, whatever they were, had escaped notice. My remarks were brief, pointless, and canted sharply downhill. Think of Bode Miller, windmilling off course, and you have a sense of it.

Now and then, we got the night off. A special guest would appear, drawn from Bill's wildly eclectic circle of friends. Henry Kissinger, the great columnist Murray Kempton, liberal activist Allard Lowenstein, convicted killer Edgar Smith. You never knew who might show up. The evening that lives in memory featured Sir James Goldsmith who was at the time (roughly speaking) the richest man in the world and (not so roughly speaking) the most pontifical man this side of Rome. Asked by Bill to suggest how the fraying Anglo-American alliance might be repaired, he bounced to his feet and declared, "It's really quite simple," by which he appeared to mean that we were unlikely to grasp its complexity without benefit of his navigational services. "It depends on whether or not we attend to twelve straightforward axioms." He then proceeded to describe each axiom at impressive length.

I had flown in on the redeye and, after a long day of back-to-back meetings, had consumed at least my share of Bill's nice Bordeaux. As Sir James's presentation rolled on I found it less and less compelling. Along about axiom No. 3, I nodded off. Not face down, gurgling-in-the-finger-bowl but chin-bouncing-off-the-chest, in the manner of the toy dog in the back window of the car in front of you. I caught a few winks. Sometime later I was shaken awake by a burst of applause. A relieved audience seemed to be congratulating Sir James on his march across the dry plains of axiom. He acknowledged the applause with a Windsorian wave and sat down, his face a rictus of frozen satisfaction. As the applause died away, WFB, who misses nothing, cleared his throat polysyllabically and announced, "Uhhhhh, responding for the United States ... Mr. Neal Freeman." In that special moment I guess I admired Bill almost as much as I hated myself.

I got to my feet, launched a few dozen words in search of a coherent idea and, finding none, did what we all had learned to do in circumstances of last resort. I pulled an O'Sullivan. (John O'Sullivan, the onetime editor of *NR*, was, like many Brits, born glib. Roused from deep slumber, he could deliver, between yawns, six chiseled paragraphs on the similarities between Gladstone and Disraeli.) I wrapped up briskly with, "I think we can all agree that Sir James's axioms speak eloquently for themselves." I fooled nobody, of course, with the possible exception of Sir James Goldsmith, who at least on the subject of his own magnificence could occasionally be fooled. Bill found it all so hugely amusing that I entertained the idea of hating him, too.

As will be apparent from this small episode, the board dinner worked at several levels. At the threshold level, it served to separate the women from the girls. Aspirants who failed the ordeal by rhetorical fire tended to disappear, airbrushed from institutional memory. Those who remained were ushered into Bill's inner circle, which was always a fun place to be. And where, I might add, people tended to settle in for the long haul. After 38 years on the *NR* Board, I ranked no higher than third in seniority.

At the operational level, the board regulars became *NR*'s ready reserves. Most of the time, to be sure, the *NR* Board was corporate in name only. Bill as the controlling shareholder would call the shots and the rest of us would say more or less with one voice, "Attaboy, Bill." He owned the stock and we were all theological capitalists. But when the finances of the magazine took a Dickensian turn, as they did from time to time, the NR Board was there, pre-briefed, bonded to the enterprise, and ready to heave to. (I can remember serving on one of those "special committees" with Joseph Donner, a savvy Wall Streeter who had acquired a Ph.D. in German history in his spare time. In the course of an afternoon, Joe dashed off a turnaround plan for which Booz Allen would have charged six figures.)

By far the greatest benefit of these dinners, however, was the opportunity to calibrate *NR*'s center of ideological gravity. To even close readers of the magazine, it no doubt seemed that the magazine spoke with the distinctive and authoritative voice of WFB—the one man in our one-man, one-vote editorial regime. But for all his gifts of insight and expression, not to mention his hierarchical dominance, Bill was always factually hungry and intellectually humble. He rarely imposed his view at the outset of discussion, preferring to hear from others before refining and declaring his own position. In the dialectic of the magazine, he rarely advanced thesis or counterposed antithesis. His natural mode was synthesis. That is, while he may have been uncomfortable watching James Burnham and Frank Meyer batter each other—and their showdowns in my own staff days could turn into draining Borg-McEnroe five-setters—he was happy to learn from them.

As the dinners evolved, then, they were rarely the occasion for issuing encyclicals in matters of conservative faith and almost always a con-vocation of the likeminded in pursuit of fresh doctrine. At the end of most of those evenings, with his thoughts neatly gathered, Bill would say goodnight, go upstairs, and write a column, sometimes spiced with unattributed quotes from his dinner guests. A few days later we would open the newspaper to find Bill's elegantly synthesized position on the issue of the day. If you want to perceive in this process a right-wing con-spiracy resulting in a party line, be my guest. There are worse ways to run a political movement.

And so we came to 9/11. On that unforgettable Tuesday morning, a series of ugly events occurred. Unspeakable death and destruction that produced terror and fear and, soon thereafter, the birth of a pernicious cliché. It was said and then repeated and then echoed and then chanted that "9/11 changed everything." Never underestimate the power of cliché to sweep all argument before it. In Washington at least, 9/11 *did* seem to change everything. Less than a year earlier, George Bush had been elected President on a foreign policy platform with three planks: (1) that the U.S. would not act as the world's policeman; (2) that the U.S. would be humble before the nations of the world; and (3) that the U.S. would not engage in nation-building. Taken together, these three planks added up to a con-ventionally conservative approach, a platform that had been roundly en-dorsed by *NR*. Now, with a 180-degree whiplash, the Bush administration began to rumble about "regime change" and "going it alone" and "build-ing a democratic Iraq." Call this 9/12 approach whatever you will—utopian, neoconservative, Wilsonian—it could not fairly be characterized as "conservative." And thus was set the agenda for every board discussion from the fall of 2001 through the summer of 2004. We would talk about Iraq.

In the early rounds of the running debate, I would guesstimate that sentiment ran three-to-two in favor of the Iraq invasion. (I should note that the subject of Afghanistan was quickly put to one side. It was a straight-line projection of long-standing *NR* policy that we should respond to 9/11 with disproportionate force and to disproportionate effect. If there was reservation within the circle about the assault on Afghanistan, it was no more than quiddity.) I was at first opposed to the Iraq invasion based on my skepticism about the presence of weapons of mass destruction. What information I had was not first-hand and dispositive. It was more interstitial and suggestive.

Over the years, I had served on the boards of a number of defense contractors all of which did classified work. Two of them had provided information that, it's not too much to say, proved vital to U.S. security interests. A third developed technology that, perhaps second only to nuclear weaponry, tipped the balance of terror against the Soviet Union. A fourth was the only private entity I'm aware of whose employees came under attack in all three 9/11 buildings—a clandestine office in one tower, a protective service post in the other tower, civilian contractors at the Pentagon. A fifth company ran supplies to America's unacknowledged allies in sundry twilight struggles. I spent a lot of seat-miles with these people.

Additionally, as a journalist I had produced for many years the PBS foreign affairs series, *American Interests*. In the course of an average week, I talked to a score of sources professionally engaged in matters of national security—defense, diplomacy, intelligence. I stayed in touch with these people. Finally, as a resident of northern Virginia's high-tech corridor for 20 years, I rubbed elbows with members of "the community" all week long—at the gym, at school events, at overpriced coffee bars. If you happen to reside in Kohler, Wisconsin, I suppose that the chat turns to sinks and tubs. In Vienna and Reston you talk shop, too. What struck me was that, over the course of the 18 months between 9/11 and the invasion of Iraq, I never encountered a single professional who *knew* that the case for WMD had been established.

The editors of *NR* were unafflicted by such doubts. Along with the rest of the commentariat, right, left, and center, they seemed to take it as a given that Saddam had built a serious WMD arsenal. When I would press them on this point at meetings, their impatience would show: "Oh please, he used them on his own people" or "Come on, why do you think he threw out the arms inspectors" or some other such non-responsive response. I wondered then and wonder still how so many people—all of them bright and journalistically trained people—could have been so trusting of secondary and partisan sources. My best guess is that it was an example of what psychologists call rational herding, which is the modeling of your beliefs on the beliefs of others whom you presume to be better informed. Rational or otherwise, there was much herding. By January of 2003, as we rolled up the ramp to war, I was the only director who spoke against the invasion. Eleven people spoke in favor, with the rest in tacit concurrence.

It has become fashionable in recent months to say that the U.S. invaded Iraq "for lots of reasons." It has been said, variously, that we were seeking to establish an island of democracy in an unstable region; (more nobly) that humanitarian principle obliged us to free an oppressed people; (more crassly) that we had no choice but to protect the flow of oil; (more colorfully) that the President was driven to avenge old man Bush; (more tendentiously) that we were manipulated into advancing Israel's interests. Pick your ax and grind it. The notion that we invaded Iraq for "lots of reasons"—like so much else in the discussion of Iraq—misses the point. There was only one "reason" that *permitted* the president to take the country to war: the presence of weapons of mass destruction. The American people were and are viscerally opposed to the idea of pre-emptive war. In the absence of a threat, pre-emptive war looks to them very much like naked aggression. (In the absence of a threat, even the argument from principle would collapse. The administration's stated preference for democracy was based on the asseveration that democracies don't attack other countries.) It's important to remember that WMD was not just one of a cluster of fungible "reasons" for war. It was the only reason for war.

Another statement that has been swapped-out by the fashionable in recent months, most famously by Sen. Jay Rockefeller of the Senate Intelligence Committee, is this: "If I knew then what I know now, I would have opposed the war." With great respect, Senator, we know now *exactly* what you knew then. And to my knowledge not a single datum of U.S. intelligence has been changed over the past three years. There have been additions and reassessments as information accumulated, but the veracity of the data file at the time of the Senate vote has not been challenged in any material respect. (I hope not to confuse the term "data" with the broader term, "intelligence." The latter comes in two forms. The first is data—the hard artifacts of intelligence including pictures, voice intercepts, alphanumeric files snatched from ocean-bed cables, and such like. The other form is human interpretation, an attempt to tell the customer what the data mean. These assessments vary widely in quality, ranging from brilliant analysis and actionable extrapolation to bureaucratic cant and partisan spin. Over time, the data record stands motionless. The interpretation swings freely in the Beltway breeze.)

In our final meeting before the balloon went up in Iraq, I pleaded with my *NR* colleagues to reconsider their drum-beating for war. I rehearsed my old arguments and added the prudential point that we should husband our resources to meet the *real* threats in Iran and North Korea. I thought then and I think today that if *NR* had opposed the invasion it could have made a decisive difference within the conservative movement and, radiating its influence outward, across the larger political community. There were no takers for my brief. For all involved, I suspect, that last pre-war evening was difficult. I probably pressed too hard against the carefully tended fences of collegiality. In an overwrought phrase that I regretted instantly, I characterized the decision to invade Iraq as "stupid, dangerous, and hubristic." (I recall the phrase only because it was tossed back at me repeatedly in the early months of the war, as if it had been memorialized on a plaque in the Hall of Crazy Sayings.) For all the sense of estrangement between me and the magazine I now barely recognized, though, there was in the air a hint of reconciliation. We were marching to war after all and as soon as American boots hit Iraqi soil, there would be no more debate, no more policy differences. It would be our guys, right or wrong. We would all be in it together. Right?

As America went to war, *NR* gave its warm endorsement to the invasion but then—rather than rallying reluctant conservatives to flag and cause—it turned abruptly to the settling of intramural scores. In the issue immediately following the invasion, *NR* ran a long cover story excoriating what it called "Unpatriotic Conservatives." The principal villain of the piece was, of all people, Robert Novak.

I had a history with Novak. Back in the 1960s when I opened *NR*'s Washington bureau, there weren't many established pressies who wanted anything to do with our little right-wing magazine. Novak had opened doors and offered friendly counsel. As his career and influence waxed, he became a mentor to many conservative journalists. Fred Barnes, John Fund, and Kate O'Beirne, among others, are in his debt. By the time that

Reagan came to town, Novak was the most important conservative journalist in the nation's capital—as important to the D.C. network as WFB was to his in New York. (The other giant in town was my old *Washington Star* colleague James Jackson Kilpatrick, but Kilpo was not by temperament a team-builder.) I will admit that the cover line had arrested my attention. In what way had Robert Novak—U.S. Army veteran, indefatigable Cold Warrior, true-believing supply-sider, the man on whose shoulders so many *NR* editors stood—in what way had Robert Novak suddenly become "unpatriotic"?

The case against Novak focused on the four pillars of his reportorial skepticism about Iraq. In his columns and television appearances he had opined: (1) that the case for WMD had not been made; (2) that the occupation of Iraq might not be a "cakewalk" (in the neocon phrase of the day); (3) that democratic values might not easily take root in the sands of the Middle East; and (4) that global terrorism might not be deterred by the invasion of the U.S. military. For making these points unabashedly, Novak had, in the judgment of *NR*'s author, revealed his true feelings and base motives. Robert Novak "hated" America. Robert Novak was "unpatriotic." (The author, David Frum, seemed to be an odd choice as lead investigator for *NR*'s Committee on Un-American Activities. Only recently naturalized, Frum had spent most of his life as a Canadian.) My own response to Novak's reporting was mixed. As noted, I shared his view on No. 1. About No. 4 I was agnostic. Most of what I knew about No. 2 and No. 3, which was not much, came from my reading of T.E. Lawrence's dispatches. The young officer had informed his Colonial Secretary (Winston Churchill, as it happened) that the sprawling territory that would one day be called Iraq was in fact three distinct entities with natural capitals in Basra, Mosul, and Baghdad. It was the estimate of Lawrence of Arabia that the three Ottoman provinces could be held together only at the point of a gun. That estimate proved to be durable. Even Saddam's long tenure offered no evidence to the contrary.

Rereading some of Novak's columns, I concluded that he had made a plausible case and a wholly responsible contribution to the public conversation. The historical record has now confirmed that judgment. On each and every point Novak had been right and his opponents had been wrong. In opinion journalism, you would hope that the quality of opinion would count for something. But in those poisonous days, truth was no defense. "Unpatriotic." It was the cruelest cut you could inflict on a conservative of a certain age. When I put down my copy of *NR*, I felt a genuinely new sensation. For the first time in my long association with the magazine, I was ashamed. If only in an attenuated way, I felt somehow complicit. All of the moral capital we had accumulated over the years, all of the credibility we had earned by weeding out the Randians, the Birchers, the racists, the anti-Semites, and the 24-hour nutbars—all of it was used to leverage an ad hominem attack on one of our oldest friends.

I instigated a campaign to pressure *NR* to print an apology. Novak's many friends chimed in and the editors agreed. I wasn't asking for any rending of garments. What I had in mind was a brief, boxed editorial saying, basically, "We made a mistake and we regret it." I should have known something was afoot when the process dragged on for some weeks. What finally appeared was a lengthy "collection" of responses to the Novak piece—some blandly complimentary to Novak, others sharply critical. The latter pieces for the most part skipped over the work product and dwelled speculatively on dark motivation. (Frum was allowed to review his own performance and found it flawless.) The impression created by the "collection" was that Novak was a controversial and deeply divisive figure within the conservative community. The reality was that he was, after only WFB himself, the most admired and influential conservative journalist in the country. In my eyes, the original felony had been compounded by the "apology." (From time to time I have reminded *NR* editors that conservatism means that it's never too late to say you're sorry.)

I continued to attend board functions, holding a grin-and-bear-it pose as the editors reported, early on, how swimmingly the Iraq campaign was going and then, in a later analysis, how Rumsfeld's inept tactics were botching Wolfowitz's brilliant strategy. I hung in there because I had enjoyed a great run with the magazine. Hell, Bill and our little gang had repainted the map of the known world. I had deep reserves of affection for the magazine and for my band of brothers and I just didn't have it in me to tell Bill I was quitting. When in July of 2004 he announced to a hushed Board meeting that he was withdrawing as proprietor, my colleagues were stunned and disappointed. I have to say that I was relieved. It gave me a chance to go out the way I came in—with my man Bill.

The Wall Street Journal
November 5, 2011

BUCKLEY, IF NOT GOD,

RETURNS TO YALE

What the late, great controversialist would have said to Mitt Romney, Rick Perry and today's conservative talking heads.

Editor's note: We replace our regular Weekend Interview feature this week with an essay adapted from remarks by Neal Freeman, delivered yesterday on the 60th anniversary of the publication of William F. Buckley Jr.'s "God and Man at Yale." Mr. Freeman is chairman of the Blackwell Corporation, served on the board of National Review magazine for 38 years, and is a director of the William F. Buckley Program at Yale, which brings speakers to campus and sponsors for-credit courses.

—*New Haven, Conn.*

It was my good fortune to be the guy standing next to Bill Buckley when he became Bill Buckley. When I went to work for him in 1963, he was a fiery polemicist in the world of the little magazine. Less than three years later—after the Buckley newspaper column had spread to every city across the country, after the Buckley for Mayor campaign in New York City, and after the launch of the *Firing Line* television program—he had become a large and influential presence on the national stage.

What I remember most vividly from those transformative years are three things. The first is his extraordinary personal courage.

When Bill Buckley set out to change the world, the ideological forces arrayed against him permeated the media, the academy, the political establishment and popular culture. As just one measure of the correlation of forces, consider the situation on the Yale campus.

As my own class approached graduation—that glorious June day when our commencement speaker, John F. Kennedy, got off the lambent line, "I now have the best of both worlds, a Harvard education and a Yale degree"—we conservatives sought to make a show of support for our emerging champion, Barry Goldwater. From a class of 1,000 young men, we managed to secure the support of five classmates. In addition to myself, one of our number is now an academic in California, one is a lawyer in New York, one is deceased and one is a lobbyist for the legalization of marijuana. Barry would have been proud of at least one of us.

Not included in our number, I should note, was our hard-drinking classmate, Richard B. Cheney. As God is my witness, Dick Cheney was a 160-pound scatback on the football team. Also not included was a quiet economics major named Arthur Laffer.

As scrawny as were our ranks in the undergraduate college, they dwarfed our support among the Yale faculty. Within the approximately 700-strong faculty, we enjoyed the support of two professors. One was a feisty lecturer in the law school, Robert Bork. The other was an Asian scholar named David Rowe. The odds on the Yale campus were, in rough approximation, the same odds that Bill Buckley faced across the broader culture—and Bill Buckley was undaunted by them. (My apologies. Bill would have found a way to include the word "synecdoche" somewhere in that last sentence.)

In the matter of physical courage, those of you who sailed through rough seas with him, or darted through New York City traffic on the back of his motor scooter, will know something of his fearlessness. What I remember is his demeanor during the mayoralty campaign. The public square could be a dangerous place during the 1960s. Political figures who stirred passions beyond the edge of consensus tended to attract not just controversy but gunfire.

As a political candidate, Bill Buckley stirred those same passions, but we were blessed with a first-rate security detail. It was called the

NYPD. That year in New York, it seemed that every cop—white, black and Hispanic—was for Buckley for mayor. It was the first known sighting of what psephologists would later identify as the Reagan Democrat.

At the first threat-assessment meeting, Bill listened patiently to the cops' presentation and then thanked them politely. On the way out, he issued two directives. The first was that he would not be attending any subsequent security briefings. Reports that he could be shot the next morning did not concentrate his mind. They bored him. And second, he instructed me to make sure that threat reports never reached his wife, Patsy. The campaign was in its early weeks and Bill was still hopeful of winning her support.

The second Buckley trait that stands tall in my recollection is excellence. Bill resolved early on that every speech he gave, every column he wrote, every edition of the magazine he edited must not be just competitive with, but superior to, the products of his liberal counterparts.

It was a humbling experience to be edited by Bill Buckley. I still have the original of the first editorial I wrote for *National Review*. We used Royal typewriters in those days to pound out copy on yellow foolscap: Here and there, one of my black words peeks through a blaze of red ballpoint ink. It was his conceit that if you couldn't write, you couldn't think; and that if you couldn't think, you were unlikely to prosper in his friendship.

The third trait is joy. The sound that rings in memory is that of Bill's laughter. Bill with a colleague in the office. Bill on the phone with a delicious story. Bill on the boat in the company of his many best friends. All Buckley ventures, be they commercial, political or simply for the good of the order, were aimed at high purpose but pursued in high spirit. When I left Bill's employ to start climbing the corporate ladder in New York, I took with me, for as long as I could, the privilege of editing his thrice-weekly column. An evening phone call from my star columnist would go something like this:

WFB: *Mon vieux*, I will be filing three columns within the hour. Do you know what that means?
Me: A particularly long and difficult evening for your editor?
WFB: Of course not. The copy will be pristine as always. It

means that we can be at the boat by eight in the morning.

Me (cautiously, remembering a previous occasion when I had agreed to meet him at the boat only to learn later that it was docked in Miami): Where is the boat?

WFB: Stamford.

Me: Where is the boat going?

WFB: Nova Scotia. You'll love it this time of year.

Me: Bill, I'm running a commercial organization. I can't just leave a note for my secretary saying that I've sailed for Nova Scotia.

WFB: Why not? Secretaries at *National Review* handle that sort of thing all the time.

And so they did. The joy that Bill Buckley brought to any room lingered long after his departure. Years after the event, I obtained excerpts of Bill's interview with the FBI on the occasion of my appointment to a federal position. At the end of such field investigations, the agent typically asks an omnibus, fanny-covering question: Would I, candidate Freeman, be likely to embarrass the administration? Replied witness Buckley, under oath: "I should think that the reverse is much more likely."

How then would Bill Buckley have addressed today's question: "Buckley's Legacy: How Would the Patron Saint Turbo-Charge Conservatism?" He would have begun, of course, with the obligatory quibble.

"Ontologically speaking," he might have mused, "how could conservatism ever really be said to be turbo-charged, as you so infelicitously put it?" After rejiggering the question to his satisfaction, he would have marched through the following agenda.

First, he would have summoned the Republican stalwarts for catechismic instruction. Mitt Romney, invited to dinner at 73rd Street, would have been given a pass on gun control, abortion, immigration and universal health care. Bill believed that every human being is endowed by his Creator with the unalienable right to flip-flop, though Bill might have regretted, in Mr. Romney's case, that it had been exercised so vigorously.

Instead, Bill would have bored in on what he perceived to be a lacuna: namely, the widespread presumption that Mr. Romney can fix our broken economy with an economic plan that is manifestly inadequate to the challenge. Mr. Romney would have squirmed through the evening. Bill would have barely survived it. He hated to drink alone.

Rick Perry's visit would have triggered the full WFB charm offensive. Tales of the original WFB and his wildcatting days in Mexico would have spiced the evening. Mr. Perry would have responded with a Dan Rather-sized Texasism, an impenetrable aphorism involving parched land and poisonous snakes. Bill would have been befuddled no more than momentarily—and segued quickly into a mini-lecture on why contemporary international affairs call for a somewhat less, uhhhh, parochial foreign policy than the governor has heretofore advanced.

When Sarah Palin came to lunch, Bill would have been on his best behavior. Patsy might even have persuaded him not to eat the salad with his fingers. After an hour and a half, Bill would have concluded, under the unbending terms of the Buckley Rule—which, as you will recall, holds that conservatives should support for election the rightward-most viable candidate—that Mrs. Palin was sufficiently rightward but insufficiently viable. As they parted that afternoon, Bill would have accepted an invitation to go spear-hunting for large mammals deep inside the Arctic Circle, a commitment that neither Sarah nor Patsy would ever let him forget.

The session with Newt Gingrich would have caused Bill to remark on the Speaker's X-ray insight, his barbed wit, his broad range of reference and allusion. It might also have caused Bill to remember an observation by the late Herman Kahn: "Some people learn through the eye by reading, others through the ear by listening. I learn through the mouth by talking." Bill would have counseled the Speaker to add to his senior staff an editor with plenipotentiary powers.

The summit meeting with Herman Cain would have excited high anticipation. Bill would have relished the prospect of a Cain-Buckley alliance for its sheer theatricality. During their time together, Bill would have spent his time much as he had with Mrs. Palin, in a quiet inventory of the intellectual warehouse. What does Mr. Cain know? What has he read? Is he . . . up to it?

I should also note—as long as we're channeling dead conservatives—that, had Bill ultimately endorsed Mitt Romney, *National Review* publisher William Rusher would have dashed back to the office to dictate his letter of resignation.

Beyond the political arena, Bill would have had advice for two other constituencies critical to his conservative enterprise. To the hardy band of right-leaning scholars beavering away in the American academy, he would have said: "Be brave, but until you have secured tenure, be no more brave than conscience demands. Concentrate your careerist energies on the edge of evolving scholarship, but celebrate loudly and redundantly the core values of the Western canon."

To the stewards of his movement's public diplomacy—the editors and publishers, writers and producers, the bloggers and talking heads—Bill would say: "Keep handy the metrics of fusionism and appreciate the vital contribution to our coalition made by each major strain of conservatism. Avoid sectarianism. Adhere strictly to principle, but polish to a high shine the fresh formulations of our timeless proposition. Labor without pause to coin language that will fire the imagination and ignite commitment. And along the way, please, have a little fun. Try to be a little less, uhhhh, constipated."

Let me close by saying why I have chosen to support the Buckley program and to serve on its board alongside Jim Buckley, my boss in several implausible political ventures, and Priscilla Buckley, my savior-editor when I was a columnist for *National Review*. There are two reasons. The first is to keep alive a longstanding but fragile tradition here at Yale. Decade after decade, Yale has done almost nothing to encourage but just enough to permit a culture of conservative dissent. I like to think of Yale's posture as a grudging but honorable acquiescence to the true spirit of academic freedom. I became a conservative while a student at Yale. Some of you in this room did as well. It's possible. Not likely, but possible.

The second reason to support this program is that Bill would have loved it. Bill Buckley had the most complicated relationship with Yale of any student since Nathan Hale. Starting off as a golden-boy student, very much in the line of Potter Stewart, Sargent Shriver, George H. W. Bush and such, Bill quickly became, with the publication of "God and Man," Yale's designated apostate. Yale's memories of the book, as Bill once described them, were "long and censorious." The relationship between the precocious graduate and the historic university was marked for many years by simmering tension interrupted occasionally by awkward confrontation.

The ice eventually began to melt and ultimately Yale invited Bill to join the faculty. His course in English composition, which debuted in the fall of 1997, became popular with both the students and their instructor.

The process of reconciliation was completed in the spring of 2000 when Yale awarded Bill an honorary doctorate. How pleased was Bill? When word began to spread of the award, I called to congratulate him. He picked up the phone saying, "Dr. Buckley here. Any metaphysical problems I can help you with today?"

National Review
February 13, 2013

The Buckley Rule—According to Bill, Not Karl

What supporting "the rightwardmost viable candidate" meant in WFB's lexicon.

T he Buckley Rule has been much invoked in recent weeks, in this space and elsewhere, and on almost every occasion it has been both misquoted and misapplied. As one who was present at the formulation, I feel obliged to record the "originalist" intention.

It was the winter of 1964 and the unresolved question at *NR* editorial meetings, week to week, was this: Whom should the magazine support for the Republican presidential nomination? To outsiders, the question would have seemed all but settled. Issue by issue, *NR* gave every appearance of being all in for Barry Goldwater.

Heck, there were those who thought Bill Buckley's merry band had invented the Goldwater candidacy. Our publisher, Bill Rusher, was a prime mover in the Draft Goldwater committee, which had propelled Goldwater to an early lead in the delegate count. Senior editor Bill Rickenbacker, a polymath, amused himself by ghosting remarks for Goldwater and then hailing them in the magazine as "brilliantly insightful." (*NR* was not in those days a conflict-of-interest-free zone.) I was the Washington correspondent, and my own weekly reporting files were more than occasionally one long leak from the Goldwater campaign. Beyond the editorial staff, WFB's brother-in-law Brent Bozell had written *The Conscience of a Conservative*, Goldwater's bestselling book that had consolidated his leadership of our fledgling political movement. Team Goldwater was well represented at the editorial meetings.

And it was not outnumbered—if, that is, you counted James Burnham's as only a single voice. Facing Rusher, Rick, and me across the conference table was Team Rockefeller. In the first chair sat Jim Burnham, a senior editor and the most potent intellectual force at the magazine. Next to him was Priscilla Buckley—Bill's older sister, Burnham's soulmate, and the magazine's managing editor. And next to her was Arlene Croce, a fine writer who went on, somewhat implausibly, to become the nation's premier dance critic at *The New Yorker*.

I will not do justice to Burnham's argument. Nobody could. His was a superbly analytical mind, powered by a mesmerizing boardroom presence. (It was the common judgment of the staff that if you were ever caught standing over a lifeless body, with smoke still wafting from the gun in your hand, you should bypass the defense bar and call Jim Burnham. He would get you off, the presumption held, with an abject note of apology from the arresting officer.)

The basic elements of Burnham's brief were these. Some of them will sound familiar. First, Rockefeller was running well ahead of Goldwater in the trial-heat polls against incumbent Lyndon Johnson. Second, Rockefeller was an Ivy Leaguer, a well-connected establishmentarian, a sophisticated candidate who could expect more positive treatment from the eastern press. Third, Rockefeller had the financial resources. (Even Rusher conceded this point.) Fourth, the influence of Rockefeller's family was marbled through institutional New York—Wall Street, medicine, the real-estate moguldom, big philanthropy, a rainbow array of well-endowed ethnic and racial groups, the cultural centers. (Every New York museum worth visiting seemed to be chaired by one Rockefeller or another.) Burnham's political point? As governor of a northeastern state, Rockefeller could put at least parts of the region in play, a rare and highly valuable asset for any GOP hopeful.

Burnham's most powerful argument, his closer, was that on the overriding issue of the day Rockefeller would stand with us against our mortal foes: the capitulationists in the twilight struggle with international Communism. In Burnham's telling, Rockefeller had shown himself to be a reliable anti-Communist in his tenure at the State Department. His family's businesses around the world had cooperated with what were euphemistically known as "agencies of the U.S. government." And most significantly for Burnham, Rockefeller had retained as his principal foreign-policy adviser a young academic with impeccable anti-Communist credentials named Henry Kissinger. Burnham concluded by suggesting that, because of the depth of his experience and the range of his contacts, Rockefeller might be even more effective in prosecuting the Cold War than the boisterously anti-Communist Goldwater.

Well, there you had it. The gauntlet had been flung. Team Goldwater's response rolled out this way. First, the polls were to be dismissed. As well as he ran against Goldwater, Rockefeller was still trailing Johnson by open-water margins. There was little chance that the American people were going to want a third president in less than a year: Johnson was the beneficiary of a halo effect as the country came together in the aftermath of JFK's assassination a few months earlier. Second, Goldwater would make our brand-new conservative case—a case that most Americans had never heard—with verve and impact. Third, a Rockefeller nomination would mute both the social issues and the limited-government issues and, as a consequence, might stunt or splinter our fragile fusionist coalition. (Rockefeller was a social liberal and, quintessentially, a big-government Republican.) Finally and most important, we argued that Goldwater would advance our cause strategically. He would rip the Republican party from its roots in the eastern establishment and push it into the future— toward the West and toward the South.

These intramural arguments, as I say, were protracted, begun in the winter and carrying on into the early spring. WFB sat at the head of the table, encouraging others to speak, keeping his own counsel. In early June, after Rockefeller had won the Oregon primary and Goldwater had won California, after all of us had had our say, after rumors had begun to creep out of 35th Street that *NR* might shift its support to Nelson Rockefeller—the equivalent, today, of word leaking out of 15th Street that the *Washington Post* might endorse Michele Bachmann—Bill, who rarely proposed, decided that it was time to dispose. With each of us in our assigned seat and with six pairs of eyeballs staring at him unblinkingly, Bill announced that "*National Review* will support the rightwardmost viable candidate."

Victory for Team Goldwater! We all knew what "viable" meant in Bill's lexicon. It meant somebody who saw the world as we did. Somebody who would bring credit to our cause. Somebody who, win or lose, would conservatize the Republican party and the country. It meant somebody like Barry Goldwater. (And so it came to pass. For the next 40 years, the GOP nominated and elected men from the West and the South. Nixon won twice, Reagan twice, the Bushes thrice. Only in recent cycles has the GOP reverted to its habit of nominating "moderates" favored by the establishment. Dole, McCain, Romney—all of them were admired by the fashionable media until they won the GOP nomination, at which point they were abandoned in favor of the liberal nominated by the Democrats.)

Bill Buckley was careful with words. If he had opted on that June day for the words "rightwardmost electable candidate," we would all have recognized it as a victory for Team Rockefeller. And life might look very different today. If there had been no Goldwater, *National Review* might not have become so influential, and if there had been no Goldwater, no *National Review*, there might have been no Reagan.

I did not check back every five minutes over the next 50 years to see if Bill had amended his formulation of the Buckley Rule. But in the following year, 1965, he reaffirmed his position by running in New York City as a third-party conservative against a highly electable Republican. I can tell you as the manager of that campaign that there was never a single day, from our first planning meeting in February until the polls closed in November, that Bill considered himself even remotely electable. But viable? Absolutely. He was the best candidate in the country to carry the conservative message into the heart of American liberalism. And for those who needed further reinforcement of the point, five years later Bill's brother, James, ran for the U.S. Senate as a third-party candidate against a mainstream-Republican *incumbent*.

We all understand that it is Karl Rove's mission to promote the Republican party. It was the mission of Bill Buckley to promote the conservative cause. There should be no confusion between the two.

National Review
June 8, 2009

FINDING MUM AND PUP

A review of Losing Mum and Pup: A Memoir *by* Christopher Buckley

I f you have read the *New York Times* excerpt from Christopher Buckley's new book, you must read the book itself. Context is not always everything, but in this case it most certainly is. The *Times* excerpt catalogues parental sins committed against Christopher by Bill and Pat Buckley, and thus misleads readers by misrepresenting the underlying document.

Christopher has written an honest book, and there are those who will say that the last thing we need on this subject is an honest book. WFB's memory is golden, a statue glistening in the sun, intimidating even the pigeons who circle at a respectful distance. Why not just declare the Buckley legacy a no-fly zone and be done with it? Easy for you to say, gentle reader. Not so easy, apparently, for Christopher Buckley, the only child of William Frank and Patricia Taylor Buckley. Not so easy, either, for their devoted fans, I'm learning. There are those who will say angry things about this book to Bill's friends, who are assumed by the act of friendship to have taken up NoDoz sentinel duty on the parapets of his reputation. (And yes, it's incontestably true that, had these WFBPTB stories been spun by a political opponent, we Friends of Bill would have fallen on the poor bastard with an assault evoking shock and awe.) But here we are, confronted with the revelation from an unimpeachable source that both Bill and Pat were on more than a few occasions (to use Christopher's word) . . . impossible.

I don't know about you, but that revelation hits me with the impact of a Nerf ball hurled by a three-year-old. Take the most widely quoted instance of Bill's allegedly abusive behavior, the time he walked out on Christopher's college graduation ceremony. That classic "Bill being Bill" moment hurt Christopher, and it will hurt you as he relives it. It's inexcusable. But it was not, alas, without either prequel or sequel. It was agreed by all who knew him that Bill Buckley was the world's most impatient man. And it was acknowledged almost as widely that, if you're going to write 50-some books and 5,000-some columns, edit a fortnightly magazine, host your own television show longer than Johnny Carson, build a political organization, and then use it to change the nation and the world, then it follows as Monday does Sunday that you're not going to sit through many canned speeches. That's the way the croissant crumbles and Christopher, in context, makes clear that he has come to appreciate The Man in full.

Then there's the "chic, stunning Pat Buckley," she of the three first names, a stylistic tic first observed by media historians in the primo Evans & Novak leaker, "tough, shrewd Mel Laird." Pat was tall, dark, and gorgeous, salty of tongue, sharp of wit, and—at least on those memorable *occasions*—a bit short on the warmth and fuzz. I had a crush on her for years and she did me the kindness of flirting back. She was, in the full Bette Midler sense of the term, a piece of work, and utterly entertaining. But an evening with Pat Buckley was not all rum punch on a sandy beach. In the House of PTB, if you listened closely, you could usually hear a lit fuse hissing somewhere. I recall an *occasion*. Over the years I had reviewed in one publication or another many of Bill's books, maybe 20 or so. Without exception, these reviews were rendered in the ecstatic mode: hyperventilationary variations of "I laughed. I cried. It changed my life."

One of those many books disappointed me for some reason, however, and, as I had committed to review it for a California newspaper, I said so in print, thoughtlessly dropping the word "trivial" along the way. Well, you would have thought that I had rented a billboard across the street from Zee Maisonette and painted the offending word in six-foot-high block letters. Two days after the review appeared—two days—Pat plowed through a passel of dinner guests and growled at me, "Trivial! Is that what you think of Bill's work—trivial?" Then, to the undisguised delight of the transfixed dinner guests, Pat proceeded to, as they say in the urological literature, rip me a new one. It was a magnificent turn, played in dudgeon higher than high, quite the best performance art this reviewer had seen in many seasons. After which I picked myself up, stuffed what remained of my dignity in a back pocket, and went home, still nursing a crush on the Canadian Firecracker.

The problem for Christopher, of course, was that he was already home. He had to stay for breakfast, and the mortification he experienced on various *occasions* did not always dissipate overnight. I remember my first impression of him. Bill would bring him along on the campaign trail, asking me to "show Christo the ropes" (which I translated from the Bill-speak as "Don't lose track of the kid because I'm never returning to this nether region of Queens you somehow sneaked onto the schedule"). Christopher was 13 then, a sweet young man, fun and precociously ob-servant but something of a nervous wreck, the result, perhaps, of being airmailed repeatedly from home to home, parent to parent. I wondered at the time how—or even whether—he would be able to find his way in life, billeted as he was with two people who routinely sucked up more than their share of the available oxygen.

Not to worry. In this small, well-formed, keenly observed book, Christopher Buckley makes it all the way home both as a writer and as a man. This is expository writing of the first rank, as finely crafted as any-thing WFB ever produced. It's no more than surmise on my part, but I've long thought that Christopher took up the comic novel as a way to avoid invading his father's airspace; that he sought shelter in the explicit dis-tinction that Christo did his thing, Pup did his, with never the twain to meet. What we see in this book is that Christo can do Pup's thing, too, and as readers we can only hope that he will do more of it in the years ahead. He's good, very good. And as for those *occasions*? Well, what the *Times* didn't tell you is that Christopher deals with them one by one, wrestles them into context, and walks away proud and privileged to have been the son of two loving parents. Not perfect people, to be sure, and manifestly not people gifted in the parental arts, but, in their son's loving estimate, extraordinary people who richly blessed his life by sharing theirs.

By my count, only one *occasion* remains unresolved. When Christopher publishes his novel *Boomsday*, Bill brushes it off with an e-mailed postscript: "This one didn't work for me. Sorry." That stung and Christopher admits as much, at least twice. Writing a book is sweatstained work (for everybody but Bill, that is, who wrote them faster than anybody could read them) and Christopher was looking for something . . . more. Believe me, we've felt his pain. Everybody who got close to Bill knew that, while he was generous quite literally to a fault, when it came to writing, he wouldn't give an inch—not on quality, not on style, and, *oy*, not on vocabulary. It was Bill's conceit that if you couldn't write you couldn't think and if you couldn't think you were unlikely to prosper in his friendship. I still have somewhere the first editorial I ever wrote for *NR*. Only a few of the typewritten words peek through the blaze of red-ink emendations scratched over the yellow foolscap. Every young writer whose copy fell under Bill's jackhammer ballpoint can tell a similar tale. We *NR* alums, we know sting. What's remarkable about Christopher's literary career, then, is that his other 13 books *did* work for Bill. That was the judgment not of a loving father but of the finest editor of his generation. The ultimate praise.

Now Christo, about that Obama thing . . .

The Newseum
April 17, 2008

An Appreciation of
William F. Buckley Jr.

T hank you for this opportunity to say a few words about my friend Buckley.

Most of you knew him as an opinion journalist. Many of you knew him as a novelist. A few, not necessarily the most fortunate among you, knew him as a harpsichordist. Now, thanks to the copious coverage of his death this winter, everybody knows him as an American hero, the man who did so much to save the nation from socialism and the world from Communism. I will not recite his resume but, rather, speak of the roles he played in the lives of some of us here tonight—his roles as mentor and friend.

The word "mentor" does not do justice to the full Buckley embrace. If the term were not usefully employed elsewhere, I would describe his approach as the Heimlich Maneuver. Bill pushed, he cajoled, he demanded that you produce your best work. When you succeeded, he was delighted and promoted you shamelessly to his well-connected friends. I have been told that every Republican White House since 1968 has relied upon the speechwriting services of a *National Review* alumnus. Every one of those writers had been mentored by Bill Buckley, which may explain the disparity between Republican oratory and Republican practice. Behind every one of those appointments, I can assure you, stood a Buckley recommendation so artfully composed, so powerfully seductive that the president, any president, had little choice but to bark at his assistant—"Quick. Hire that guy before somebody else does." The same can be said for the nation's great conservative publications, beginning with the *Wall Street Journal*'s Paul Gigot, who cut his teeth at *NR*, and moving on through the world of newspapers, magazines and books. Just in my own publishing career, I had the privilege of editing not only Bill but John

Chamberlain, Jack Kilpatrick, Jeffrey Hart, Stan Evans and other *NR* regulars.

Just one story, to give you a sense of Buckley the mentor. In 1964 *NR* sent a four-man team to the GOP convention in San Francisco. Bill, of course, as principal correspondent and de facto commander-in-chief of the Goldwater movement, a conflation of roles, I would suppose, not encouraged by the tablet-keepers here at the Newseum. William Rusher, who carried the title of publisher but was in fact head of the provisional wing of *NR*, executing daring political sorties into enemy territory. Me, the kid editor, by then schooled rigorously in the *NR* style book. And a freelance reporter who was to be our eyes and ears around the convention floor. At the end of a very long first day, I proudly presented Bill with the full daily file for his approval. I watched as he read through the copy, pleased that he was making only a few changes with that deadly red ballpoint—when suddenly he stood up, snatched a few sheets of paper, marched across our tiny newsroom and, holding the offending copy with his fingers extended, as if they were industrial tongs disposing of some particularly toxic substance, cleared his throat in that polysyllabic way and said, "Uhhh Neal, Dos is allowed to roll his own." I had converted into bland, standard-issue *NR* style a column by our freelance reporter, John Dos Passos, one of the most celebrated prose stylists of the 20th century. I spent the next half-hour restoring syntactical eccentricities . . . and learning for a lifetime an elusive concept known as the exception to the rule.

If Bill was the best editor of his generation—as Prof. John Roche and others had described him—he was a better friend. He wove the fabric of his friendships so finely as to make of his life a work of art. Fishing around in my attic the other day I came across two photographs of the National Review Board—one taken in 1970 and the other in 2000. That's a long time in the life of any enterprise. While new faces had of course been added in the interval, there had been remarkably little change. The only people who had left the board had either died—like Dan Mahoney of the Conservative Party, or Roger Moore, the legal brains behind every conservative salient between the Draft Goldwater Committee and the election of Ronald Reagan, or Jim McFadden, the father of the pro-life movement. Or they had been called to public service. Jim Buckley to the

U.S. Senate, or Van Galbraith to Paris as our ambassador. The rest of us—Bill Buckley, Joe Donner, Bill Rusher, Priscilla Buckley, myself—we look ready to take on the world in that 1970 photo and there we still are in the 2000 edition, albeit looking as if the world may have won a few rounds in the intervening years. Those photos suggest Bill Buckley's notion of friendship: till death or the federal government do us part.

Last year his e-mail traffic slowed to a crawl. His pace for years had been that of a tobacco auctioneer, so I thought to check in on him. We had a house in Maine up the road from York Harbor, which during his sailing days had been one of his favorite anchorages. I've always assumed he favored it precisely because of its reputation among sailors as one of the most perilous on the East Coast. I called and said "why don't you come up for a few days, we'll watch the boats, have a lobster, and sketch out your next six books." He didn't respond. I tried again, "There might even be an apology for *Firing Line* in it for you." That was an inside joke. I had been the first producer of his television show. He hated the name *Firing Line* but consoled himself with the thought that it would be forgotten after an initial 13-week run. In the event, the show became the longest running series in the history of television. Still no response. And then he said, "*Mon vieux*, I have terminal emphysema." Bill Buckley did not use words imprecisely. I thought a bit and said, "All right. We'll bring Maine down to you. Hold lunch for us Tuesday." We pulled some lobsters and scavenged some of his favorite Chardonnay and barreled down to Stamford. It was a beautiful, chilly day at Wallacks Point and we sat out on his lanai overlooking Long Island Sound. My wife Jane was with us. She had worked for him in the early days and he had in fact introduced the two of us. We drank some wine and laughed and talked about the good times, of which there had been many. As the golden afternoon wore on he tired and his tone turned serious. He was mortified, as he put it, to learn that among the books he had given me there was one he had borrowed from a British friend. Could I be sure to get it to him? He was troubled by some cross words that had passed between him and a former colleague a while back. Would I remember to tell her he loved her? One by one, this man who had shaped so much of the history of the second half of the 20th century worked his way through a list of slights unattended and courtesies unreturned, none of them rising even to the level of social misdemeanor. But these were important matters of which we spoke. These were his friends.

On February 27th, I found a letter in the mailbox forwarded from my Maine address. It bore the familiar blue corner card on the cheesy stationery. It was Bill, thanking me for some forgettable favor and for a lifetime of friendship. A few hours later I received the call with the news that he had died that morning. It was utterly characteristic that he should expend some of his last breaths dictating expressions of gratitude. Bill Buckley's life with words was one of legendary promiscuity, but his attachment to the word "gratitude" was steadfast. Indeed, it was the title of one of his favorite books, which took the form of a long love letter to the United States. He was grateful to his family, to his friends, to his Church and to his country. It is of some consolation to his friends that over the past few years, as he made what amounted to a valedictory tour across America, he heard so many of his countrymen say what I invite you to join me in saying here tonight—Thank you, Bill.

National Review
December 4, 2013

THE GOP CIVIL WAR

A longtime combatant looks at the GOP, and conservatives' place in it, from the early days of NR on.

I understand that you've been involved in the GOP civil war for some time.
    Only 50 years or so. I came in late.
How did you first become involved?
I headed Youth for Goldwater in New York.

Wasn't Goldwater's principal opponent for the Republican nomination, Nelson Rockefeller, governor of New York at the time?

I had grown up in New York and at some point began to fear that Rockefeller would be governor for life. Mine, as well as his.

Why didn't you support Rockefeller?

His big-government Republicanism was 'roided up. He treated the municipal-bond market like an ATM machine. If he had stayed in office another term—he served three and a half, before being named vice president by Gerald Ford—he would have bonded trash collection, not just landfills.

He's been called a supply-side bureaucrat. What's that?

It's somebody who borrows money to build a huge development in the middle of nowhere in the expectation that government workers will fill the space available. They did, of course. The result was Albany, N.Y., which makes the Soviet-era parts of Bucharest look good.

You're referring to his famous "edifice complex."

Every conservative knows in his bones that the threshold question in politics is whether or not to enlarge city hall.

How would you characterize Rockefeller's politics?

A classic liberal cocktail of class privilege with a splash of ideological presumption.

Explain, please.

He wanted to open opportunities for all people to advance, he said *urbi et orbi*, but only in tiny, mincing steps that would never permit low-born types to approach his own station in life. The freezing of privilege seemed at times to be bedrock principle for him, unlike his other principles, which were ethically situational.

And the ideological presumption?

That he and his heavily subsidized entourage of academic experts, minority-group leaders, and nonprofit executives could design, implement, and enforce social arrangements superior to any that might arise organically from a benighted citizenry.

He must have done something right.

He hired competent people. If Rockefeller had been in charge of Obamacare, it would have been up and running and wrecking the health-care system on schedule.

Did he do anything else right?

Well, some people said he died heroically.

I thought he died in the arms of his 20-something mistress.

That's never been confirmed, but he was 70 years old.

What was your relationship with Goldwater?

We were not close in the '64 campaign. He seemed to think my name was Fred.

What drew you to him politically?

He was not a student of Madison, much less Tocqueville, but he was dead right *attitudinally*. He carried a giant chip on his shoulder about the intrusions of government. Over the years I heard him say dozens of times about one government program or another, "It's none of their goddamn business!" Barry used a lot of exclamation points.

Did he make a lasting contribution?

Indisputably. It was Goldwater who reminded us that, if it is the natural tendency of government to metastasize, it is the obligation of the citizen to join the resistance.

Goldwater seemed to lose favor with conservatives later in his career.

Over the years, conservatives came first to suspect and then to conclude that Goldwater was really not Brent Bozell, who under Goldwater's name had written the bracing manifesto *The Conscience of a Conservative*. That was a whale of a campaign book, but it got out in front of the candidate a bit.

What was your take on Goldwater, all in all?

Toward the end of his career, he and I became colleagues on a board overseeing classified projects, which meant that the two of us spent a lot of seat-miles wrapped in a security cocoon. What I can report authoritatively is that, when it came to defending America's interests, Barry Goldwater was both reliably testudinal and aggressively forward-thinking. Our enemies were right to fear him.

What happened to the civil war after the Goldwater–Rockefeller campaign?

It continued, but in mutated form. The GOP civil war is by its very nature a war without end. It's not a tactical skirmish, but a dynamic contention between the political haves and want-to-haves.

Did Nixon and Reagan become engaged in the civil war, too?

Yes, in different ways. Nixon was a close student of political archi-tecture. In his political life, he was a full-spectrum fusionist—social con-servative, free-market man, national-security hawk. In choosing his speechwriting staff, he cued up the perfect singer for every number on the conservative jukebox, from the Irish tenor Pat Buchanan to the Ivy League crooner Ray Price to the New York saloon singer Bill Safire. But that was Nixon's political profile—all fusionist, all the time. His policy profile was altogether different. His uncontained enthusiasms ran from EPA and OSHA to arms control and welfare to—and, after all these years, I still find this hard to believe—wage and price controls. Unfortunately for Nixon, Lincoln proved to be correct in the matter of fooling people. Conservatives turned sullen and then mutinous and at the end refused to save Nixon when his campaign people got into the breaking-and-entering business.

I'm guessing that you think Reagan then declared peace in the intra-party war.

Not at all. He declared victory. He welcomed moderates into his ad-ministration, beginning with George H. W. Bush and running through Baker, Darman, and the other media favorites. But it was a marriage as morganatic as it was convenient. Reagan made it clear that it was *his* ad-ministration and, lest anybody forget, that it was *his* party. Reagan's great contribution was to demonstrate that a right-center coalition could com-mand majority support in modern America. He proved that a principled fusionism was, not at all coincidentally, a formula for political success.

Was there any downside to what you call Reagan's great contribu-tion?

Only that some conservatives came to believe that Reagan-style gov-ernance was the natural order of things. It wasn't. It was a case of an ex-traordinary man meeting an extraordinary opportunity—and then taking the steps necessary to realize it in full measure.

Where do you place Bush 43 in terms of the GOP civil war?

With George W. Bush, conservatives voted for Reagan and got Nixon. In policy terms, Bush's signal "achievements" were longstanding left-De-mocratic goals: federalizing education, creating a new drug entitlement, breaking the fiscal discipline of the Clinton years. Bush adopted the old Nixon formula of rhetoric for the Right, policy for the Left. Inevitably, though, everything Bush did or tried to do was overshadowed by 9/11.

What about Bush 43's politics?

Like Nixon, Bush was a party stripper. He left the GOP depleted and sliding inexorably toward defeat. Nixon's demise left the door open for Jimmy Carter, and Bush 43's departure for Barack Obama. Contrast those exits with Reagan's. In 1988, Bush 41 was elected to what voters openly embraced as "Reagan's third term."

Did Bush 43 leave a political legacy?

The wisdom of the Iraq adventure will be debated for years: Many conservatives applauded it; others thought it was butt-stupid. Scholars will sort it out one day. But in political terms, the Bush 43 legacy is already set in stone. He nurtured, promoted, and helped entrench a consultant class that maintains a chokehold not only on party structure but on much of the donor base that funds it and the commentariat that promotes it.

Whoa! Are you talking about Karl Rove & Co.?

I have great respect for Karl Rove & Co. as campaign technicians. As navigators for the conservative movement, not so much.

And are you talking about some of the conservative pundits, too?

To thrive over the long haul, a political commentator has only two viable options. He can be a party guy or a movement guy. That is to say, he can speak in a partisan voice or a principled voice. Bill Buckley chose the latter option, and most conservatives would agree that he chose wisely. It is useful to remember that, to underscore his commitment to the principles business as distinguished from the elections business, Buckley launched the magazine as a pitbull critic of Dwight Eisenhower, who was, perhaps after Coolidge and Reagan, the most popular and conservative president of the 20th century.

But didn't Buckley himself become a darling of the establishment?

Very much so, but only after taking down their pants and paddling their fannies in public debate, after which many of them became docile, even affectionate. To borrow wisdom from the car bumper, the beatings continued until morale improved.

Is it likely that conservative pundits will recover their balance?

I hope so. The movement will always need navigators more than party operatives. Buckley's injunction, never refuted by experience, was that principles should always precede politics.

What, then, should conservatives do now?

Conservatives must acknowledge their role in contemporary America. We are the permanent insurgency.

And how does that translate into political action?

It may seem counterintuitive, but it remains demonstrably true: For conservatives, devotion to principled fusionism is more likely to be rewarded with policy success than any partisan accommodation, however cleverly contrived.

You're not talking about that same-old, same-old Eighties approach, are you?

We need a new idiom, not a new paradigm. The principles are timeless. It's the clichés that are tired.

What form would the new idiom take?

It would include a robust new federalism running across the domestic agenda—more Mitch Daniels and less Kathleen Sebelius. It would include tough but stable regulation for the corporate economy and radical incentives for the small-business economy—more mom and/or pop capitalism and less buddy capitalism. It would include a national defense re-scaled and re-shaped to meet probable threats—more rapid response and less massed armament in the Fulda Gap. It would embrace the politics of reality and raise the retirement age for entitlement benefits to 70—more data and less cant. It would proclaim a civic morality of personal responsibility and citizen service—more Tim Tebow and less Nancy Pelosi. And it would incite a full-scale public revolt to save our schools—more mentors, more rote learning, more tech and trade schools and less administrative support, less union privilege, less help from Washington. Thematically, the new idiom would celebrate unabashedly the virtues of work, faith, family, freedom, and country. And it would carry the day.

National Review
September 4, 2014

THE CONSERVATIVE MOMENT

GOP leaders squelched the opportunity offered by the Tea Party, but it's not too late to get it right.

Mitch McConnell is a man of his word. He said that he would crush the Tea Party, and he did. He not only got himself renominated in Kentucky, but he helped renominate fellow GOP senators who, like him, had been primaried by tea-party opponents: Lindsey Graham (S.C.), Pat Roberts (Kan.), John Cornyn (Texas), Lamar Alexander (Tenn.), and Thad Cochran (Miss.).

Those could turn out to be expensive victories.

I followed the Mississippi campaign from early on. The first thing you notice about Thad Cochran, if you haven't seen him in a while, is that he's adopted an old man's shuffle. There's nothing wrong with that. I'm working on one myself. But it's not a good look when you're campaigning at the age of 76 for a six-year term. And then there's the short-term-memory thing. It doesn't matter a hill of beans whether you happen to be in Smithtown or Jonesville, but the locals tend to fuss over the distinction.

Cochran told friends late last year that he was packing it in after 36 years in the Senate. Enough was enough, he said. Then he reversed himself and filed for reelection. He may have been right the first time.

The second thing you notice is how different Mississippi is from her neighbors. I live in north Florida, which is about as far south as you can get. We share a political culture with extra-Atlanta Georgia and much of Alabama, a salutary blend of small-business Republicans and disaffected southern Democrats that produces a rich, red soil. Put it this way: My home county went bigger for Romney-Ryan than did either Romney's or Ryan's home counties. We don't just preach the limited-government gospel. Some of the time, anyway, we practice it.

All of that private-sector buzz stops dead at the Mississippi border, where the dominant economic and political player is your federal (and apparently unlimited) government. Drive down Magnolia Boulevard, any Magnolia Boulevard, and everywhere you look there are government complexes, defense contractors, welfare dispensaries, all of them fueled by a D.C. pipeline serviced diligently over the years by Democrats (James Eastland, John Stennis) and Republicans (Trent Lott, Thad Cochran). Lott is speaking for this bipartisan effort when he explains, "Pork is federal spending north of Memphis." If the states can be divided between givers and takers, count Mississippi as a taker and, dadgummit, proudly so.

You have probably heard that Cochran ran second in the GOP primary to an obscure state legislator from the Jackson suburbs. That was an upset. Big time. But then the wiliest political operation in the state, Haley Barbour's, went to Plan B and brought in enough Democrats to put Cochran over the top in a runoff.

Some dust kicked up. There were those who thought it wasn't right for the Democrats to nominate the candidates for both parties. Others thought it wasn't right and maybe borderline illegal to toss walking-around money into black precincts in the Delta and center-city Jackson, which benefactions seemed to have had the effect of spiking Cochran's support in those areas from roughly "none" to roughly "all."

There was something else that may not have been right. I'm skeptical of the notion that, for 15 bucks a head, you can get large numbers of black Democrats to vote in a Republican primary for an old white guy. Some of those blowout precinct numbers suggest a top-down deal more than store-bought deference to the white power structure. My surmise is that there was a sit-down and that the black leaders didn't open the conversation by saying: "Mr. Thad, we're worried sick about the national debt. How can we return to fiscal discipline?" More likely, it was something along the lines of: "Mr. Thad, we understand that you're in line to chair the Appropriations Committee. Should that blessed event occur, what tangible form might your gratitude take?"

What we know as a matter of public record is that, for his big finish, the six-term incumbent rolled out his former colleague and current lobbyist-sidekick, Trent Lott, to make the point the candidate might have preferred not to make himself. Said Lott, directly and repeatedly: Cochran's defeat could cost government jobs. That's right. In the closing days of a Republican runoff in the deep-red state of Mississippi, the airwaves were filled not with cries of "Jobs! Jobs! Jobs!" but with cries of "Government jobs! Government jobs! Government jobs!"

Now, none of us here at Conspiracy Central is a stickler for doctrinal conservatism, but let's be clear: It's time that we checked our ideological coordinates.

To ask where we went wrong.

And to set a corrected course.

Sub specie aeternitatis, it could be said that we went wrong with that first bite of the apple in the garden, or indeed, at almost any point along the bumpy road of the human story. But for the present purpose, let's throw a dart at the calendar and take a look at the turning point of 1985.

Ronald Reagan had come to the Oval Office in 1981 having promised to a) prosecute more vigorously the Cold War against the Soviets, b) revive what was then diagnosed as a stagflationary economy, and c) push back against an ever-encroaching Leviathan state. History's preemptory judgment is that he succeeded splendidly on the first two commitments and whiffed on the third.

The dispositive test, for some of us at least, was the debate over the Department of Education. During his campaign, Reagan had promised to abolish it, and, in the flush of his sweeping victory, a shutdown seemed well within his grasp. The department was brand-new—it had been launched hurriedly in 1979 as a Jimmy Carter/teachers' union concoction—and it was moving ahead with all the speed and coherence of an Obamacare website launch. Conditions were thus optimal for a real-world test of constitutional conservatism: Could the federal bureaucracy actually be rolled back? Could a government agency that had not even found its purpose, much less outlived it, be discontinued?

The answer, at that time and in that circumstance, was: apparently not. At first, Reagan waffled, appointing a placeholder as secretary of the DOE while he mulled his options. But then, in a wobbly moment, Reagan was seduced by the statist conceit—namely, that government can be a force for good *if only we can put the right people in power, if only we can put our people in power.*

The right person in 1985, for Reagan as well as for everybody to the right of the hard-Left, was William J. Bennett. Roundly educated, morally grounded, stunningly articulate—the day that William J. Bennett was appointed secretary was a great day for the Department of Education. He excelled at the job and, in doing so, assured the new agency of eternal bureaucratic life. The problem for the rest of us was that Secretary Bennett did not himself achieve eternal life, at least not in his corporeal form.

It's useful to remember that the process of bureaucratic evolution is not easily analogized to the progress of the human race. We've all seen that graphic representation of human evolution that begins with a hirsute ape squatting at the far left, who then transitions into a close relative of Piltdown Man, who then finally elides at the far right into Mr. Perfect, rising resplendently from all fours to his hind feet, well-formed and smooth of brow. Upward, ever upward.

That's not typically the arc of bureaucratic evolution. A bureaucracy can just as easily begin with a William J. Bennett, wise and leonine, and then morph into a Kathleen Sebelius, imperious and unapologetic, before taking final form as a Lois Lerner, riled and eager to inflict pain on her adversaries. Our cicerone Hayek could have predicted it all, and in fact he did.

In 1985, to skip to the bottom line, we came eyeball to eyeball with Leviathan, and we blinked. Even worse than the lost opportunity was the fact that we were persuaded to learn The Lesson, which went like this: If not even Ronald Reagan, the sainted Ronald Reagan, could trim or pinch or crimp the edge of bureaucratic sprawl, well then, nobody could. The Lesson to be learned, in other words, was that ours was an impossible dream: The cause of limited government was lost, and men and women of sound mind would be well advised not to waste their time blowing on the embers or sifting through the rubble.

That proposition, dubious from the outset but puffed assiduously by the Beltway chirpers, held for a generation and might have held for several more but for two signal developments. First, the government went broke—not in the sense that it was unable to pay its bills, but in the sense that it could continue to cover obligations only by cooking the books and fudging the statements issued to creditors. The second development was that a group of citizens came together to protest the cooked books and the fudged statements.

This new citizen group was, in political terms, both unconventional and asymmetric. They were a genuinely grassroots organization, spontaneously combusted. They sprang, most of them, from the managerial class, with large contingents from small business and the military. And most of them, serendipitously, were either too old to remember or too young to have learned The Lesson. What was most striking about them, in fact, was their unshakable belief in core Republican rhetoric about low taxes, sensible regulation, and balanced budgets.

The response to the arrival of these concerned citizens by the media was comical. It reminded me of nothing so much as those network reporters, back in the mid Seventies, doing stand-ups from the nicely trimmed lawn of the Baptist church in Plains, Ga. These drop-in correspondents would interview Jimmy Carter's fellow parishioners and report, with a mixture of smirk and befuddlement, "Many of these Carter supporters, David, say they have been 'born again.'" The network types might as well have been saying: "Many of these Carter supporters, Walter, say that they arrived last night from the Planet Dweebo." There are certain political stories that only political reporters are perfectly equipped to misunderstand. This was one of them. Those supporters who said they had been born again were the base of the Carter campaign, and, in the tens of millions, they carried him to the White House.

Just so with the new citizen group. The media refused to believe that the new group was a genuine political force. Why, they had no headquarters on K Street. They had no talking heads. They didn't even have a PR guy. "Heck," said the cable talkers to each other. "They can't be that important. I've asked my neighbors in Georgetown, and nobody knows anything about them."

For the national media, the concept of American citizens assembling freely to exercise their constitutional rights was beyond their ken. These citizens were off the media grid, every bit as invisible as those born-again Christians 40 years earlier. And so, as we have seen over the past few years, the national political press, its analytical powers exhausted, slipped into default mode. These concerned citizens, whoever they were, must be . . . racists. The ones, that is, who weren't homophobes or domestic terrorists.

The response to the arrival of the concerned citizens by the Republican party was not comical.

Imagine if you would a prayer breakfast in Washington attended by the leadership of the GOP—Messrs. Boehner, McConnell, Priebus, and their associates. They drop to their knees, bow their heads, and invoke divine intercession in the country's troubled affairs, and in the party's parlous condition. Would it be too much to ask Him to deliver unto them a mass political movement, self-financed and benignly led, God-fearing and well-mannered, almost all of whose members believed in the literal version of the Republican platform and almost none of whose members wanted anything from the federal government but constitutional restraint?

Yes, it would have been too much to ask, but, yes, it has been given unto them, anyway. The Tea Party arrived in vast, friendly numbers and said to the GOP, "We're not from the federal government and we're here to help."

What happened next was not pretty. Or smart. The GOP brass responded with insults, attack ads, collaborative media trashing, and, finally, over the past six months, the charge of McConnell's geezer brigade seeking to "crush" the Tea Party. And here we thought congressional Republicans were too prone to compromise, too quick to split the difference.

Our colleague M. Stanton Evans once said of the two-party system: "One is the evil party and the other is the stupid party. I'm proud to be a member of the stupid party." I am as well, but sometimes party stupidity asks too much. Here we have before us an epochal opportunity to revive the national enterprise, and we are woefully (and smugly) ill prepared to realize it. As we look forward to 2016, where do we find ourselves? We find ourselves, in my estimate, with no candidate, no message, no coalitional unity, and a thoroughly rusted party machine. Only this question remains: Can we rally in time to save the country from a terminal identity politics that could over the next few cycles bring us not principled and experienced leaders, but (regardless of their qualifications) the first woman president, the first Hispanic president, the first gay president?

I wouldn't bet the rent money on us. But I know that we have no chance whatsoever unless we divide the labor and begin to engage now. So let's roll.

To our friends at the Republican National Committee and its affiliates: You've told us that you have closed the digital deficit (by which you mean the technical capabilities to identify potential supporters, micro-target messages to them, and deliver them to the polls). You've told us that you have learned how to poll effectively in a wireless world. You've told us that you will eliminate the fundraising gap between the parties. Effective November 5, please commission an outside, independent audit of your performance in these three program areas.

To our friends at National Review: Please develop and promote a fusionist foreign policy. All we have now is Rand Paul's demobilization, Marco Rubio's interventionism, and the vast chasm between them. What we need is a policy that will a) serve national purpose, b) abjure ideological abstraction, and c) command majority right-center support.

You have done it before. Former *NR* editor Willmoore Kendall once memorably said: "An emergency phone call between [Frank] Meyer and [Brent] Bozell is one that interrupts the regular call between Meyer and Bozell." The product of that endless phone call—a fusionist conservatism that conjoined Meyer's freedom and Bozell's virtue—was so compelling that William F. Buckley Jr. signed on for life.

To our friends at AEI, Cato, and Heritage: Please develop and promote a pedal-to-the-metal program for economic growth. No meliorism, thank you. And we are looking for some pride of co-authorship.

To our friends on Capitol Hill: The Obama administration reports that fewer of its senior appointees have come from private industry than in any previous administration. Please confront this managerial solecism. A good place to start would be to call up, at least monthly, Obama's new and astonishing choice to head the Veterans Administration—Robert McDonald, a West Point graduate and former CEO of Procter & Gamble.

Mr. Speaker, please don't pummel McDonald with sound bites. Work with him, encourage him, wrap him up in a big, teary, bipartisan hug. The mistreatment of veterans is both a national disgrace and an egregious management failure. Seize it as a teachable moment, Mr. Speaker, an occasion to remind every government executive that the essence of the job is to *allocate limited resources*.

And to our friends in the GOP: Make nice, Mitch. Nobody likes a sore winner.

National Review
November 11, 2016

WHAT TRUMP AND TRUMPISM
REALLY MEAN

A Firing Line *conversation with Neal B. Freeman.*

Q. Congratulations! You have now covered more presidential elections than anybody else in *NR* history, even more than the sainted WFB himself. To what do you attribute your longevity?

A. To my resolve never to get mad about politics.

Q. Well, yes, but have you ever managed to get even?

A. Not yet.

Q. Whom did you support in the recent unpleasantness?

A. After passing through all five of Ms. Kubler-Ross's stages of grief, I supported Donald J. Trump.

Q. Don't I remember you writing anti-Trump pieces for *NR* and elsewhere?

A. You do. I had met Trump in another life and regarded him as bad news for the conservative movement. In the summer of 2015, I described him as an existential threat to the cause and urged conservatives to take him seriously.

Q. What was the reaction?

A. I was too early. Most of the opinion writers who take in each other's laundry thought Trump was a joke. By the time *NR* published its "Against Trump" issue in the winter of 2016, it was too late. It just may be true that conservatives have no sense of rhythm. I once attended a conservative ball and entertained that notion.

Q. Why did you finally fall in with Trump, knowing what damage he could inflict on the cause?

A. For two reasons. The first was formalistic. I had been part of the effort to impose a loyalty oath on the candidates. I have long believed that, when a candidate seeks his party's nomination, he accepts the implicit obligation to abide by the result of the process. I regard the Kasich-style pocket veto as unacceptable.

Q. And the second reason?

A. I have never confused a political election with a beatification. It's a messy process that produces deeply imperfect candidates. With the exception of the Reagan campaigns, every election in my lifetime has posed some form of the lesser-of-two-objections dilemma.

Q. That's not the view of the Never Trumpers.

A. I admire the principled stand of my colleagues, even when some of them conflate cause with party. The problem for the political purist is that he tends to be disappointed with democracy itself whenever Pericles declines to run. The Founders would have been neither disappointed nor surprised to learn that Pericles wasn't on the ballot this year. The genius of the Madisonian system is that it doesn't require a genius to run it.

Q. Did you follow the Trump campaign closely?

A. I hung around long enough to get to know the Trump voters— most importantly, that the animating message of their campaign, delivered in the many indigenous dialects of our vast polity, is: "I don't like what's going on here." The Trump voters sense American decline and cultural erosion and the evanescing of opportunity and, to them, much of it appears to be the result of conscious decisions by the Obama-Clinton coterie. The media call the Trump voters "angry." That's only part of it. They are heartbroken.

Q. Any specifics?

A. Trump voters are miles ahead of conservative intellectuals in appreciating the salience of political corruption at the IRS and the DOJ.

When both the tax power and the police power of the state are turned against citizens for thought crimes, we have crossed a bright red line. In that circumstance, government, at least in its small-r republican form, is unlikely to survive.

Q. And Trump voters think Trump might be the answer to that question?

A. They are supremely confident that Trump will clean out both agencies. They were almost as confident that Hillary would use them as models to corrupt other agencies.

Q. Was that the issue that sold you on Trump?

A. I have a larger ambition for him. I think he has a puncher's chance to break the grip of the Iron Quadrangle that controls our political culture: the one-party government bureaucracy; the pay-to-play rent seekers; the tax-exempt Left; and the symbiotic media class—roughly speaking, everybody who's ever thought of associating themselves with the Clinton Global Initiative.

Q. Why do you think he has even a puncher's chance?

A. He's instinctively anti-bureaucratic. And highly skilled in the recriminative arts.

Q. What else did you learn from the Trump voters?

A. I learned that conservative intellectuals have failed them, redundantly, on the issue of immigration. The first-level effects of incumbent policy, both cultural and economic, fall on rural America, border America, and deindustrializing America. The Acela corridor, by contrast, has felt only third-level effects, none of them material. My view has long been that the core mission of the conservative movement is to protect the inherited culture and bolster the opportunity economy. We blew it.

Q. What should our immigration policy be now?

A. We should adopt a pro-American policy. Border security first, and then if an applicant can help us—if he's clean legally and medically and brings needed skills or capital investment—we want him. If he wants to spend more time with his relatives, that's an argument for a guest permit, not citizenship.

Q. Have conservative intellectuals failed in the same way on the trade issue?

A. No, we've failed in a different way. The case for free trade is intellectually unassailable but politically indefensible. We offer no comfort to the two guys who've just been fired when we report that three other guys have just been hired. It's the classic squeeze—concentrated pain in tension with dispersed benefit.

Q. What should conservatives do now?

A. We should make the case for the free economy aggressively, but consider it a legitimate activity of state government to help those whacked by the swinging door of free trade. In other words, we should palliate individual pain while spreading the general prosperity.

Q. Was that Trump's position?

A. For a time. He sensed the power of the idea early on, but then bent it out of shape. By the end of the campaign, he seemed to be supporting the proposition that companies exist not to make salable products but to preserve high-paying jobs.

Q. What's ahead for the conservative movement?

A. With nuances aplenty, there are two basic options. The first is to withdraw to the castle, pull up the drawbridge, and labor to defend market share in what has become a tax-privileged and well-upholstered Conservatism, Inc. I was at one D.C.-based shop this week that took all of 45 minutes to adopt this "strategic plan." That was a very Beltway thing to do.

Q. And the other option?

A. The other option is to recognize that the game has changed, thanks in large part to the inadvertent contribution of Donald J. Trump. He has identified and at least semi-organized a large constituency previously unreachable by Conservatism, Inc.—soft Democrats, fallen Republicans, distracted moms, disheartened vets, category-averse minorities, regulation-strangled business people, country-class patriots, and more, many more. The only common denominator among these disparate groups is their values. They're pro-family, pro-enterprise, and pro-America—pretty much the kinds of people our movement has claimed to represent these many years.

Q. And you're suggesting that conservative intellectuals should make common cause with the Trump voters?

A. It's the kind of coalition-building opportunity that comes around once in a generation. Think of the religious conservatives. Think of the neoconservatives. This opportunity is knocking loudly enough for even the hearing-impaired.

Q. What are your personal hopes for the movement?

A. My hope is that I'll wake up tomorrow and be 48 years old and the editor of *National Review* magazine. It's the best job in the country right now.

RONALD REAGAN
(WITH A NOD TO
BARRY GOLDWATER)

The American Spectator
July 1, 2005

REAGAN AT FIRST GLANCE

I first met Ronald Reagan in the early '70s. It was not, as they might have said in one his B-movie scripts, an auspicious beginning.

At the time I was the editor of King Features, the Hearst-owned syndicate that then billed itself immodestly but not all that inaccurately as the "world's largest newspaper syndicate." We syndicated everything you were likely to find in a metro newspaper, from comic strips (Blondie, Beetle Bailey) to self-help gurus (Heloise, Dr. Joyce Brothers) to wisdom-dispensing pundits (Bob Considine, William F. Buckley Jr.). Then there were the real moneymakers—the crossword puzzles, horoscopes, stock market tips, news photos, dress patterns, architectural drawings and such like. Each day we distributed to thousands of papers around the world a firehose-spray of editorial copy. We also distributed a steady flow of features that we labeled "gossip," which was what we called the spicy stuff that we wanted to use but had been unable to verify. The reigning monarch of King Features gossip when I arrived was the legendary Walter Winchell, he of the police radio, the ubiquitous tipsters and the staccato, three-dot prose style. Walter had been a dominant figure in both print and electronic media for 30 years, a classic newspaper columnist and a brilliant radio commentator. For decades, Mr. and Mrs. America, as he called his audience, couldn't seem to get enough of his brassy, apparently inside dope. But that had been more than a few years back during his salad days. As it happens to all writers sooner or later, he had begun to repeat himself and, even more problematic for his boy editor (me), he had begun to make stuff up. Bad stuff. About people who could afford to hire lawyers. Toward the end of his career, and the beginning of mine, Walter had become a litigation-breeder—a money-draining, time-devouring lawsuit magnet—and it became my unhappy duty to retire him after one of the most spectacular careers in the history of American journalism.

Thus was born the career of one Robin Adams Sloan, a saucier-than-thou gossip columnist who not only succeeded Winchell but quickly became the rage of the syndication business, appearing in hundreds of newspapers around the country. Robin Adams Sloan was a flat-out hit. Every column produced hundreds of letters, praising, yelping, goading us on. Unlike Winchell, however, Sloan was a dream to work with—no creative differences, no deadline crises, no hassle. Sloan quickly became my model employee because, I now confess, Sloan did not exist. Like a general fighting the previous war, I had resolved to syndicate the un-Winchell, and in Sloan I found an androgenous byline behind which lurked no personality quirks whatsoever. After wrestling with such cantankerous personalities as Jimmy Cannon, Jim Bishop, Westbrook Pegler and the other talented members of the Hearst stable, I had at last under my supervision a productive but completely malleable columnist. (On one occasion I even gave an interview to the press on behalf of the "absent" Sloan.) Most of the actual writing for the Sloan column was done by three well-placed sources in the media and entertainment worlds to whom I gave assurances of anonymity. Not a good idea. These well-informed sources were thus invited to let go with the full force of their private furies—and it would be left to me to stand behind their copy. Only later did it occur to me that this arrangement amounted to a kind of moral hazard, a journalistic version of the system that gave rise to the S&L crisis of the 1980s. That is to say, whenever A's risk is underwritten solely by B's credit, A is likely to slip the bonds of discipline.

Well, Robin Adams Sloan slipped the bonds of discipline early and often. We went after celebrities with gusto. We gave it to them, as a former president used to say, with the bark on. And we went after them in a crowd-pleasing way that made the column the talk of the business. And then perhaps inevitably, with the cheers of the crowd echoing in our ears, we went too far. One day my sources reported and I released an item stating that one of Hollywood's best known figures had ordered up a pubic merkin. Why, you may ask, would responsible journalists distribute such an item? What were we thinking about? To this day I have no explanation, but I do remember regretting the decision almost immediately, and then waiting apprehensively for the inevitable wave of criticism and quite possibly legal complaint.

For some reason, no doubt providential, there followed nothing but silence. While even innocuous filler about an upcoming movie would draw heavy-breathing mail for Sloan, about our lapse into monumentally bad taste there was no comment whatsoever. (A colleague pointed out helpfully that abridged dictionaries usually omit the word merkin.) But we had learned a lesson, nonetheless. We had to tighten up and we did. The moral hazard was dissolved, the editorial lines were untangled and the column was set on a more responsible course. Robin Adams Sloan settled quickly (and, for those of us who had reveled in the rock-em, sock-em days, a bit sadly) into journalistic responsibility. But even as we locked the barn door we learned that at least one horse had escaped.

One of the items we published in the Sloan column reported that Ronald Reagan, then recently re-elected as governor of California, had taken to dying his famously chestnut-brown hair. I noted the item when it came across my desk, called Robin (I thought of my three sources as, respectively, Robin, Adams and Sloan) and asked where she got the item. She replied that the item was hard, that it had in fact come directly from Reagan's barber. That was good enough for me. It seemed scarcely man-bites-dog news that a middle-aged man with a background in Hollywood and a foreground in politics would color his hair. No big deal. Soon after the story was published around the country, however, we began to hear a distant rumble from southern California. To at least one member of the Reagan family, it appeared that the story was at least a medium-big deal. The governor's wife, Nancy, passed word to us that the story was untrue and that she would appreciate it if we corrected the record as soon as possible. I checked again with our source's source, the barber in question, and he reaffirmed his account. He said he even had clippings to prove the point. Thus reassured, I brushed aside Mrs. Reagan's objections with what I hoped was a polite but professional and case-closing note. No big deal. What I then encountered, however, was not Frank Sinatra's Nancy with the laughing eyes, but rather Ronnie's Nancy with the sharpened claws. In a series of escalating moves and feints, she began to make it clear that the deal was not only big but that it wasn't going away. Not only was

Nancy Reagan a resolute and resourceful infighter, but she happened to be married to the governor of a state in which the Hearst Corporation owned major media, real estate and other politically sensitive properties. On one occasion, she deftly brought it to my attention that the Reagans counted among their personal friends the publishers of Hearst newspapers in Los Angeles and San Francisco, both of whom, as luck would have it, were named Hearst. I began to see my young corporate career flashing before my eyes. I was not at all sure that the Hearsts' professed admiration for fearless newspapering extended to coverage of their highly placed political friends.

It was against this background that I received, out of the blue, an invitation to lunch with Ronald Reagan. A mutual friend, a conservative publisher, called to suggest that it might be good for me to meet the rising political star and, in a bit of forced symmetry, that it might be good for him to get to know me. I jumped at the chance. The arrangements were set for a quiet, elegant restaurant on Manhattan's East Side, and I arrived promptly at the appointed hour. Just as my friend and I sat down in the private room off the main dining area, Reagan strode in. I didn't actually see him—my back was to the door—but I felt him. As I was to be reminded many times over the following years, Ronald Reagan brought with him to every encounter a magnetic field of personal charisma. Amid a cloud of bonhomie and rosebud cheeks, with the hanky squared and his suit just back from the dry cleaners, you would have no trouble casting him as . . . the rising political star. He greeted us as soon-to-be old friends and introduced us to his two bodyguards, who then stationed themselves at the door to block any unannounced visitors. The sight of these two large, crewcut men with plugs in their ears, motionless except for darting eyes that followed every clam perseille to every pair of thin lips, would have chilled most dining rooms. Not this one. It was an international hotspot just a few blocks from the United Nations and favored by ambassadors, high-powered emissaries and security details. Probably a third of the men in the room were concealing firearms. (That's not a sexist remark, by the way. In those days, the ladies who went to lunch did so unarmed.)

We took our seats with Reagan in the middle, I to his right. And the investigation commenced. Every time that Reagan turned to speak to my friend, I would lean in and squint at the hairs on Reagan's neck. Conditions were good. The lighting was lunch-bright and not dinner-intimate. And Reagan had one of those 1950s buzz haircuts up the back and over his ears. By the third squint, I was convinced. Dammit. There was but a single grey hair peeking from his neck, just the touch to lend verisimilitude to Nancy's claim. Whatever his other vanities might be, Reagan was not dying his hair. ("Thank you, waiter, I'll have the braised crow in a light mustard sauce.") With that piece of business completed, I then joined the conversation in progress and was soon engulfed by the legendary Reagan charm. First, the jokes. The wide world has heard many of them, some several times. The private versions tend to be only a little more politically incorrect and thus involve more Poles and priests and fat girls and horny guys and other unmentionables. Even so, nothing truly scandalous. But over the years people from every corner of the human condition have found the experience thoroughly enjoyable—partly because the jokes are oldies but goodies, partly because Reagan's rendition of them is so polished and most of all because few people can resist the very idea that Ronald Reagan is taking the trouble to entertain them.

After the jokes and the appetizers, we got down to what politicians refer to as The Substance. Issues. Goals. Tactics. Extended conversations with politicians, of course, tend to be heavily autobiographical and in this respect Reagan proved to be no exception. From both his comments and his questions it was clear to me that he wanted to be president and that he was prepared to take risks to achieve that objective. But his ambition for the office seemed to be neither palpable nor ravenous. In a way it was not even personal. As many observers have remarked over the course of his career, he was comfortable with who he was and, unlike many politicians, he did not crave political eminence merely to validate his sense of purpose or self-worth. He was in politics, it seemed to me on this first meeting, for the right reason: he saw his political career as an efficient vehicle for advancing important ideas. Much to my surprise, the longer he talked the more plausible his White House ambitions began to sound. Surprise, indeed. Remember, I was living and working close to the heart of the Eastern media world where it had long been established wisdom that Reagan was a lightweight cowboy actor who would never be a serious national figure. I like to think that I began to form my own opinion of Ronald Reagan that day.

But first I had to fix things with the missus. In a series of calls, letters and public grovelings that will one day win me at least a footnote in the history of sycophancy, we finally secured Mrs. Reagan's forgiveness. It had to be done. We had made a mistake and we had to make it right. For Mrs. Reagan, even in victory it was still a big deal. She had won one for her man, she was greatly relieved and, toward me, she was in the end thoroughly gracious, as if we had worked together toward a mutual goal. We never became friends—this was a much larger episode in my life than hers—but we established a working relationship that carried on into her White House days when, by that time a television producer, I helped produce spots for her Just Say No anti-drug and Foster Grandparents programs.

As for the governor, he and I began a long distance, very one-sided political courtship. I would look for opportunities to build up our tenuous relationship, sending him clips and speech ideas from time to time, pointing out a media opening here, a fundraising salient there. He or his associates would respond just often enough to keep the channels open. By the time of his bold and nearly successful challenge to incumbent Gerald Ford in the Republican primaries of 1976, Reagan had made it clear to all who would see that he was no mere cowboy actor. He was, rather, the finest piece of political horshflesh that most pros would ever have the chance to see and he had established himself as the odds-on favorite to win the Triple Crown in 1980—the primaries, the nomination and the White House. By the late '70s I had become a political columnist, openly and ardently pro-Reagan (and not infrequently the beneficiary of leaks from his organization). And by the time he was sworn in as president in 1981, there remained for me only one more question to be answered about Ronald Reagan. Would I help his "revolution" by working inside the administration, or by continuing my work in the private sector?

As so often happens in political life, the answer that finally emerged was, "none of the above." After a series of stop-start talks with White House aides, I became both an independent contractor and a political appointee. The contract called for me to provide video production services to the White House. Loosely translated from the bureaucratese, I was hired to produce the president's video messages—everything from his New Year's greeting to the Soviet people to his salute to the newly elected President of Peru to his toast to Mr. and Mrs. Lew Wasserman on the occasion of their 50th wedding anniversary. This type of "video message" is now a standard item in the communications toolbox. At the time, however, it was new and different and born of necessity. Pressed for time in the presidential schedule—and always eager to avoid the marginal plane ride—Reagan began to travel to ceremonial events "by television." And what was seen at first as a poor substitute for the President's personal appearance became in time what political observers regarded as still another brilliant innovation by the Great Communicator. You have probably consumed a few of these messages yourself. At a ballroom dinner—and not infrequently at simultaneous ballroom dinners at the far ends of this large country—the lights would dim, a baritone voice would intone, "Ladies and gentlemen, the President of the United States . . ." and there, on a 50-by-30-foot screen, would appear the reassuringly familiar face of the Leader of the Free World. In the early days, we would send or satellite these tapes with quasi-apologies, stressing that only history-sized events had prevented the president from joining the fun that night in Omaha or wherever. As the program rolled out, however, it was soon demonstrated that the impression he made by videotape was far more powerful than if he had walked on stage, appearing ant-sized to those in the back row, and delivered a few weary remarks at the end of a long dinner program tacked on to the end of a long flight. It turned out to be a win-win-win. The president got his sleep. The diners got a star turn. And the host organization got a professional videotape for promotional use.

By the second term, Reagan was turning out these video messages by the dozens. On most Thursday afternoons, if he was in Washington, he would devote several hours to this outreach effort, perceiving in each video the opportunity to win friends and influence people for his program. It was often said of Reagan by some of the journalists who covered him and virtually all of his political opponents that he was inattentive and unfocused in the conduct of his office. I can say with authority that, when it came to articulating his ideas and radiating them to important constituencies, there is no basis to the charge. He edited professionally, he practiced conscientiously and he advocated brilliantly. He is reported to have said, when asked to respond to the charge that as an actor he was unqualified to be president, that he could not imagine discharging the duties of the office without the skills he had learned as an actor. Just so. Reagan reminded us that the office itself has few powers if the incumbent cannot rally the people to his cause.

By 1983, I was pleased to be offered a presidential appointment to the Board of Directors of Comsat (short for The Communications Satellite Corporation), which was the principal U.S. provider of global communications to many voice, video and data customers. The appointment was satisfying at several levels. It engaged my career-long interest in communications technology; it afforded me the opportunity to represent the president in national affairs; and, inasmuch as it was a part-time assignment, it permitted me to pursue my private business interests. I accepted with genuine pleasure.

How did I get the job? Any presidential appointee who tells you he knows the definitive answer to that question is either under-informed or less than candid. All of the pertinent discussions are held, and all of the critical decisions taken, at meetings to which you have not been invited. Such was the case with my appointment. I like to think that the president summed up the discussion by saying, "Neal Freeman is one of the truly outstanding communications executives in the world today. Our policy initiatives, the administration and indeed the future of the American economy will benefit greatly from his service in this key post." But then again, he might have said, "Comsat, schmomsat. How much damage could he really do?" I'll never know. When the presidential aide called to give me the news, of course, he trod carefully along the former line. And then he closed the conversation with a reference to our earlier conversations about international telecommunications, reminding me to stay in touch about "that privatization thing."

National Review
May 2, 1980

WAITING FOR RONNIE

We liken the mood of your nation's capital to the mood of Greater New York in November of 1970. In that dark hour for the Republic, a moment of electoral aberration in which James Lane (Fangs) Buckley was elected to the United States Senate, the suburban daily *Newsday* epitomized the icy fear that gripped the metropolis. "It crept in during the night . . ." began *Newsday*'s day-after election report. The story went on in a prose style usually reserved for promoting drive-in movies. To *Newsday*'s half-million readers, mild-mannered Jim Buckley became The Creature That Ate New York.

We were reminded of this great moment in journalism by recent coverage of the Reagan campaign. It has changed, we note, from casual disdain to agitated concern, from a smirk to a growl. The Reagan campaign, just another road show a few months ago, has become The Problem That Won't Go Away. The premonition has crept into Chevy Chase that Ronald Reagan just might be our next president.

As the chimerical candidacies of Ted Kennedy and John Anderson drift off into the media ether, the stark reality obtrudes. Hear Joe Kraft stammering the godawful truth: "The depressing prospect of having to choose between Jimmy Carter and Ronald Reagan this fall forces a Job-like question. Why? Oh Lord, why?" Poor Joe. Having endorsed the two-party system and ruled Jimmy Carter unacceptable, Joe is scraping the bottom of his option barrel. It may be time to scramble for the rhetorical lifeboats, men.

A third-party effort by John Anderson provides a way-station, of course, for those who *simply refuse to believe* that Ronald Reagan can be elected. Some will stick with Anderson, no doubt, as the only acceptable candidate in this year's thicket of Job-like questions. But as his poll ratings start to slump, as he is disqualified from the ballot in major states, and as he reveals the petulant side of his personality, his support will disappear: the cry of "all the way with JBA" will echo down the empty streets of Madison, Wisconsin. Thus the central question of the 1980 campaign: How to deal with Reagan?

One response, peeking up here and there, is the hint that Reagan isn't what he seems; that he may be, in fact, something of a closet liberal. This hint has surfaced in Ellen Goodman's syndicated column and, at the other end of the spectrum, in *Human Events*. Mrs. Goodman reminds us that Governor Reagan signed a "liberal" abortion law, that he once supported the ERA, and that he signed 66 bills "supported and/or initiated by the California State Commission on the Status of Women." Dream on, sister. For its part, *Human Events* has launched a preemptive strike against Reagan's logical choice for vice president, Howard Baker; the Tennesseean is so liberal that his selection would amount to a "betrayal" of conservatives, says the Washington weekly. Shades of 1964. If Reagan can't reach out as far as Howard Baker, a man smack dab in the middle of a deeply conservative GOP Senate caucus, now comes (Bill) Miller time.

Another response, more widely evident, is a redoubled effort to cut Reagan down before his campaign gathers undeniable momentum. This faction of the press has no love for Jimmy Carter, but it answers the call to the Higher Pragmatism. Consider Stephen Rosenfeld, who covers foreign affairs for the *Washington Post*. Way back in 1976, Rosenfeld perceived in candidate Carter the virtues of fresh perspective and the gritty experience of executive office. The "outsider" could make contributions of great value to the incestuous community of foreign-policy experts. By 1980, with admirable candor, as they say, Rosenfeld tells his readers that he now sees things differently. What is clearly needed is an incumbent's savvy.

Rosenfeld is clearing the decks in preparation for what, we guess, will be a sustained attack on Reagan's inexperience in foreign affairs. Already moving to the offensive is Lou Cannon, the *Post*'s political reporter, a Californian who, it is hoped, cannot be accused of regional bias. Cannon has no patience with the cliché arguments about Reagan's age or ideological extremism. He has traveled with Reagan's campaign often enough to know that the candidate runs men half his age into the ground. And he was close enough to Reagan during his years in Sacramento to know that the former governor is a moderate, fair-minded man. The charges of kookery will not stick, however often they may be re-applied. Cannon has, instead, minted a new argument against a Reagan presidency—the man is not too old, he's not too right-wing, he's too *dumb*.

Cannon's line has already been picked up elsewhere—*The New Yorker* magazine and CBS News have played variations on the theme. Over the next month we can say with some assurance that it will pop up *passim*, tracing the influence lines of the media system with all the precision of a barium test. The line will spread for two reasons. First, because it's a line with which the best and the brightest are utterly comfortable. It plays directly to the presumption of the Eastern elite about an ex-actor from California. And second, the line will spread because it is so difficult to rebut. (One remembers poor Senator Scott of Virginia. He was named by *New Times* as the dumbest member of the U.S. Congress. When he held a press conference to deny the charge, he appeared to confirm the estimate.)

It's been an interesting year already. The idea of a Reagan candidacy was plainly meant to frighten us. Back in January, it was because he was too old—Do we want William Henry Harrison's finger on the button? Then in February, it was because he was too docile—Do we want John Sears's finger on the button? By March the real threat was Reagan's extremism—Do we want J. R. Ewing's finger on the button? Now, come spring, we're told that he just doesn't have the smarts—Do we want Chauncey Gardiner's finger on the button?

Ronald Reagan, clearly the smartest of this year's candidate crop, has 'em just about where he wants 'em.

National Review
September 19, 1980

THE FIRST HUNDRED DAYS

G eneral Tooey Spaatz is best remembered at the Pentagon for two things. The first is his name. It is said that during his long career he was never confused with another Tooey Spaatz. The second is the set of rules he laid down for Air Force officers testifying before congressional committees. After years of refining them, General Spaatz gave his boys these simple, practical instructions: 1) Don't try to be funny. 2) Don't lie. 3) Don't blurt out the truth.

Tooey would have made a helluva campaign manager. A columnist observing the current campaign thinks wistfully of the possibilities: suppose, just suppose, that the Republican candidate in each of his meetings with the press had observed not one, not two, but all three of Tooey's rules? If he had done so, Dr. Gallup and Dr. Harris would be meeting under the Central Park aqueduct at midnight, making furtive arrangements to restore their reputations for psephological probity. The race would be over, with Carter and Anderson fighting for last.

Recent campaign developments suggest otherwise, however. They suggest the possibility—*the possibility*—that our long national nightmare may not be ended on November 4. It may on that account be useful, even therapeutic, to look across the valley of the autumn to the hilltop of the winter and contemplate the shape of a Ronald Reagan administration.

Even his critics agree that Reagan has the ability to select outstanding subordinates and the strength of personality to give them broad discretionary powers. We can expect with confidence that a Reagan Cabinet would be exceptional, led by such men as George Shultz (probably at State, the only portfolio he would accept), Paul Nitze (Defense, an appointment long overdue), Donald Rumsfeld (at Treasury, for both personal and political reasons), William Simon (World Bank, a turnaround situation), and William Casey (CIA, likewise). Perhaps the most exceptional appointments, however, would turn out to be the "unknown" members of the Cabinet, men and women plucked from the business and academic worlds for temporary duty in Washington. Reagan's California record in this regard is unassailably impressive.

In terms of government operation, several important consequences would flow from such a personnel strategy. First, with strong leadership at the department level, the vise-grip of the White House staff on policy development would be loosened if not broken. Meanwhile—the other side of the coin—we would not be shocked to see Cabinet secretaries establish offices in the Executive Office Building next to the White House. And there would be more than symbolism involved in the move: The secretaries would be working for the White House, not for the departmental bureaucracy they "represent."

Second, with the establishment of Cabinet government, or something resembling it, there would follow a proliferation of contact points with the policy-making process. If the White House staff slams the door, there would be an appellate mechanism at the department level. The president and his senior staff would then be obliged to arbitrate the disputes. Cabinet meetings would thus become decision-making sessions rather than photo opportunities (in the Nixon mode) or discussion groups (in the Carter mode).

Along with the organizational changes in the Executive branch, a new Reagan administration would try to change the mindset of top-level bureaucrats. One can imagine a freshly inaugurated Reagan announcing to the Senior Executive Service a first-year goal of 10 percent reduction in all federal employment.

One can just as easily imagine first-year reviews in the media dwelling on the fact that Reagan, for all his bluster, had come up short. What those reviews would have missed—and in fact what all the critiques of Reagan's years in Sacramento have missed—is the change in mindset. To persuade a bureaucrat even to think in terms of force reduction, rather than of irresistible growth, is a heroic management achievement. Reagan's amiable personality would help to lubricate the organizational gearshifts. Unlike Carter, he is not stubborn, he is not standoffish. While playing the political game may not be his favorite pastime, Reagan demonstrated in California that when he had to do business with the local Tip O'Neills he could do it effectively.

The same degree of specificity would distinguish a first-hundred-days call for budget cuts. We can hear it now. Eliminate Amtrak. Close the spigots at the National Endowments. Repeal Davis-Bacon. *Cut back the school lunch program!* The media would gasp, the Hill barons would do a slow burn, and the bureaucrats would say, "No way, boss. Can't be done." Again, those year-end media reviews might turn in poor grades, but they would have missed the point that, superb communicator that he is, Reagan had fundamentally altered their perception of political success.

Perhaps the boldest stroke of them all would be General Reagan's Inchon Landing on Capitol Hill. Reagan would open an office on the Hill and begin courting congressional allies in both parties. Congressional figures would be recruited for the Cabinet, Democrats among them. Others would serve as whips building bipartisan coalitions around clusters of social, economic, and international issues. Reagan would try to break through the institutionalized hostility that now controls the Executive-Legislative relationship and make common cause against the forces of fragmentation—the special-interest lobbies, the single-issue groups, the innumerable "communities." Responding to a recognizably patriotic impulse, he would attempt to create an environment in which a sense of renewed national purpose could take root.

What do you say, gang. Let's win this one for the Spaatzer.

National Review
May 15, 1981

Winning One for The Quipper

I n Evelyn Waugh's novel *Scoop*, there is a wickedly satirical scene, one of many, in which William Boot, confused with an illustrious journalist of the same surname by Lord Copper of Fleet Street, is dispatched to cover the hostilities in far-off Ishmaelia. Appointed a "special" for the daily *Beast*, Boot fumbles through a briefing with His Lordship's managing editor before inquiring finally, "Well, there is one thing. You see I don't read the papers very much. Can you tell me who is fighting who in Ishmaelia?"

The managing editor, Salter, replies: "I think it's the Patriots and the Traitors."

To which Boot responds: "Yes, but which is which?"

Waugh's delicious bit of dialogue does double duty for us today. It reminds us not only of the pretensions of so-called investigative, so-called reporting, but also of the importance of political definition. For the struggle is always and everywhere, is it not, between the Patriots and the Traitors, and the semantic trick is to affix the proper labels before the belligerents engage. If one is interested in limiting union power, for instance, one might champion the "right to work." If one wishes to trivialize the Afghan resistance, for another instance, anti-Soviet forces can be designated "rebels." If one wishes to maintain monopoly profits in media businesses, one can hold high the banner of "the people's right to know." And yes, if truth be told, if one wants to give the productive class a tax break, one is well situated to witness the birth of a new social science called "supply-side economics." Our journalism has become a child's garden of rhetorical conceits. All of which is a roundabout way of explaining why the coming of Ronald Reagan has been an event of such significance.

Let us say first off that we did not fully appreciate the power of his voice or the gift of his leadership until he was struck down. It is only in the last few weeks, during the period of his recovery in hospital and his recuperation at home, that we have noticed the slackening pace of his revolution. So amiable has he been, so reassuring was his manner in assuming the "burdens" of the presidential office, that we scarcely remarked the speed with which familiar scenery was passing our express-train window. It is only now in the relative quiet of his convalescence that his ambition becomes apparent. He means to carve out a new role for government at home and a new role for America in the world. Frankly, it had never crossed our capitolized mind that he intended to do *exactly* what he said he would do. But there is the plan, his plan, for all the world to see. It's a revolution, quite evidently, but he *says* he is shoring up our defenses and revitalizing our economy and it sounds like just a little more of the same, only better. Who could oppose common sense? he asks with a shrug. And virtually nobody does.

Then comes the Hinckley bullet, time stands still, and, while the president rests in Nancy's solarium, other men good and true are left to carry on the battle: George Bush, Jim Baker, Dave Stockman, and Ed Meese. They push hard on the staff and hard on the Hill and hardest of all on themselves. They want desperately to win this one for The Quipper. But the results are slow in coming and the first gossamer lines of political opposition begin to form. In the battle for spending cuts, precious momentum is lost when three conservative senators, two of them beneficiaries of Reagan's coattails just a few months ago, jump ship. On the House side, a Democratic member senses an opening and produces an "alternative budget." Instead of sweeping all before it in a tidal wave of political inevitability the administration now finds itself locked in a line-by-line debate with a balding congressman from Oklahoma named Jones. The revolution cools and the chapped-finger crowd recalculates the odds. More time is lost. On the foreign policy front there is more trouble. The Senate Foreign Relations Committee, which must pass on all of Reagan's nominees for policymaking jobs, goes into a deliberative trance. The president's man for African Affairs, Chester Crocker, is too liberal and the president's man for Law of the Seas, Jim Malone, is too conservative, and as for Ernest Lefever and Tom Pauken and Lawrence Eagleburger, well, they're all too something. April turns into May and the Senate has still not given the president the help he says he needs.

For the first time, the White House staff begins to put the knock on the Senate. Howard Baker is to blame for settling for a 9 to 8 Republican-Democrat ratio on Foreign Relations. With 9 to 7 or even 10 to 8 we would be home free, they say. And Chuck Percy, the chairman, is to blame for letting Cranston call the committee tune. We're the majority now. Let's act like it. And what about Mathias? Who let *him* become the swing vote on that committee? Are we going to be held hostage for four years to his private agenda? And so on and so on. Loser's talk, all of it. The kind of talk that the president, were he in the room, would silence with a casual wave of the hand. Without looking at anybody in particular, he would duck his head to one side, smile, and say, "You fellas sound like the guys we voted out of here last November." It is the president's cruelest cut but it draws no blood.

George Bush does his best, which, just now, in these extraordinary circumstances, is not good enough. He gropes for but cannot locate the fresh formulations that redescribe and thus redefine the choices in political life. He seeks instinctively the familiar ground of code-word rhetoric and the opposition, reassured and emboldened, moves in its customary way to confront him. How very different from wrestling with the political chimera of Ronald Reagan! That same chimera who with a sad smile could dismiss an incumbent president as a petulant incompetent—mute his quest for a radically transformed America into an old-shoe summons to common sense—and, in a moment of personal heroism, call back a nation of believers from the edge of cynicism.

National Review
June 28, 2004

One of Us

Ronald Reagan gave me the worst job I ever had. He awarded my firm a contract to produce his video appearances from the White House. I thought it was a dream assignment until the first time I sent a crew into the Oval Office. That's when it dawned on me. There were only two possible outcomes to every shoot: The public would whistle appreciatively, "That Reagan. What a great communicator!" Or they'd snarl, "Who did that to him? What's the name of that nitwit producer?" We considered it a small triumph that we managed to labor for years in fearful anonymity. The alternative was to find instant fame as the guys who managed to make Ronald Reagan look bad on television.

For all its high anxiety, the job had its moments. For openers, we got to hang out with the Leader of the Free World. We were under strict Jim Bakerly instructions to discuss only the shoot itself, no freelance "face time," in the phrase of the day. Fat chance. We chatted up the president on sports and comics and, finding him completely approachable, moved on to personnel, policies (where there was a distinction), and other radioactive matter. He had, as has been noted by another commentator or two, a winning personality.

On one of these occasions, I crossed that broad line between cheekiness and chutzpah and asked the president if he would attend the premiere of a film I was then finishing. It was called *Conservatives* and it was the kind of piece about which people tended to form strong opinions. Not to put too fine a point on it, the film was being trashed by the trendier media, and even the hint of a presidential endorsement would help me regain lost ground. Reagan listened to the request, gave me one of those nods, and said, "Would it be all right if I said a few words?" Only my Welsh genes restrained me from hugging the man.

Shortly before the great event, Reagan was diagnosed with colon cancer and underwent major surgery. He was sent to Camp David to recuperate, which meant that doctors, and Nancy, were controlling events. His condition was serious, whatever the press releases might be saying. I was frightened for Reagan and disappointed that my "Special Guest" would not be making an appearance at the Kennedy Center premiere. The morning of the event, as I was still scrambling to assemble the program, the Signal Corps called to ask whether they could string a line from Camp David into the theater: The president wanted to say a few words. I replied that they had my permission to dig up Pennsylvania Avenue from end to end.

On the way home that night, I told my wife that there may be few better feelings in life than sitting in front of 500 of your friends listening to the President of the United States tell them what a helluva guy you are.

I tell this story because, obviously, I like to tell this story. Who wouldn't? But I would be willing to bet that there are hundreds, perhaps thousands, of people reading this page who had similar encounters with Ronald Reagan. Vivid, personal encounters that organized your impressions of the man and fixed them in your calculation for all time. He was always described by the media middlemen as the Great Communicator, a technician in the arcane field of mass persuasion. What those analyses always missed was that he built his circle of colleagues, and then his circle of admirers, one relationship at a time. Sure, he mastered television, but he used it only as a time-saving device: He still spoke to his listeners one by one. And when he did, we came to realize, it was only after he had listened carefully to what was on our minds.

Smart Washington used to make fun of Reagan's note writing and phone calling. He would send a check to a sick child, give a pep talk to an unemployed worker. He was a sucker for a hard-luck story. The smarties never seemed to figure out that he was one of *us*, and that he had no secret ambition to be one of *them*.

Think back to some of the moments that define your own memory of him. Foremost, perhaps, the assassination attempt. Breathes there an American boy who has not dreamed of taking a bullet for the flag? Who has not hoped against hope that, when the day came, he wouldn't whimper and feel a tear slide down his cheek? When Reagan was wheeled into the operating room, looked up at his doctors, and joked, "I hope you're all Republicans," he took the pressure off them, and then off us. He closed the emotional sale with the American public: He acted the way we hope we would act in that moment, and fear we wouldn't.

Or go back to his first turn on the political stage, his speech for Barry Goldwater on October 27, 1964. Goldwater is on the last lap of a landslide defeat. Reagan wants to make it clear that he stands with Goldwater, a clarity upon which few were then insisting. The rats had already checked out of their staterooms. Reagan strides onstage and rips through riffs on welfare, taxes, the Commies—and then says, directly to the camera: "You and I have a rendezvous with destiny. We will preserve for our children this, the last best hope of man on earth, or we will sentence them to take the last step into a thousand years of darkness." You heard him: a rendezvous with destiny. Jimmy Carter could arrange a get-together, Bush a power breakfast, Clinton a bull session. But this was something *bigger*.

Or slip forward to January 28, 1986. The space shuttle *Challenger* has just exploded and awkward silence has fallen over every conversation in America. It is 5 P.M. here in the East and I happen to be holding the hand of my terrified 13-year-old daughter. Reagan scraps the State of the Union speech he had planned to deliver that night and, instead, goes live with this statement from the Oval Office: "And I want to say something to the schoolchildren of America who were watching the live coverage of the shuttle's takeoff. I know it is hard to understand, but sometimes painful things like this happen. It's all part of the process of exploration and discovery. It's all part of taking a chance and expanding man's horizons. The future doesn't belong to the fainthearted; it belongs to the brave. The *Challenger* crew was pulling us into the future, and we'll continue to follow them." He said it for the rest of us.

And he did it again and again. As we fumbled for the words, he found them. As we sorted through our feelings, he felt them. By creating this intimacy between himself and his fellow citizens, he generated an extraordinary rhetorical power: He was the only public speaker of his time who could make grown men cry, with tears of patriotic joy. Ronald Reagan saw us Americans as heroes with a high calling. And for seeing us that way, we loved him.

Privately Published
October 1992

Comsat

When I got to Comsat in 1983, it was more of a small large company than a large small company. It was doing a few hundred million in revenue, placing it in the bottom half of the Fortune 1000. But it was a large company in defining ways—large in ambition, large in corporate manner, large in bureaucratic appurtenance. It was also the largest single shareholder of Intelsat, Ltd., the global satellite system.

Comsat's ambition could not have been larger. An idea born in the ebullient days of the Kennedy-Johnson Sixties, the company proposed to knit together the human family by building a global telecommunications network. In those days, one could not just pick up a telephone and let one's fingers do the walking from one end of the known world to the other. Data networks were a sometime, somewhere thing and e-mail was a term not yet coined to describe a phenomenon that existed only in the fevered imaginations of futurists. When you made a phone call, or transmitted alpha-numeric information, you could do so only along the prescribed pathways of dedicated pipelines. Most of these pipelines were the famous "twisted pairs," the copper lines strung by the great national telephone companies, and they were directed for the most part from one population center to another. That is, the networks transmitted signals only from one point to one other point, not from one point to many other points. If the pipelines didn't happen to go where you wished to send your message, you had an alternative, but it was slow, expensive and not altogether reliable. It was called the U.S. Postal Service. The Comsat proposition was thus both large and galvanizing: suppose you could use high technology to allow businesses to become global, to allow families to reconnect with each other, to allow information to flow freely, so as to open minds and spread ideas and lift spirits? Suppose, in sum, that you could communicate as easily with somebody halfway around the world as you could with somebody halfway down the block? Suppose you could shrink the world to neighborhood scale?

As with all new and large ideas, the Comsat proposition was met with initial skepticism. Some technologists said it couldn't be done. Some financiers said it would be too expensive. Some bureaucrats said it would be impossible to secure the necessary intergovernmental approvals. And some economists said that, even if you managed to overcome all of the launch obstacles, an insufficient number of customers would show up to support the system—if you built it, not enough of them would come. The skepticism was so thick that prospective investors were scared away from what appeared to be a very high-risk start-up. The Comsat proposition was, to use the ugly word of the day, unbankable. With no takers in the private markets, entrepreneurial ideas of the great-next-thing variety seldom make it out of the pediatric ward of economic life. Comsat got lucky. These were the heady days of the New Frontier, remember, and the U.S.

was in full bear-any-burden, pay-any-price mode. Comsat seemed to hit all of the hot buttons of the new Kennedy administration. It was new, it was big, it was high-tech, it would project American leadership and, not incidentally, it would make the post-Sputnik Russkies look like a bunch of techno-klutzes. The decision was thus taken by the White House to make a global satellite network happen.

In 1962, under heavy lobbying from the administration, Congress passed the Satellite Act. Its approach was innovative but straightforward. If the newly chartered company—called The Communications Satellite Corporation, or Comsat for short—could build or midwife a global satellite system, the company could keep the profits from its U.S. operations. To entice private investors to back the risky venture, that is, the government gave Comsat a commitment of U.S. exclusivity to the system. This commitment proved to be the needed catalyst. With its risks thus modulated, Comsat gained access to the private capital markets and proceeded to float what became one of the most ballyhooed initial public offerings in market history. More than a mere financial transaction, the Comsat IPO became almost a rite of patriotic affirmation. Parents were moved to buy shares for their children not just as an investment in Comsat but as an investment in America's future itself. As it happened, the first stock I ever owned was a handful of Comsat shares given to me by my father. He was a fairly sophisticated investor, but in this case he was acting as one of the men who won the Second World War and were not about to let the Soviets run off with the peace. Like dads everywhere I suspect, mine advised me to put the shares away for the long term.

As a congressionally chartered corporation, Comsat was born as a fully private company with its shares soon listed on the New York Stock Exchange, but it came with a few strings attached. One of them was that within the 15-member board, only twelve directors were to be elected by the holders of common stock. The other three were to represent, in addition to the shareholders' interest, the national interest embraced by Comsat's global mission. (The basic business of the company was the provision of voice, video and data communication services to customers around the world. But along the way, as you can imagine, we became privy to some sensitive information. We didn't talk much about that side of the business.) These three directors were to be appointed by the president with, as the Constitution prescribes, the advice and consent of the U.S. Senate. It was for one of these seats that President Reagan had nominated me. As far as the Senate was concerned, I anticipated no major problems with either advice or consent. I had been through the confirmation process a decade earlier following my appointment to the Corporation for Public Broadcasting and the ride had been fairly smooth along the winding road from form-filing to final floor vote. (It can warm even the chilliest morning to read in the Congressional Record that your nomination has been confirmed by a vote of 96 to 0.) What I did not appreciate in the Eighties was that Washington's atmospheric conditions had changed since the early Seventies. A third-rate burglary called Watergate had occurred in the interim and the politics of presidential appointment had become a bit more lively.

The confirmation process began with what is known as a full field audit by the FBI. Think of this exercise as the emotional equivalent of a colonoscopy. Scanning across the nation, the Bureau talks to dozens of people who knew you back when. The agents want to know about your education, your professional life, your character, your family and your habits. Lots of questions about habits. The agents have a special interest in people who were on the other side in a business, legal or political dispute. The agent tells the interviewees two things: first, that they are legally obliged to tell the truth; and second, that their identity will never be revealed. In other words, the interviewees are invited to take their best shot with no chance of reprisal. As far as I knew, I had no nomination-killers lurking out there—no ex-wives, no ex-partners, no former cellmates. But could there be a neighbor who didn't like my dog, or a former employee who knew a once-in-a-lifetime opportunity when he saw it, or a relative who suffered still with the thought that Mom always liked me best? I was not so sure. What do people really say about you, I found myself wondering, after they have been guaranteed anonymity by the Federal Bureau of Investigation?

Some years later, amazingly, I found out. Using the Freedom of Information Act, and outlasting a notably uncooperative bureaucracy, my wife managed to obtain a copy of my FBI file and presented it to me as a

Christmas present. Without reservation, I now recommend FBI files as the perfect gift for those difficult-to-buy-for guys and gals on your list. For while I think of myself as no more self-fascinated than the next person, I must report that I found my FBI file to be a real page-turner. For openers, it was redacted, which is to say that most proper names were blacked out to protect the Bureau's anonymous sources. For instance, the report of an interview might begin, "Blank Blank, a partner in the Boston engineering firm of Blank Blank and Blank, reports that he did business with the subject between 1968 and 1973." You will note that Blank is fully protected here. If my file happened to fall into the hands of an enterprising journalist or a business competitor, he would find it extremely difficult to discern Blank's identity. But when the file fell into my hands, I had no such problem. I knew exactly who Blank was. The file had been redacted, conveniently, for everyone but me.

As I say, it was a real page-turner. That file taught me much not just about how others saw me and my career but more generally about life in these contentious political times. First, it was reassuring to learn that most people tell the truth. Yes, memories fade around the edge and perspectives shift and spin happens. But when asked by the FBI to tell it straight, almost everybody does so. Even the co-workers you had to fire and the neighbors whose fence was crushed by your falling maple tree. For our fragile democracy, it seems to me, this is big news. Our civil society relies for its survival on the honor system and at least in this controlled ministudy the citizens passed with colors flying. The second lesson I took from the file was that paranoia is a waste of time and a thief of psychic energy. Most people are good at heart and large in spirit. If you have accomplished anything in life, there will be a few grumblers trailing along the path, but they are few in number and should be weighed light in memory. Even more important to my eye were the interviewees whom I regarded as no more than Rolodex acquaintances who revealed themselves, under oath, as committed friends. I record it as one of the deeply satisfying experiences of life to listen to friends, assured that their words will never reach your ears, declare their solidarity with you. The FBI file helped me make a few new friends for life.

With the audit complete, my "papers" went to the Senate. In addition

to the FBI file, the papers included highly detailed reports of business activities and financial holdings, along with a virtually month-by-month account of professional developments and residential movements. Taken
together, these papers represented an almost unimaginably comprehensive
and intrusive record of my life and work. (The word Orwellian really isn't
quite up to the job here.) There then followed a series of meetings with
both senators and staff members. The former were brief, ceremonial and
cordial. Senators tend to be charming people, after all. The latter were detailed, contentious and partisan. We spent several weeks, for instance, dis-
cussing the details of my financial life. The "vast Freeman fortune," as my
wife and I took to calling our modest, middle-class stake, was picked over
with the diligence of a CSI unit looking for trace amounts of toxicity. In
the mantra of the day, the staffers conceded that there were no genuine
conflicts embedded in my portfolio, but said they, repeatedly and portentously, "even the appearance of a conflict" could be equally important. (It
was not and could not be nearly as important, of course, but fighting rooted
Beltway clichés, I had learned, is a fool's errand.) The Democratic staff
members, who showed no inclination to leap to positive conclusions about
my nomination, enjoyed a tactical advantage, as well. At that point, they
knew what was in the FBI report and I didn't. They had facts and I had
anxieties. When negative items about me began to appear in the trade
press, I had no doubts about the source. It was clear to me why over the
years, for dozens of accomplished men and women in my circle, the confirmation process has become a red neon sign hung over the prospect of
government service blinking, "Do Not Enter." It is a commonplace insight
by now, but no less true for being so: To make public service unattractive
to experienced citizens is both stupid and counterproductive.

As the old clock on the wall continued to tick, working against me
day by day, my best option was to move the process into open session,
where I could force my opponents to identify themselves and make their
case. I was more than eager to make mine. I thus pressed repeatedly for
an early committee hearing. Just as repeatedly, I was assured that it was
in the works. Even as one man's Mede can be another man's Persian,
however, the word "early" seems to mean different things to different
tribes. Now, I know that I am not the only presidential nominee in history

whose so-called fast-track nomination seemed to be moving with the speed of molasses running uphill in Vermont. And I understand that I experienced only a fraction of the frottage of a major nominee—say, for a Cabinet post or a Court appointment. But when you have put at least part of your life on hold, and nameless sources are using your reputation as a dartboard in your own professional world, time tends to move slowly. There were more than a few nights when I would come home and say sweetly to my wife, "Why the hell did you let me do this?" When at last the Senate Subcommittee on Communications scheduled a hearing to consider my nomination, it was a good night at the Freeman home. (Or as we had come to think of it by then, the stately Freeman manor.)

Senate hearings are not what the consultants like to call a win-win situation. There is no conceivable upside for the nominee other than survival itself. The negative possibilities, by contrast, are without number or limit. The nominee is a stationary target while the Senate examiners, like the Crimson Tide defensive unit, are agile, mobile and hostile. When the whistle blows and the action starts, the successful nominee is the candidate who can make himself important to his supporters and insignificant to his opponents. If I needed instruction on this point it was provided in the hearing room of the Senate subcommittee. I was scheduled as the first witness of the day, to be followed by a hearing for Sharon Rockefeller, who as chance would have it had been appointed to my old seat on the Corporation for Public Broadcasting board. As I took my place at the witness table and began to review my notes, senators began to wander in. They appeared to be either bored or distracted, with aides whispering in their ears and pressing papers into their hands. Despite my eager efforts, none of the senators favored me with eye contact. Then Sharon arrived with a small but fast-moving entourage and headed directly for the dais. As if cued by an off-stage choreographer, each of the five senators present leaped to his feet, grinning, waving, calling out her name joyously, save for a quite senior senator who addressed her in honeyed drawl as "darlin'." Sharon was gracious and charming, favoring each senator with a vaguely aimed airkiss. A bit pressed for time, she agreed to take the first questions. Of the brief interrogation that followed, I think it could be fairly said that only I was disappointed by its perfunctory nature. Deeply impressed as I was by now with the importance of financial conflicts, I was looking forward to an ex-egesis of the Rockefeller family holdings and the appearance of any con-flicts that might possibly lurk within. But, alas, senatorial curiosity was left unexcited. There was not a single question for Mrs. Rockefeller on the subject of money. The Rockefeller holdings, it thus appeared, posed none of the analytical challenges, none of the accounting complexities that had riddled the vast Freeman fortune. Instead, most of the questions sprang from the senatorial wonder of it all: how could the Republic ever hope to express its gratitude to Sharon for agreeing to serve? After five U.S. sen-ators in succession dwelled semi-puzzled on this point, I began to wonder myself. Perhaps it was all a bureaucratic snafu, perhaps the administration would have to improve its offer—a major ambassadorial appointment, per-haps. In just a few moments, it was over. Amid a torrent of effusive thanks from senators left and right, Sharon waved to the committee members and was gone. The nation's business had been swiftly done and her nomination sent forward. It occurred to me only later that Sharon had done so swim-mingly because she had prepared so carefully, even comprehensively. Sharon Percy Rockefeller was the daughter of a Republican senator and the wife of a Democratic senator.

I was neither, of course. As soon as Sharon departed, four of the sen-ators stood up abruptly and left the room. Disconcerted for the moment—I had gotten all dressed up for the rhetorical prom, for gosh sakes—I quickly realized that their departure was a good omen. The Democrats had taken their best shot at me in the staff process ("meat tenderizing," as it was then and may still be called) and had come up short. It was time for the senators to move on to venues where the stakes were higher and the photo ops more bountiful. The balance of my hearing was thus con-ducted by the chairman, Barry Goldwater of Arizona, who, apparently reading my file for the first time, found it to be generally agreeable. He seemed to be particularly impressed with my record of volunteer activi-ties, including a short and stunningly unproductive term as New York state chairman of Youth for Goldwater. Hearing no objections, the chair-man supported my nomination and secured approval from the full Senate shortly thereafter. I was thus confirmed as a director of The Communica-tions Satellite Corporation.

For me at least, Comsat was a new world. Just how new is captured in a boardroom photo, taken in May 1984, that I am looking at even as I write these words. I am there in the back row, far left, a position befitting my junior status on the board, as also my relative chronological station. In this picture I am 43 and most of the other 14 directors are in their mid-60s. As I gaze across the line I recognize my former colleagues—the chairman of JP Morgan, the chairman of Bethlehem Steel, the chairman of Goodyear Tire, the president of General Motors, and the chairman of Alcoa. Over the next few years, I would serve also with the chairman of Eastman Kodak, the CEO of Apple Computer, the chairman of Metropolitan Life and the president of Martin Marietta, not to mention the former Secretary of Defense and the former Secretary of Commerce. I was running a different kind of organization. At the time the photo was taken, I was Chief Executive Officer of Jefferson Communications, an entrepreneurial start-up in the business of syndicating editorial features to newspapers. We had a staff of eight and, at the end of a good week, we were able to make payroll and, as our Scottish friends say, put a little siller in the kist. (I bemused myself with the thought that Jefferson was growing rapidly and calculated that, if we maintained our current growth rate, we would be overtaking Goodyear Tire in annual revenues along about the middle of the 22nd century.) In the business press the Comsat board was routinely described as "distinguished" and it was true that in almost every case Comsat was the smallest corporation on whose board its various directors sat. These were the fabled captains of American industry and, I soon discovered, they inhabited a world all their own. At the physical level, surprisingly, it was a small world, at least along the axes of time and space. Most of the industrial captains had their own airplanes—in fact, most of them traded up regularly to maintain air superiority—which tended to both shrink distance and expand reach. A company plane can be and no doubt is in many instances an unjustifiable extravagance, but when used properly it can add a full day to the executive work week. My early judgment was that most of the Comsat directors put in work weeks that would satisfy even the Scroogiest of shareholders. Being a captain of industry is a full-time job and then some.

If their lives were more compressed than the rest of ours, though, they were also more limited and ingrown. They tended to know and work closely only with people like themselves, bound as they were by a common culture and governed by a sense of institutional hierarchy. Chairmen did not associate uncomplicatedly with presidents, for instance, nor presidents with vice presidents. In those days of the early Eighties, long before the words "corporate governance" snapped off salutes in the corner suites, chief executives were unembarrassed by and indeed looked with special favor upon the propagation of interlocking directorates, by which handshake arrangements they would serve on each other's boards and, together, on third-party boards. I noted that there were entire fortnights when some sub-grouping of our Comsat directors would pack themselves into somebody's plane and airmail themselves around the country to a series of two- or three-day board meetings. Not surprisingly, these executives would wind up using the same buzzwords, supporting the same causes, joining the same clubs and finding the same recreational release. One Friday morning in Washington, with board business put to bed an hour or two earlier than expected, four of our colleagues dashed off to make an afternoon tee time at one of their favorite golf clubs—Augusta National.

As with most clichés, there seems to be some truth in the observation that it is lonely at the top. For all the power and wealth that comes to chief executives, there is if not exactly loneliness then at least a striking singularity visited upon the person who carries ultimate organizational responsibility. (Over the years photojournalists have time-sequenced the record of U.S. presidents coming to terms with this singularity. Lyndon Johnson, Jimmy Carter and George H.W. Bush are all examples of executives who seemed to age two or three or five years for every year in office.) As a practical effect in today's webbed and litigious world, there is nobody within his own organization with whom the chief executive can speak freely about sensitive issues. Such is the power of the modern myth, and the inflation of expectations, surrounding his office. It is for this reason, I think, that two figures have attained central importance in the development of a big-time corporate career—the spouse and the peer. They are usually the only two sources of sympathetic counsel and personal support that remain available to a top executive, his mentor by this time being long gone. It was my observation, based admittedly on little more than anecdotal observation, that captains of industry can draw real friends from only these two shallow pools. Of the two, the spouse is doubtless the more important figure but customarily less visible. The peer is a cherished friend, an indigenous tribesman from CEO-land who speaks the same dialect.

As a cultural flatlander I moved into this world with small, tentative steps. At board meetings I tended to speak only when spoken to. At dinners and receptions and the other highly structured occasions that passed for corporate informality, I deferred to my seniors and to what I thought at least in the early going were probably my betters. I read all of the voluminous material distributed to directors, becoming quite possibly the only corporate director in history to do so. I voted reliably with the leadership—with committee chairmen reporting to the full board, with the CEO seeking support for actions taken or initiatives contemplated, for financial managers filing reports to pertinent governmental agencies, and so on. I was the classic new guy trying to find a role for himself. As the meetings rolled by and the routine took hold and the comfort level—both mine and theirs—began to stabilize, I was able to pick out individuals from that class picture of fungible big-business types. I got to see these men in different moments—buoyant in victory, dog-tired from constant travel, confounded by esoterica, ego-propelled on rhetorical tangents, heavily stressed, a tad too relaxed at cocktails. I got to know them one by one and to understand that they were all unique, as different in their own ways as any group of overpaid middle-aged white guys could be. And one day I realized that I had made a new friend.

Committed as it was to the imperial style, Comsat had one of the most drop-dead board rooms in all of corporate America. Heavily carpeted, darkly paneled, theatrically lit and wired for every conceivable electronic velleity, it was to the eye of some beholders a thing of beauty. To others the question might not unreasonably occur: why would anybody spend so much money on a room used only a few days each month? The board room was dominated by a huge, hand-tooled table made of blond wood and gleaming metal, sweeping in a half-circle in front of a

Cinemascope-worthy multimedia screen and grand enough to seat 20 people along its outer edge. The chairman and the CEO sat at the top of the half-circle with the other directors arrayed in descending order of seniority out along either side. Senior executives of the company sat at the far ends of the table next to the juniormost directors. The layout of the board room, it would seem to the amateur anthropologist, was designed not so much to encourage lively exchange among peers as to concentrate control in the hands of the leadership at the head of the table. The point was accentuated by the electronic console embedded discreetly at the CEO's seat, from which microphones were activated, slides displayed and videostapes cued.

As the juniormost director I sat at the end of the table alongside the next-to-juniormost director, who happened to be Eliot Estes, the president of General Motors. An engineer by training, Pete Estes had climbed the greasy pole at GM by adding superb sales and management skills to his executive inventory. He was an engaging, hands-on sort who despite his lofty corporate status did not easily suffer ostentation or pretense. It is probably also true that he was more discomfited than I with our treatment, in subtle ways, as second-class board citizens. Pete Estes spent most of his working days sitting pretty close to the head of the table in whatever room he happened to occupy. His natural affability was thus occasionally interrupted with sidebar grumbling about our "mushroom" status—in Pete's view, management kept us in the dark most of the time, cracking the door open now and then only to shovel some manure on us. Within a few months, Pete and I had formed the Mushroom Caucus in which development, looking back, I can discern the roots of my own subsequent career as an independent director.

Pete, through long experience, and I, through entrepreneurial instinct, came to share a primal view that the mission of a board is to help create economic value so as to reward shareholders for their investment. This may sound obvious, even lapidary, but during my service on seven public company and many more private company boards over the next 20 years, I rarely encountered such an unadorned view of corporate governance.

Well, if they were going to assign us back-row seats, so be it. Our of-fline conversations kept us alert and entertained. For example, an endless, aimless, fee-justifying presentation on the mission statement would prompt an exchange like this:

> Freeman: By the way, Pete, what's the corporate objective of that little car company you run?
> Estes: We're just trying to match the profit margins chalked up by that Jefferson Communications outfit. You're my role model, man.
> Freeman: I'll give you the secret of our success in just two words. Avoid unions.
> Estes: Wish you'd told me that earlier.

Or if management was recommending a merger that seemed calibrated more directly to trigger executive bonuses, or befog a company unpleasantness, than to enhance shareholder value, our below-the-salt conversation would go as follows:

> Freeman: What do you think of a merger between GM and Jefferson Communications?
> Estes: No question, it would create a powerhouse.
> Freeman: What kind of combined revenues could we do?
> Estes: I figure we could do about $10 billion a quarter—as long as we could count on you for half a million.
> Freeman: What synergies do you think we could effect?
> Estes: Well, only the obvious one. We'd have to fire you, of course.

If Pete Estes's asides were inadvertently didactic they were critically important to my education as a board-room neophyte. I learned from him the most valuable lesson any board member can learn: Be collegial, be optimistic, be quick to support management when they deserve it—but never leave your skepticism at home. The most important tool of the director's trade is a well-tuned BS detector.

A few years later, I was walking through Boston's Logan Airport when I stopped to catch the news on a taproom TV. Pete Estes' smiling face was flashing on the screen and the voiceover brought the news that Pete had died a businessman's death. He had dropped dead of a heart attack while rushing through the Detroit airport. Still another lesson from a man who, too briefly, had been my mentor and my friend.

National Review
February 10, 2004

One Last Win for The Gipper

The *Washington Post* reported last week, in a routine business-section story, that Intelsat Ltd. will float a public stock offering in the next few months. Just another garden-variety IPO, it would appear, except for the *Post*'s throwaway line that Intelsat "has an unusual history."

Well, yes.

From Kennedy to Johnson to Nixon, a series of U.S. presidents made the global satellite system happen. It was a rare triumph of government-sponsored enterprise that, at the macro level, empowered businesses first to multinationalize and then to globalize, even as it permitted friends and families, at the micro level, to connect and reconnect. Looking back over the decades, the Intelsat system stands out as one of the more important public initiatives undertaken during that period.

But flash forward, if you will, to 1983. Ronald Reagan is now in the White House and feeling his ideological oats. His political sister, Margaret Thatcher, is shaking up the political economy across the pond with her campaigns for "privatization" of state-owned assets—with public housing, with Jaguar motor cars, and most pertinently with British Telecom, the U.K.'s version of Ma Bell. Intelsat, for its part, has by this time evolved into a very large and not very wieldy IGO—an Inter-Governmental Organization built along the lines of its bureaucratic brethren, the United Nations and the World Health Organization and the like. Intelsat board meetings lasted a full week, the organization's business was conducted in a Berlitz-catalog of languages, and the conflicting interests of more than 100 sovereign nations had to be carefully tended. Suffice it to say that at Intelsat in the '80s, cost-efficiency was not Job One.

It was against this background that Reagan appointed me to represent him in the international satellite system, asking me to look into "this privatization thing." I saluted, clicked heels, and strode off to shape up the international satellite business. That was 1983. As I remember it, I was young then. What the Great Communicator had failed to tell me was that the Intelsat organization was governed by a treaty and that privatization, accordingly, would require the approval of (ultimately) 146 signatories to the treaty. Some of those countries, I now confess, were new to me. Many of them were difficult. One was French.

Thus began the long, hard slog through the tangled jungles of diplomacy, bureaucracy, technology, and high finance that brought us to yesterday's little story in the *Washington Post*. Along that path, I should stress, I never played a particularly heroic role; my distinction was that at Day Last, I was the sole survivor of the hardy crew that had set out on Day First. A colleague described my functional role, somewhat uncharitably I thought, as "turning thousands of bureaucrats into hundreds of business people." With its forthcoming IPO, Intelsat will be a profitable, fully competitive public company with a market capitalization of $2 billion-plus and a mandate to serve customers around the world with constantly improving communications services at free-market prices. Not bad for a day's work, or even a couple of decades'. As so many other people have come to conclude on so many other occasions: "What do you know? Reagan had it right."

National Review
June 12, 1981

A Conversation with R

Mr. R is a member of the intelligence community. He reads the classified literature and he knows the players. He doesn't like what he sees. This is his story.

"Let's talk about collection first, what we pick up on the other side. You have to understand that, despite all the Church committee noise, we've never really had a clandestine service. Almost all of our agents abroad have official cover—political officer at the embassy, or whatever. Now that journalists have gotten religion, as a matter of fact, the only non-official cover left is commercial agents, and commercial agents account for less than 15 percent of our field presence. So . . . operating under official cover, our agents are known to be representing the government and they are treated accordingly by foreign nationals. We thus tend to collect what others want us to report to Washington, and those reports, in turn, tend to become indistinguishable from diplomatic reports. Where's the clandestinity?

"Now what about technical collection? Satellite photos, sensors, and the rest. Some of it is marvelous, and thank God for that. But most of it, by definition, is meaningless, and much of it—like any snapshot of a dynamic process—is subject to misinterpretation. Additionally, there are *enormous* gaps in our knowledge—so enormous, in fact, that we're not at all sure what we don't know. And finally, since technical operations are run by engineers, there are large analytical blindspots. The bells-and-whistles people tend to be uninterested in unquantifiable concerns. Such as why our telemetry picks up some Soviet signals that are encrypted and some that aren't; which message is intended for which audience?

"But collection is only part of the problem. Once you collect the data, somebody has to analyze it, and in our system that task falls to the Director of Central Intelligence. He is responsible for what they call 'national products'—National Intelligence Estimates—for the president. And you know how they produce those estimates? By committee—in a political process dominated not by area specialists but by people who are good at 'coordinating.' To give you an idea of what kind of people we're talking about, think back a year to the campaign. One of the claims George Bush used to make was that he was one of the most respected directors in the history of the CIA. He was. The CIA is still a social club, and it's teeming with would-be Ivy Leaguers who want to marry blondes named Muffie. They want to be more like George Bush than George Bush. One of the reasons that Bush was so respected, of course, was that he dug in his heels against Team B, Dick Pipes's group that finally focused some attention on the Soviet threat.

"I'm not suggesting, understand, that Bush is insufficiently anti-Communist. I'm merely noting that he was inordinately pro-bureaucracy. For that matter, so is Bill Casey. He's an old boy from the OSS days, and he went to Langley thinking he was going to 'unleash the CIA.' It's sad to say, but I don't think he's found out yet that there's nothing to unleash. He's relying on the supergrade bureaucrats and most of them were put in place by David Aaron and Bill Miller—the crowd that tried to discredit Team B.

"As for counterintelligence, I tend to think that a great deal of the problem is structural. The FBI runs the domestic show and the CIA runs the foreign show. They both have some good people, but those people are being asked to do the impossible. You see, the very core of counterintelligence is the central file, the *comprehensive* information, that allows an analyst to see a problem whole. There is no such thing as an intelligence operation that is entirely domestic or entirely foreign and, under our divided system, the Soviets can maneuver in the bureaucratic interstices.

"The fourth element of our intelligence system is covert action. As you know, we're all but out of business in this area. Sure, we have conducted some operations the last few years and they have been, almost without exception, successes. But there's a reason for that. The agency bureaucracy has run so scared that they are taking on only the small, sure-thing operations that make no difference in the overall balance. See, the bureaucracy doesn't like covert action for two reasons—first, they lose control over attenuated command structures; and second, failed operations tend to be conspicuous. That's bad for business. So the agency would much prefer to run to the Hill with news of a letter-perfect operation that doesn't amount to a hill of beans.

"I'll give you a story to illustrate how bad the fanny-covering has gotten. You remember Nosenko, the defector? We knew—I mean, we knew rock-hard—that he was a wrong number. And we would have squeezed him hard but for one problem. Some of our best agents in the field supported his story. What does that tell you? That some of our best agents were also wrong numbers, right? But the bureaucracy wasn't about to admit a mistake of that size, so the agency refused to drop him. To this day he's still on the payroll.

"Let me give you another story. You've probably read in the right-wing press that the CIA has been demoralized. That's true, but not in the way you think it is. The people who are demoralized are the solid guys who have a grip on reality in world affairs. Among the senior people at the agency—among the social climbers and the coordinators and the bureaucratic warriors who prevailed over the Helms faction and the Angleton faction—morale is too high. That's right, too high. These people have actually consolidated their control over the agency since the election. One of the political godfathers to this crowd was Birch Bayh, the chairman of the Senate Intelligence Committee. You know what the CIA did when the Republicans took over the Senate and Bayh was forced into retirement? They laid on a fancy affair at Langley last winter and gave him a goddamn medal."

National Review
June 12, 1981

As Shevchenko Sees It

He lives in a quiet, older neighborhood. The houses are well maintained, the lawns neatly trimmed. Graceful trees throw shadows over the sidewalks where the kids tool around on tricycles and the pets are meticulously curbed. His pretty wife, a daughter of the Confederacy, tends the fine backyard garden and keeps a warm and happy, appliance-bedecked home. From first appearances, Arkady Shevchenko is all but indistinguishable from your average American.

It was not always that way with Shevchenko, of course. Up until April 1978 he had been considered indistinguishable from his colleagues in the top echelon of the Soviet foreign-policy establishment. A protégé of Foreign Minister Andrei Gromyko, Shevchenko, still only 50, had advanced quickly through the bureaucratic thicket to the post of Ambassador Extraordinary; he also became Under Secretary General of the United Nations, taking charge of Security Council affairs, disarmament issues, and, as he says, "other political matters." Some Kremlinologists had him pegged as Gromyko's successor. When Shevchenko broke with the Kremlin three years ago, then, the china commenced to rattle in New York, Moscow, and other world capitals.

After an unseemly struggle for proprietary rights between "the Agency" and "the Bureau," Arkady Shevchenko settled down to an extended dialogue with American intelligence agents. Authoritative word has it that Shevchenko has not disappointed his interlocutors. As a world-class talker, he is both conceptually imaginative and anecdotally revealing. His "conversations with the authorities" continued for 18 months. (Persistent rumors that Shevchenko had been working for Uncle long before 1978, and that his defection thus represented a setback for U.S. intelligence, will be confronted in a book that Shevchenko is now writing for a New York publisher.) Now that he has paid his dues, so to speak, to his host government, he seems ready to offer his views to a wider audience. His agreement to discuss issues with us is one indication.

Speaking a nuanced, idiomatic English, his fourth language, Shevchenko made these points in our long interview:

On Afghanistan. Western press coverage has been "unrelieved nonsense." The Soviet invasion had nothing to do with petropolitics or Moscow's hunger for a warm-water port. The Afghan Communists were fragmenting, with the pro-Chinese faction gaining power. Such a flanking movement "to the left of the Soviets" could not be tolerated. The Soviets had to go in, but in doing so they made a tactical mistake. They didn't realize they would have to use regular troops to put down the rebels.

On the Soviet Mission to New York. There are 800 Soviet personnel in New York attached to various offices. Of these, 400 are either KGB or GRU (military intelligence).

On "The Spike." Part of it, according to Shevchenko, is on the button—the part that describes Soviet disinformation activities. "That's exactly the way the Soviets do it." But the part about the Soviet timetable for taking over the world is "absurd." "The Soviet foreign ministry doesn't know what it will do next month."

On Castro. In the early days of the Cuban revolution the Soviets did not trust Fidel Castro. It was not until Khrushchev came to New York in 1960 for the Harlem meeting that Castro managed to pass muster. Whereas Raúl Castro had always been highly regarded, and whereas Che Guevara was "out in front of the Soviets" in revolutionary fervor, Fidel, Shevchenko maintains, might have evolved with careful American cultivation into a social democrat "whom the Communists would have considered a traitor."

On Central America. Che had accused the Soviets of not being "real Communists" because of Moscow's caution in the Caribbean. Proceeding incrementally, the Soviets had counseled Fidel to rebuild Cuba before undertaking to export the revolution. According to Shevchenko, "In Latin America today, the Soviets have caught up."

On the CPUSA. Ambassador Anatoly Dobrynin is obliged to turn in periodic reports on the performance of the party here in the States. It's a frustrating task for the Soviet diplomat. The last report he saw, Shevchenko giggles, summed up the situation as "dismal."

China. At the time of our interview, Alexander Haig had just returned from Peking. Shevchenko was highly enthusiastic about the way in which the Secretary of State had played the China card and argued for additional American initiatives in the Far East. Given Soviet problems in Afghanistan and Poland, "now is the time to move."

Poland. Quite simply: "A disaster! Yesterday, today, and tomorrow—a disaster for the Soviets!" Groping for ways to convey the hugeness of the problem for the Soviets, he adds, "Afghanistan is not even comparable." And then again, "Poland affects everything—the empire [!], the economy, ultimate Soviet goals." If the Poles diminish the role of the Party, if they loosen ties to Moscow, if they permit free trade unions, they will succeed in establishing independence from Moscow. In just a year or two the *entire* Polish army could break away from Soviet command. In a year or two a new nation could begin to take shape: if the Soviets don't move now they could soon be confronting "a nation like France." But invading Poland is altogether different from invading Hungary or Czechoslovakia. Poland is "a huge country, the largest in the Warsaw bloc: the population is anti-Russian—the Poles will never forget 1939—more religious, more international. Not even the elites are doctrinally orthodox." Additionally, the Poles are "more clever than the Hungarians. The U.S., will never come to Poland's rescue—but the Poles know it."

Arkady Shevchenko is beginning to share his opinions on a number of subjects . . . just like any other American.

The Weekly Standard
November 27, 2006

AuH2O in '64

A review of A Glorious Disaster: Barry Goldwater's Presidential Campaign and the Origins of the Conservative Movement, *by J. William Middendorf II*

There's much to like about J. William Middendorf II's new book. First, of course, is the title—*A Glorious Disaster*—which is dead on and may finally help to strip away the Velcro long stuck between the name "Goldwater" and the noun "debacle." Then there's the author, Bill Middendorf, who bolts into politics with typical businessman swagger and, atypically, stays to create his own space, develop survival skills, and do much good. And finally, there's the candidate, Barry Morris Goldwater, without whom there would have been no campaign and no movement and maybe no magazine quite like this one.

Glorious is the memoir of a working executive, not a philosopher-king. Arrived on the political scene from early success on Wall Street, Middendorf already knew what he believed—he was a Goldwater Republican—and he concentrated his considerable energies on the political process and how it worked. With no need for ideological infusions from the policy wonks, he was free to focus on operational details: the governing regs, the people who could get things done, the sources of funds and the fine art of campaign bill-paying. He became an expert in political money, which saved him a place at every meeting he chose to attend. And he became that most feared of all meeting-attenders: the note-taker. The reader benefits here from Middendorf's encyclopedic files. The subjects of those files benefit only intermittently, which adds seasoning to this most unusual campaign book.

It seems almost inevitable that Middendorf would become a close associate and warm admirer of the Draft Goldwater Committee leader, F.

Clifton White. One of the few professional politicians of his era—someone, that is, who devoted his full working life to the practice of campaign management—Clif White was a man of schedules and time tables, agendas and reviews. Wise enough to know that he could never impose lasting order on the chaos of politics, White was still determined to control as much of the process as he possibly could.

Middendorf felt a sense of order, comfort, and shared purpose. Along with his mentor Jeremiah Milbank Jr., he signed on with White to be the money men for the Draft Committee. (Among the other key figures were *National Review* publisher William Rusher, who set the ideological compass for the group, and John Ashbrook, a young congressman who emboldened and energized the effort. Ashbrook, no son of 1994, seemed to harden in his views once he was elected and moved inside the Beltway.)

The story of how Clif White's crew drafted Goldwater and took over the GOP has been told elsewhere, including in White's own memoir, *Suite 3505*. The story of the "first genuine draft" is a great yarn, and not just for lovers of the political yarn. What Middendorf brings to the grand old party is those damn notes. He remembers who said what, and when, and then how they tried to tidy up the after-action reports. As a storyteller he's not going to make anybody forget Alexandre Dumas, but for political junkies, there's a fix waiting here.

I never knew, or had forgotten, that J. Edgar Hoover, on LBJ's orders, was bugging Goldwater headquarters. Or that the CIA man running traps on the Goldwater staff was our old friend E. Howard Hunt. Or that brand-name pols really thought that the selection of William Miller as the vice presidential nominee might lock up the electoral votes of New York. Middendorf is particularly good on the ouster of the Draft Goldwater crew—White and company, as well as William F. Buckley Jr. and the dreaded "intellectuals"—just as Goldwater secured the GOP nomination.

Middendorf, by then the indispensable fundraiser, was the only Clif White man to survive the purge, and he provides a peer's-eye view of the incoming "Arizona mafia." The just-nominated Goldwater, with his political life flashing before his eyes, decided to bring in three old friends from home—Arizona lawyers Denison Kitchel, Dean Burch, and Richard Kleindienst—to run his general-election campaign. He might as well have brought in Larry, Curly, and Moe. None of the three had any experience in national politics, and a campaign against an incumbent president was not the best place to start.

By Labor Day—in those days the traditional start of the campaign—it was all over but the shouting. Historians would later note, of course, that it was precisely the shouting that was much the best part of the campaign. Barry traveled to terminal sun colonies and informed oxygen-gulping oldsters that Social Security ought to be voluntary. He went to Tennessee and told the rent-seekers packed in around the federal trough that the Tennessee Valley Authority was a waste of public money. He reminded effete Eastern audiences that an efficient way to uncover North Vietnamese trails was to tactical-nuke 'em.

Not everybody found the candor refreshing. When Barry, in West Virginia, launched an attack on the War on Poverty, there was an eerie quiet as the audience searched his remarks for subsurface meaning. (My lingering campaign image is of a mid-sized cutter headed through rough seas toward a looming iceberg. On the bridge the tension is palpable. A young officer breaks the strained silence, shouting into the gale, "Skip, let's see what this baby can do." The captain replies, "Good thinking, lieutenant," and guns the engine full forward.)

Middendorf is undoubtedly correct when he laments the departure of White's battle-hardened team and the takeover by Barry's well-meaning rookies. Clif White *would* have run a better campaign and the race *would* have been closer. But Goldwater would have lost even so, and the ultimate victory of conservatism might possibly have been compromised, the paradigmatic character of the campaign somehow sacrificed. The residual value of the campaign—the themes developed, the troops bloodied, the lists compiled, the organizations framed—redeems Barry's decision to do it his way. All choice, no echo. The campaign was a lab lesson in gratification deferred, or as George Will has written: "We . . . who voted for him in 1964 believe he won, it just took 16 years to count the votes."

While Middendorf gives only brief attention to matters of policy and program, he is careful not to confuse the politics of Barry Goldwater with those of Brent Bozell. Goldwater, it will be remembered, was propelled to leadership of the nascent "movement" after publication of his huge best-seller, *The Conscience of a Conservative*. Bozell, who had ghosted the book, was a brilliant lawyer and a skilled ideologist (and yes, the father of the magisterial media-basher of the same name). A political intimate of the fusionist Frank Meyer, Bozell had woven strands of Milton Friedman's free-market programs in with Russell Kirk's traditionalist philosophy to produce a seemingly seamlesss text. Bozell was also a master of chiliastic prose. The book was a call to arms, and the first generation of movement types fled the plow for the armory. (Partial disclosure: I managed Bozell's Maryland congressional campaign to a brilliant second-place finish.)

Goldwater evinced mixed emotions about the book. He was grateful for its success, of course, but always a bit awkward in accepting praise for work not really his own. Early on he adopted the formulation that Bozell had been the "guiding hand" in preparation of the book, and over the years, Goldwater made little effort to hold Bozell close to the inner circle. Late in his life, when we had reconnected as colleagues on a corporate board, I asked Goldwater for his final reckoning on *Conscience*. The essential Barry responded, "Well, I read the book. I even agreed with parts of it."

What, then, were Goldwater's politics, if not elegantly Bozellian? Perhaps they can best be described as western ornery. Goldwater would have been a charter member of the Leave Us Alone coalition—if he had believed in coalitions. Born only a few years after the birth of his beloved Arizona, he shared the frontiersman's sleepless wariness, the bone-deep distrust of large, remote, and power-grabbing governments. His first reaction to almost any initiative on the fuzzy border of constitutional authority would have been—"It's none of the government's damn business."

It's a measure of how far we have come that there is today in Congress perhaps only a single heir to Goldwater's minimalism—Ron Paul of Texas—and that he is regarded within his own Republican caucus as somewhere between a curiosity and a kook. It is noteworthy as well that the man who inherited Goldwater's Senate seat, John McCain, has made his mark in politics by abridging speech freedoms in the name of campaign finance reform. Which seems to beg this question: Is there still room in the movement for a smaller-the-better-government conservative, a national modesty conservative? Is there still room for Barry Goldwater?

THE
PHILANTHROPIC
WARS

Speech to El Pomar Foundation
Colorado Springs, Colorado
September, 2002

WHEN FOUNDATIONS GO BAD

T hank you and good morning.

I hope that most of you were here last night to hear Jeff Coors' heartening remarks. He told a happy story of family philanthropy. A story of family cohesion, shared purpose and—most surprisingly of all—intended consequence. It was a rare story, indeed. For much more often the story of family philanthropy is a story of jammed communications—of ambitions unappreciated and motives misunderstood—of bad vibrations between generations and—most expensively of all—between first wife and last wife.

Why do so many family foundations go wrong? Why do they wind up so often frustrating rather than fulfilling the dreams of their founding mothers and fathers?

Well, one of the principal reasons is—lack of candor. Successful people find it extremely difficult to talk candidly about money—and especially their own. By comparison, sex is relatively easy to talk about. I think of my own family. As soon as our kids explained it to Jane and me, we picked up on it right away. But money is a darker, more esoteric subject—always left to a more appropriate occasion, a later date, a time that may in fact never come.

It might be useful, then, if I were to break the ice with a little candor about my own situation. First, you should know that I have been married to this lovely lady over here for more than 30 years. To our mutual regret, neither one of us was smart enough to inherit or marry any money. So, we had to make our own—the old-fashioned way, by working for it. And, if we're still being candid, we must acknowledge that the actuarial tables decree that Jane will outlive me by 8.7 years—which is to say that Jane will get to spend the balance of our lifetime earnings.

How would I like Jane to spend my money? I'm glad you asked that question. I have only three simple guidelines. First, do what's right. You, Jane, will know what that is at least as well as I. Second, have some fun. You have had fun all of your life and there's no reason to stop now. And third, don't reward my enemies. About that last point—it may sound harsh. You may find yourself reflecting one day—would my late husband, genial and warmhearted man that he was, be so petty, so small, as to carry ideological grudges with him into eternity? Let me assure you that he would and he will.

More seriously, let's talk for a moment about rewarding your ene-mies—for that has become the core problem of contemporary philan-thropy. And let me begin by outlining the dimensions of the philanthropic problem—which I hope by the end of this hopeful weekend you will begin to perceive as a philanthropic opportunity.

The first and most conspicuous aspect is demographic. We are at the leading edge of what has been called a "massive intergenerational transfer of wealth." In plain English, that means that the Reagan entrepreneurs, lots of them, are about to leave large estates, lots of them, to their baby boomer children. To put a number on it—*The New York Times* reports that between now and 2020, the baby boomers—Americans now between the ages of 35 and 53—will inherit $12 trillion. Nothing of this financial magnitude has ever happened—in this economy or any other—and its ef-fects on our society will be transformational. While these effects cannot be precisely known, it is inevitable that they will shape new social, cul-tural and political realities. This transfer of wealth will be, accordingly, a historical development of epochal consequence.

The second important dimension of the philanthropic moment is the outmoded tax code. As you are all gratefully aware, the secular trend in in-come tax rates has been downward for almost 40 years. Beginning with John Kennedy and accelerating through Ronald Reagan, personal income tax rates have been cut, at the margin, from 91 percent to a shade under 40 percent. The trends in capital gains rates have been positive, as well. The Republican Congress has cut long-term rates to 20 percent. But one part of the tax code has been left untouched for generations—estate taxes—and they remain stuck at levels that can be fairly described as confiscatory.

Let me give you a painful example. Between now and 2020, there will be tens of thousands of estates created in the $30 million range. That may sound like a lot of money to some of you, not much to others. But the historical point is this: that figure will not be out of reach for unremarkable citizens lucky enough to be healthy and productive during these golden days of the American Era. Yes, the comic's question has been answered for all time: this *is* a great country. But when that $30 million estate comes before the tax bar, bad things will happen to good people. If Mr. and Mrs. Productive Citizen have three children to share the estate, each one of them will get approximately $3 million. Bill Clinton and his friends will get $20 million. With a federal rate of 55 percent, state and local taxes, executors and lawyers—the bureaucratic take is almost two-thirds of everything you put away—after tax!

And that, my friends, is what you call a tax incentive. An in-your-face, won't-go-away, loser-take-the-foremost tax incentive. Under that kind of move-it-or-lose-it pressure, Mr. and Mrs. Productive Citizen are almost obliged to set up a foundation to preserve their resources.

And, finally, the third critical aspect of the philanthropic problem. It is the current infrastructure of foundation management. The people who run the foundations—advise the boards—manage the staffs—design the grants—pick the grantees—and evaluate the results. The philanthropic establishmentarians who describe themselves as "professionals"—to differentiate themselves from us amateurs who make the money and, if left to our own clumsy devices, would spend it in narrow, unlettered ways. This establishment, ladies and gentlemen, is a formidable construct—as impervious to dissenting views as the media establishment of the Seventies, or the academic establishment of the Eighties. Its leadership class, fashionably educated and ferociously verbal, tends to hold political opinions running the gamut from A to B.

How tightly do they have the foundation world buttoned up? Let me give you two numbers. First, a recent study of U.S. philanthropy reported that foundations giving mostly to liberal causes held more assets than foundations giving mostly to conservative causes by a ratio of 17 to 1. A remarkable number—especially when you consider the political coloration of that same money at the front end of the process—when it was donated to the foundation. I have no exact numbers, but I would be willing to bet that, out of every 18 entrepreneurs in this country, there are fewer than 17 dedicated left-wingers.

And here's the second number, courtesy of John Von Kannon of The Heritage Foundation. Von Kannon is the most diligent tracker of cause money in this country: If a political dollar has the audacity to cross a state line, it's on his radar the next morning. I asked him—how many explicitly conservative foundations are there, among the 50,000 foundations of all kinds? His answer—eight or nine. And that answer reflects not imprecision, but flux. There are nine, as it happens, but one of them may be following a well-worn migratory path to the political Left.

Numbers tell most of the story, but not all of it. To appreciate the special flavor of the philanthropic world most of us need anecdotal help. Happily, that help was provided recently in a piece in the *Washington Post* by Peter Frumkin, a philanthropic scholar at Harvard. I give you a sentence that should reverberate in institutional memory: "Philanthropy has become a controversial matter, particularly when donors make their own decisions about how and when to spend their money rather than leaving those details to professionals." Or, as the *New York Daily News* might put it—PHILANTHROPOIDS TO DONORS: DROP DEAD.

So, there you have it—the correlation of forces as the millennial battle is joined. A tidal wave of money moving between the generations. An anachronistic tax code virtually shoving new wealth into foundations. And a cohesive, ideologically aroused professional class fully prepared to take control.

How did this happen? How did we get so far up the creek with so few paddles? I have studied this question some and can offer—as they say on the 10 o'clock cop dramas—a theory of the crime. The story goes something like this . . .

We begin with that heroic figure, the entrepreneur. He looks pretty much like your average American, but he has an idea and a bit of a wild streak and an extra gland for quick energy. He also has a run of luck, which he often overlooks, and a great wife, whom he almost always overlooks. Over the course of a frantic lifetime—long, hard, head-down years—he builds a franchise business. And finally, near the end of the road, he looks up and experiences—the philanthropic moment!

Aging and improbably wealthy, and motivated by undifferentiated good intentions to "give something back," the entrepreneur sets up a foundation. He inscribes his name proudly on the front door, much as he had done in the start-up days of his own business. For his new board, he picks a handful of trusted friends, his children and a few associates who have foundation credentials of some sort. Experts. Indeed, a veritable corps of technocratic experts seems to pop up around him. They volunteer to guide him through thickets of philanthropic esoterica and he gratefully accepts. The entrepreneur may think of these helpful professionals as corporate vice presidents, subordinates primed to execute the boss' orders.

But for all the apparent similarities to his salad days in business, it soon becomes clear that the philanthropic world is different in important ways. Instead of serving customers with attractive products at reasonable prices, there seems to be no discipline in the philanthropic marketplace. Most of the decisions are qualitative, subjective—the kind of judgments the entrepreneur feels ill-prepared to make. As for the "customers," they are for the most part pre-selected by the experts—causes and people with whom the entrepreneur, frankly, may not be wholly familiar. This is a new experience for him; he sometimes feels as if he is the least well-informed person in the room. For the experts seem to know more than he does about lots of things. They even seem to know each other, men and women with impressive credentials who recommend each other roundly for important assignments.

As the process rolls forward, the incremental changes wrought by the experts become hardened, first into procedural approach and then into policy. The foundation transcends its narrow base as a vehicle for personal charity and becomes an institution. And soon enough—a year or two or ten years later—old friends of the entrepreneur notice a striking development: the foundation with his name inscribed proudly on the front door is supporting ideas and institutions of which he explicitly disapproved.

Ford. Pew. MacArthur. Packard. The stories are as familiar as the names. The great fortunes of modern capitalism turned to the service of anti-market initiatives. The great names of the American Century now fronting for the centrifugal forces of multiculturalism. The fruits of technological genius now funding the corrosive campaigns of junk science.

What's happening in the foundation world today is a kind of reverse alchemy, with free-market gold being turned into philanthropic dross.

Is the process irreversible? Are the Reagan entrepreneurs destined to turn up a generation hence as the posthumous funders of a burgeoning American Left? Will the wealth produced by the market system be deployed in an attack on the system itself? Well, as Damon Runyon used to say, "the race is not always to the swift, but that's the way to bet." Unless the forces of philanthropic reform can gather themselves and apply early, concerted effort, the creators of America's late-century boom will be picking up the tab for the Reagan counter-revolution well into the next century.

Thank you.

Palm Beach, Florida
January 17, 2003

Successful Giving in Extraordinary Times

I begin tonight with an uplifting story about the spirit of philanthropy . . . as interpreted by the plaintiffs' bar.

It seems that here in Palm Beach, the American Heart Association has a skilled information officer who, in mixing and matching databases, came up with the factoid that the individual with the largest personal income last year contributed not one dime to organized charity. The head of the Palm Beach chapter of the Heart Association, sensing a large opportunity, set up a meeting with this individual, who happened to be a tort lawyer, and made a pastoral visit to his law office. After some pleasantries, the Heart Association official said, "Mr. Tort Lawyer, our research shows that as a result of your class-action settlements against the asbestos, fast food, chemical, tobacco, tire, beer, HMO, computer, cell phone, handgun and lead paint industries that, last year alone, you earned $383 million in personal income—and yet you made no charitable contributions whatsoever . . .

And the lawyer responded, "Well, does your research also show that I have three children pursuing graduate degrees, all of them at Ivy League schools?

And the Heart Association official said, "Well, no."

"Well, does your research show that I have an 87-year-old mother whose healthcare bills run upwards of $100,000 per year?"

"Well, no."

"Well, does your research show that my sister and her five kids were left penniless when her husband was killed in an auto accident?"

"Well, no."

"Well, if I wouldn't help any of them, why would I help you?"

Thus saith the tort lawyer.

I have been asked by the management to submit a status report tonight—to establish our current position in the evolving story of American philanthropy. It's an important marker, for the critical calculation in any decision is to determine where you are in the cycle of events. To find the path ahead, in other words, you must first know where you are—and to do that you need a kind of global positioning system, a time-sequenced GPS, if you will. For instance—wouldn't it be useful to know whether the fourth-quarter uptick in the equity markets was the beginning of a sustained advance—or an evanescing opportunity to bail out before the global economic implosion? Wouldn't it be useful to know, for another instance, whether the prospective invasion of Iraq will be seen by history as the introduction of democratic values to that troubled region—or as the tragic miscalculation of those who sought to turn the American republic into an American empire?

Well, those questions are properly addressed above my pay grade. But I'm pleased to announce that they will be answered definitively at 12:30 Eastern time tomorrow, in this room, by my learned colleague, Fred Barnes.

The question for us tonight is: Where is American philanthropy—after a half-century of dynamic growth and troubled performance? After the early promise and the more recent disappointment? After the abundance of good deeds by donors—and much mischief committed by foundation executives?

My best judgment is that we are nearing the end of the bad old days.

Let me explain. Over the past generation, the performance of American philanthropy has failed to match the promise of American generosity for three primary reasons:

First is the petty larceny of the philanthropic management class. You all know the stories—the self-enrichment of nonprofit executives, the side deals and sweetheart contracts, the occasional lootings and liftings. We were even treated to our own perp walk—when William Aramony, the head of United Way, was chased down the sidewalk by the tabloid media. His walk of shame didn't have quite the showbiz flair of Tyco's Dennis Kozlowski or Adelphia's John Rigas. But it had a poignancy all its own—Kozlowski and Rigas, after all, were taking money from corporate shareholders. Aramony was taking money from undernourished children.

The second problem has been the almost total collapse of trusteeship. The idea—descended from the common law—that to accept a board appointment is to acknowledge the donor's declaration of trust in your stewardship. From the time when men marched off to the Crusades to the time—this week—when men sail for the Persian Gulf, they have said in the most careful, premeditated way, "I, John Jones, trust you, Bill Smith, to handle this matter in my absence." For centuries, if that trust was well-placed, a handshake would seal arrangements for a lifetime and beyond. Today, in the foundation world, a three-inch-thick trust agreement incites an immediate search for loopholes, for the elastic phrase, for the exploitable lacuna.

How does the foundation trustee approach his job today? How does he define the responsibility and discharge the trust? Well, I think the *Washington Post* had it about right a few months ago when it profiled one of the most influential figures in East Coast philanthropy. In one of those endless 4,000-word Style section pieces, festooned with color photos, the

Post recounted the career of a woman it described as the gold standard of nonprofit trustees. (I will omit her name on the chance that she's a major donor to your organization.) The *Post* described this trustee as open, generous, protean in her energies and, above all, passionate in her philanthropic interests. Those passionate interests, according to the *Post*? Population control groups and environmental activists. To give us just a hint of the intellectual rigor she brings to her philanthropy, the *Post* quoted her as saying, "I love the population issue because it's so human." And then, almost in passing, the *Post* mentioned that her family fortune had been built in a "global power company." Just to remind you—a global power company is a multinational corporation that consumes large amounts of the earth's resources to generate electricity. That is to say, it is the *bête noire* of population control groups and environmental activists. So there you have, in capsulated form, what the establishment regards as the gold-standard trustee—promiscuously generous, intellectually undemanding, at least vaguely uncomfortable with if not utterly guilt-stricken by the source of family wealth.

The third problem—by far the largest problem—is what I would call the ideological larceny of the philanthropic management class. Indeed, the rolling capture of America's great foundations is in many ways comparable to the wave of corruption that has rippled through corporate America in recent years—with one striking difference. In the corporate world, it is wealth that has been taken from shareholders and diverted to managers. In the foundation world, it is power that has been taken from donors and diverted to managers.

Consider. The David and Lucile Packard Foundation has become one of the largest funders of the sustainable development movement, which at its core is both Luddite and Malthusian. David Packard, the father of Silicon Valley, devoted his entire life to the proposition that technology could change our lives for the better.

Consider. Principals of the Andrew W. Mellon Foundation are among the leading proponents of a high-tax fiscal policy, including the confiscatory rates of the estate tax. Andrew Mellon, along with John F. Kennedy and Ronald Reagan, was one of the three great tax-cutters of the 20th century.

Consider. The W. K. Kellogg Foundation is among the leading funders of the nonprofit management class—supporting thousands of employees who make their living in the processing of grant applications. W. K. Kellogg, the apostle of Midwestern self-reliance, set up his foundation to help individuals help themselves.

I could go on—and on other occasions, I will. For it is a long and still not widely understood story. These *are* the bad old days—but, as I say, they appear to be coming to an end. Donors are beginning to push back. They are defining their own objectives—and setting their own agenda. Donor families are reminding trustees that they do not sit on foundation boards merely to keep the chairs warm—or to dress up their résumés. They are reminding trustees that they have not been invited to replace the values of the donor with their own. They are reminding trustees—and, occasionally, reminding them with the business end of a lawsuit—that they have undertaken fiduciary responsibilities and will be expected to discharge them faithfully. Thanks, in part, to some of the stouthearted men and women in this room, a genuine reform movement is gaining traction. And it is beginning to redress the imbalance between donors and what Professor Frumkin calls the professionals—as if foundation staffers had been sent abroad to some prestigious Swiss academy, there to have the secret tablets of philanthropy entrusted to them.

And as the reform movement—what I call the donor's rights movement—has gained momentum, the professionals have become unhappy. And you know what happens when philanthropoids are unhappy. They become . . .verbal.

Hear the president of the Fund for New Jersey decrying what he perceives to be a dangerous new trend: "I believe that we are essentially cowering before the spectre of donor designation. Our language is largely defensive—we use phrases like 'not a penny will be mis-used.' This sends a terrible message that does not honor the intelligence and integrity of our partners." Or hear *The NonProfit Quarterly*, one of the leading trade publications in the foundation world. In its current editorial, it implores foundation executives to "withstand the 'donor is God' trend and create a more democratic and inclusive form of . . . grantmaking." I suspect that the verbal escalation may have topped out last month in Bermuda. After

I spoke there on the donor's rights movement, it was reported that I had "unleashed a wave of donor terrorism."

Well, I don't think they should be so hard on themselves. Cowering becomes them.

What you hear behind all of this yelping, I would suggest, is the sound of an establishment challenged—its clichés rebutted, its cozy relationships re-examined, its settled patterns of behavior upset. What you hear, I think, is the sound of change—and perhaps, with the concerted efforts of reform-minded people across the industry, the end of the bad old days.

How, then, will we know when the good old days are finally at hand? That's easy. We'll know when the donor's vision and values are restored to their rightful and central place in foundation grantmaking. We'll know when the person who created the wealth and sought to make his world a better place is honored for both the achievement and the intention. And we'll know, most clearly, when, after the donor can no longer speak for himself, his words are accorded both primacy and high place within the foundation that bears his name.

Thank you.

Speech to The Heritage Foundation
Sea Island, Georgia
April 12, 2002

THE FORD FOUNDATION

AND ITS EXPERTS

Good morning.

You will hear later this morning from Michael Grebe of The Lynde and Harry Bradley Foundation about how one of the nation's 50 largest foundations is directed. You will hear from me how the other 49 are directed. For while Mike's story of the Bradley Foundation is bracing, heuristic and replicable, it has not proved to be contagious. Indeed, although their funds spring from the same wellhead as Bradley's—the capitalist system and the men and women who realize its potential—the other great foundations have strayed from the values that informed their creation.

In recent months I have been digging into this story. How the great fortunes of modern capitalism were turned to the service of anti-market forces. How the great foundations, born of good intention and high purpose, became the private bankers for modern liberalism. In sifting through the files, I conclude that it has happened in only two ways. You as a donor may—possibly—be reassured to learn that a full-scale hijacking can occur only if a) you trust the experts or if b) you trust your family.

This morning I want to talk about the experts. And Exhibit A is the Ford Foundation.

As you may recall, the Ford Foundation was conceived in mid century at the confluence of three emerging trends. First was the Ford family's awakening sense of charitable obligation—the undifferentiated impulse to give something back to the society that had so copiously enriched it. Second, the mounting concern among Ford's lawyers that the estate tax could dislodge the family from control of the Ford Motor Company. And third, the urgency felt by Ford PR executives to associate the family name, then clouded by controversy, with good works of the warm and fuzzy sort.

Thus was born the first American mega-foundation. At the beginning, tens of millions, then hundreds of millions and by now billions of tax-advantaged dollars secured in a charitable endowment. To give you a sense of scale, each year the Ford Foundation gives away funds roughly equal to the total assets of the Bradley Foundation. That's the correlation of forces. Each and every year for the past half-century, Ford has given away the equivalent of a Bradley Foundation.

The story of the Ford Foundation is not only the story of trust betrayed but the story of audacity rewarded. We all know audacity when we see it. When 25 years ago, a fuzzy-cheeked Ed Feulner and cherubic Phil Truluck marched into the epicenter of American socialism—Washington, D.C.—and began to proclaim the virtues of the free market—that was audacity. But consider the problem of the American Left at mid century. They had grand designs, as ever—vast plans for what other people should do with their time and their money—but they had precious few resources. The truly left-wing capitalists—the Cyrus Eatons and so forth—were famous in a man-bites-dog kind of way, but they were always few in number. The solution? To reshape the American economy in its own image, the Left resolved to use the assets of America's proto-capitalist, the man who brought mass-produced goods to the new consumer society, the first great entrepreneur of the American century—they resolved to use Henry Ford's money. Now that is audacity squared.

The patriarch of the Ford family at the time was Henry Ford II, to whom it fell to superintend not only the automobile manufacturing company but in very much of a sideline activity, the brand-new Ford Foundation. He needed help. And of all the young executives recommended to him to tend the family's philanthropy, one in particular caught his eye. His name was Wilbur H. Ferry—known to his friends as Ping Ferry. (His brother, inevitably, was known as Pong.) Over the succeeding years, Ping Ferry would become such a cultish figure among philanthropists of a certain age that he was referred to with the same one-name reverence as Hollywood in the 1980s would speak of Frank, or today, of Barbra.

What did Henry Ford see in Ping? First, like Henry, Ping was an Ivy

Leaguer. Second, like Henry, Ping had grown up in the fancy suburbs of Detroit. Most importantly, Ping was the son of a former president of the Packard Motor Company, another automobile manufacturer of the day. In other words, at least by bloodline, Ping represented to Henry Ford that highest of all human life forms—a car guy.

There were, however, a few things Henry Ford didn't know about Ping Ferry. First, he never got along with his father. Second, he had no use for the automobile business. And most importantly, he was a dedicated leftist who despised corporate America and the rapacity of its market system. He found much to admire in world socialism and would soon become a leading figure in the unilateral disarmament movement.

The key moment occurs in 1950. Let me set the scene, as it has been drawn in Ping's authorized biography. (The book, inevitably, was entitled *Ferrytale*.) Henry Ford and Ping meet for lunch in a private dining room at the Detroit Club, the downtown refuge for generations of industrial captains. Henry Ford has a couple of drinks before lunch and appears distracted by business concerns. He is, in fact, getting punched around in the marketplace by a little outfit called General Motors. Ping pulls out a huge bundle of paperwork. Ford asks, "What the Hell is this?" Ping replies that they are grant applications and that each one will have to be read and evaluated. Ford responds: "Are you crazy? Just tell me what's in them."

That is, I submit, an important moment in the history of bureaucracy. We are witnessing here the birth of the executive summary—the one-page cover sheet that presumes to distill the essence of the 40-page document to which it is affixed. In the hands of the skilled practitioner, the executive summary would become the Swiss Army Knife of modern bureaucracy. A single tool capable of performing 28 discreet operations. It was at this moment in Detroit, in that dining room, that philanthropic power—the power to advance certain ideas while starving others—passed from the donor to the nonprofit manager. And in this case from the capitalist to the socialist. Over time, of course, these summaries began to reflect, less and less, the distilled essence of grant applications and, more and more, the political agenda of Wilbur H. (Ping) Ferry.

How bad did it get? How many miles did Ping take when Henry Ford gave him that first inch? Well, by the mid '50s those same Ford PR executives who had been so happily present at the creation of the foundation were now up in arms. They were getting an earful from their network of dealers around the country. The controversy stirred up by Ping and his left-wing grantmakers was now spilling back onto the company. Something had to be done to protect the franchise. In 1956, the extended Ford family—in all its dysfunctionality—gathered its declining influence and pushed through the board a resolution forbidding the foundation's affiliates from hiring or awarding grants to members of the Communist Party. Remember: We're still talking here about Henry Ford's money.

With the keen corridor sense of the veteran bureaucrat, Ping understood that the game had changed and he turned immediately to his exit strategy. Here, again, he proved to be a philanthropic innovator. To my knowledge he was the first philanthropoid to achieve procedural efficiencies by fusing the roles of grantor and grantee—tracing smoothly the arc from benefactor to beneficiary, as if, in a baseball game, he had served as both pitcher and catcher on the very same pitch. Nice work if you can get it and Ping could. His soft landing was something called the Center for the Study of Democratic Institutions, and it was richly upholstered with millions of Ford money.

The idea was this: If you could gather in one place the greatest minds of the era, free them from the quotidian pressures of time and circumstance, and then turn them loose on the vexed questions of the human condition—well, the seemingly intractable problems of life would soon melt away before the power of sustained insight. It was, in a word, the idea that all of you came across as college sophomores—and then soon abandoned as being too sophomoric.

For the center's home they picked a hilltop in Santa Barbara overlooking the Pacific Ocean—some of the priciest real estate in the country. Each morning the fellows, as they were called, would make their way up the hill to join The Conversation—yes, some of them capitalized it. The Conversation. It proved difficult to sustain much insight early in the morning, however, so The Conversation would begin at 11 o'clock and the fellows would add uninterruptedly to the sum of human knowledge until, oh, 12:15 or so, at which time they would adjourn for lunch on the terrace. Lunch would be accompanied, first by a local wine and then, as one participant remembered, by the big wine. Some fellows found these sessions so stimulating that by mid-afternoon, back in their offices, they would be so lost in thought as to appear to be asleep. Other fellows would be hunched over their typewriters banging out interoffice memoranda, many of them attacking other fellows. They found their colleagues to be, variously, too verbose or too taciturn, too conformist or too lone-wolfish, a badge or a stain, too this or too that. These memos make for fun reading—full of wit, rhetorical flourish and personal venom. Reading them, one is reminded of Irving Kristol's classic remark about campus life: Academic politics are so vicious, Irving said, precisely because there's so little at stake. As it quickly became apparent that none of the era's great minds had any intention of showing up, the fellows began to turn on each other for keeps—voting one another off the island, as it were. Ping, of course, excelled in the composition of vicious memos and he outlasted most of his colleagues. But as it did ultimately for all of the fellows, his number came up one day—and he was expelled from paradise. Some years later, the center itself withered and died an unlamented and virtually unnoticed death. Unsympathetic observers of the center's work could say with some satisfaction that not most but all of Ford's money had been wasted.

What lessons can we draw from this short and highly unofficial history of the Ford Foundation?

Well, for Ping, the next move was obvious. He became a serial philanthropist, married a wealthy divorcée and began to give away *her* money to left-wing causes.

As for the Ford family, they came in time to understand that they had made irrevocable, multibillion-dollar mistakes in the central questions of mission and governance. In 1978, Henry Ford II resigned in frustration from the board, severing the last connection between the family and the foundation that will bear its name in perpetuity.

For the Ford Foundation, the victory was complete, establishing a model for the subsequent capture of America's other great foundations. But the episode was also sobering, at least at the margins. Henry Ford's public criticism brought unwanted scrutiny to the foundation. And for most of the subsequent 25 years, it has embraced a relatively quiet, trendy liberalism rather than the rowdy radicalism of the Ping Ferry era. Even so, the ideological enthusiasms sometimes break through the institutional restraints. Just this past February, for instance, Ford gave $500,000 to the Sexuality Resource Center in the rough Mission District of San Francisco. The purpose of the new center, according to director Gilbert Herdt—identified in news accounts as author of the book, *Ritualized Homosexuality in Melanesia*—is to "make America safe for sexuality." I have always thought that the best way to calibrate donor intent is to imagine the grant applicant making a face-to-face appeal to the founding donor. In this case, Mr. Herdt might have begun his pitch to the great automaker, "Mr. Ford, may I assume you're familiar with my classic study, *Ritualized Homosexuality in Melanesia*?" That would have warmed up the old boy.

For the rest of us—for those involved in a foundation or thinking of becoming so—the lesson is equally clear. The time to prevent a hijacking is before the plane takes off. If you get the mission statement right, if you get the inaugural board right, if you get the start-up staff right—the trip is likely to be not only safe but richly rewarding. For remember: In the second half of life there are two great joys you rarely experience in the first half—one is grandchildren and the other is charitable giving to the people and ideas you hold dear, the people who enrich your life and the ideas that inform it. We can't help you much with the grandchildren. We'll do our best with the other part.

Thank you.

NEAL B. FREEMAN

The American Spectator
May 22, 2009

JEEZ, LUIS: NEW FORD FOUNDATION CEO OFF TO A BUMPY START

There was a tizzy of speculation in January 2008 when Luis Ubinas was named the new (and ninth) president of the Ford Foundation. His résumé seemed to be of the garden variety: He was young and Hispanic, born in the Bronx, educated at Harvard, an Obama contributor, married to a professor of Human Sexuality Studies at San Francisco State. He seemed to have punched most of the tickets, eh? What set off the speculation was that Ubinas also held an MBA and had spent 18 years as a management consultant with the pinstripe firm of McKinsey & Co. (Some of his most important clients were newspaper companies, which, coincident with, but presumably unrelated to, his consultancy, plunged into death spirals.) Ubinas's management background seemed to suggest that Ford might be changing course and preparing to adopt a more businesslike approach to its vast philanthropy. It also suggested that Ford might be trying to rehabilitate the "MBA mystique"—the 1980s conceit that a skilled manager can manage anything and thus needs no grounding in the particular industry under his management. Ubinas was a textbook example of the type. He had no experience in grantmaking, but he had just been installed as the most influential grantmaker in the world. Both of these suggestions caused a *frisson* of disquietude to pass through the upper echelons of Ford and the pack of likeminded foundations that have traditionally padded along behind it.

When Ubinas arrived at Ford's rosewood palace in New York, he assumed the lowest of all possible profiles. He announced almost immediately that he would spend the next year meeting staff, touring Ford's international offices, communing with grantees current and prospective and, generally, thinking large thoughts. A listening tour, if you will, scaled to dimensions that would excite even the record keepers at Guinness. And then off he went, rarely to be seen or heard outside a tight circle of Ford associates. (At an annual salary of $675,000, some Ford executives were heard to express the preference that he flash a bit of his much-hyped chops as a quick study.)

Somewhere along the world tour, word began to filter back to head-quarters that Ubinas had experienced an afflatus. He had seen the future of grantmaking, it was rumored, and he had begun to draw the blueprint for the next great iteration of Ford philanthropy. Excitement simmered and then boiled. Nothing warms the bureaucratic blood like word of The New Plan. With roll of drum and trill of horn, the Ubinas vision-thing was released last month. The details were leaked, atavistically, to the *New York Times*, so we quote from the story by the *Times'* excellent beat reporter, Stephanie Strom:

> The overhaul will bring additional focus to what Ford calls "lines of work," which are individual initiatives managed by individual program officers that have at times numbered more than 200, by condensing them into 35 new lines of work handled by groups of program officers around the world. Those teams will report to a director with responsibility for several of those 35 areas. Thus a single line of work devoted to advancing and supporting Native American arts and culture has been melded into a new, broader line of work supporting and promoting native, indigenous and minority contemporary artists . . . the overhaul has not included a staff reduction.

There's more, but trust us, not much. Kudos to Ms. Strom for keeping a straight face. What Ubinas has given his colleagues is, yes, the old McKinsey Shuffle. In the world of management consulting, this type of an org-chart makeover has conventionally served three purposes: a) it has bought time for hapless management; b) it has asserted temporary authority over a restless staff and c) it has disguised the absence of an organizing principle behind a blizzard of boxes, graphics, pie charts and squiggly lines. The opinion is firming up that Ubinas managed to hit all three birds with the single stone. (The New Plan, we note without surprise, has been met with a deafening silence inside Ford itself, a silence owing on the one hand to a sense of anticlimax and on the other to intramural anxiety. The real power in a nonprofit bureaucracy is the power to decide who reports to whom and Ubinas has just moved everybody's cheese.)

It is said by Ubinas's supporters, of course, that since he's been on the job only 18 months he still deserves the benefit of the doubt. Perfectly reasonable, but he is off to a slow start, a career-cloudingly slow start. Indeed, there's only one bright spot for him at this point: He has developed a new and fervent political following. By restating Ford's mission as "social justice," he has begun to tilt Ford away from his predecessor's centrist-liberalism and back toward the hard-Left policies of an earlier generation of Ford leadership.

Two of his rare public appearances have excited special attention. Asked by one interlocutor what motivates him as a philanthropist, Ubinas replied that it was his sense of the "creeping unfairness" of American life. What kind of philanthropist, you might ask, would look out over the vast stretches of human misery—the continental swaths of disease and illiteracy and hunger and strife—and single out for priority attention the problem of American "unfairness"? Only a man in the grip of ideological fever, the Left seems to hope. Another interviewer asked Ubinas about his special interest in the Census. Was his interest just residue from the consultant gig, a technocratic fascination with economic trends and social patterns? Or an interest in psephology, perhaps? No and no. As Ubinas explained, "If there is any single thing a community foundation can do right now to benefit the people they are supposed to be serving, it is to make sure that every one of those people is counted because every one of those people comes with thousands of dollars in federal entitlements." Ah yes, the Census as a tool to max out government welfare spending. If you don't recognize it, folks, that's ACORN talk. And the hardcore "community organizers" think they've just received a secret handshake from the president of the Ford Foundation.

Buckle up. This could be a long, sad chapter in the checkered history of the Ford Foundation.

The American Spectator
December 29, 2009

BEWARE THE RICH GUYS
TALKING TAXES

E very time the air fills with talk of tax increases, Bill Gates Sr. is trotted out to make the case that higher estate taxes are good for philanthropy, good for the country and good for goodness' sake. Now, with the estate tax set to expire January 1, there he was again last week at a press event, joined by oil heir Richard Rockefeller and mutual fund pioneer John Bogle, the three of them singing from the same high-tax hymnal. The press, hushed as usual in the presence of accumulated wealth, responded with uncritical coverage.

Permit me a moment of skepticism.

Consider the cast of characters, beginning with Mr. Rockefeller. While he may be a source of wisdom on many matters, Americans are unlikely to seek or accept his advice on the vexed subject of inheritance. As the grandson of the great oil man, he was trust-funded at birth and has had little influence over the primary course of his own financial life. It seems safe to say that, to the vast majority of Americans, his experience will seem more alien than instructive. Mr. Bogle makes a more credible witness. He not only built the great Vanguard financial services firm from the ground up, but he was in large part responsible for democratizing and demystifying the financial markets for America's middle class. Whenever he has something to say on the subjects of savings, investment, philanthropy or taxation, we should listen respectfully. And when he says, specifically, that the tax exemption for charitable gifts is a "huge incentive" for him and will result in the donation of a "substantial part" of his estate, we have no reason to doubt him.

Then there's Mr. Gates. It is no slight to Messrs. Rockefeller and Bogle to point out that, had they shown up without Mr. Gates, their conference would have registered a zero on the media Richter scale. Mr.

Rockefeller's fortune has been barricaded for generations, which places his tax situation somewhere beyond the range of general curiosity. And Mr. Bogle, for all his business success, probably made less money in a half-century of service to Vanguard than a few 29-year-old hedge fund managers will take home to Greenwich this year. As the man said, life is unfair. No, it is Bill Gates's presence at these high-tax rallies that gives them snap and crackle. It is Bill Gates's presence, carrying as he does the name of the most successful entrepreneur of the age, that midwifes the headline, "Rich Guys Seek Higher Taxes," a contrarian tease lodged squarely in the long journalistic tradition that began with the query, "Say, is that a man biting a dog?" If Bill Gates's' name happened to be, say, Walter Gates, he would be dismissed as just another tax lawyer hyping tax increases because they're good for business.

Why then is it problematic to call Bill Gates Sr. as a witness in this case? For openers, he's not really a rich guy. He's *related* to a rich guy, a fate that has befallen many an American and ruined more than a few Thanksgiving dinners in the process. Then there's the fact that he's the father of the world's richest child, which makes him uniquely unqualified to speak to the dynamics of inheritance. He will never know either the difficulty or the satisfaction of leaving the family business to his children—his family business was created in the *successor* generation. Nor will he face the challenge of passing on the family farm—if he bequeaths the family farm, assuming he has one, it will amount to no more than a rounding error in his son's real estate portfolio. And he will never understand the emotional importance of smoothing life's path for his children and grandchildren—life's path for his children and grandchildren is freshly Zambonied each morning.

That's on the personal side. On the professional side, Mr. Gates's background is more question-begging still. Now retired, he was for most of his career a partner in a Seattle law firm called Preston Gates. Back when Bill Jr. was starting to build his software company in the Seattle suburbs, Preston Gates employed 13 attorneys: it enjoyed a solid reputation, but it was nobody's idea of a legal powerhouse. Then Bill Jr.'s company began to grow and grow and Preston Gates grew along with it, not as exponentially as the Microsoft miracle, but fast enough to become a substantial regional firm with a presence in Washington, D.C. One could thus say that Bill Sr. became one of those demographic oddities—a parent who, in effect, inherited wealth from his child. But that would make the story too pat. In his legal practice, Bill Sr. never really immersed himself in intellectual property rights or antitrust issues or any of the legal esoterica critical to Microsoft's future. His specialty at the law firm was estate planning, which is to say that he made his living advising clients on how to avoid paying estate taxes. By all accounts, he was good at it. It has long been a poorly-kept secret that top-tier lawyers regard the estate tax as a "voluntary tax," in that it is actually paid only by taxpayers who are ill-informed or under-advised. The clients of Bill Gates Sr., by all accounts, fell into neither category.

So whenever Bill Gates Sr. starts dispensing advice on estate-tax policy, aren't we entitled to ask—to whom should we be listening? The high-paid professional who helped his clients avoid the tax? Or the public moralist who advises the rest of us that it is our civic duty to pay it?

Paper for the Bradley Center for Philanthropy and Civic Renewal
The Hudson Institute, Washington, D.C.
January, 2009

THE *ROBERTSON V. PRINCETON* CASE: TOO IMPORTANT TO BE LEFT TO THE LAWYERS

I t's a pleasure to participate in this program at the Hudson Institute. Back in my New York days, I spent memorable days at your original headquarters on the banks of the Hudson River. Your founder, Herman Kahn, would convene for marathon conversations an eclectic group of business leaders, journalists, academicians and military brass. Conversations with Herman tended to be highly autobiographical and on one of these occasions, Frank Cary, then the president of IBM and the only one of our number with the stature to do so, chided Herman for dominating the proceedings. Herman wheeled around—at almost 300 pounds, he was the world's largest physicist—and replied, "Frank, you don't understand. Some people learn through the eye by reading, others through the ear by listening. I learn through the mouth by talking."

Who knows, sometime during the course of these remarks I may become a wiser man myself.

You are all generally familiar with the *Robertson v. Princeton* lawsuit, the most important donor rights case since the Buck Trust case a generation ago. I will try to add some color and emphasis to accounts that have appeared in the press. I do so after stipulating that I am speaking only for myself and not for the Robertson family, nor—much as I'd like to—for Princeton University.

The story begins 48 years ago this month when a young and charismatic president exhorted his fellow Americans to bear any burden, pay any price in the cause of freedom. Two of those fellow Americans, Charles and Marie Robertson, patriots both, answered the call. They devised with officials at Charles' alma mater, Princeton University, a program to develop young Americans for government service in the international arena—Foreign Service officers, trade and development officials, intelligence analysts and such like. In 1961, to launch and sustain the program, the Robertsons made a contribution of $35 million. Inside the Beltway, that may sound like loose change spilled from a bailout bill. But it was at the time the largest contribution ever made to the university. It is thus useful to remember as this story unfolds that the Robertsons are one of Princeton's most generous donor families. It should also be noted that the Robertsons were private people who were assured by Princeton that their contribution would remain anonymous.

The new program, housed on campus at the Woodrow Wilson School of Public and International Affairs, got off to a promising start. So promising in fact that the rumor began to spread, and then take root, that the lavishly funded program was in actuality a CIA front. Fearing damage to its academic reputation, Princeton then asked the Robertsons for a second contribution—this time, the gift of their privacy. The Robertsons consented, their patronage was publicly acknowledged and Robertson Hall, designed by the eminent architect Minoru Yamasaki, became the visible symbol of the school.

Over the decades that followed, the Wilson School grew in reputation and influence, becoming both an ornament to the university and a resource for the nation. The initial Robertson gift of $35 million grew just as impressively. After giving away hundreds of millions to support the Wilson School, the Robertson Foundation—the supporting organization set up to administer the family contribution—had amassed assets of approximately $930 million by late 2007. This stellar investment performance, in perfect symbiosis, fueled the ongoing academic excellence. The Robertson Foundation—directed by a board comprising four university appointees and three family members—was regarded as an unqualified success; indeed, as a model of collaboration between a donor family and an academic institution.

Over time, of course, the founding generation gave way to successors. On the family side, Charles and Marie passed on and were succeeded in family leadership by their four children and a cousin. Leadership turned over periodically at Princeton, too, bringing in people who had not been present at the creation of the foundation and seemed to the family to be less collegial and, ultimately, less committed to the founding vision. As the years passed, squabbles over procedural issues began to harden into principled disagreements. In the view of the second-generation Robertsons, the foundation was falling victim to mission creep. They became particularly concerned that the Wilson School was no longer turning out enough first-tier candidates for the Foreign Service. In one cohort of 66 Wilson students, for example, only three had entered the Foreign Service. More from that same cohort had gone into management consulting, more into investment banking, more into exotic quarters of the financial services industry. While those professions may have been warmly esteemed in the offices of the Princeton Alumni Fund, they were taken as warning signals by the Robertson family. The Wilson School seemed to be morphing into some hybrid form of business school. As the data crystallized year to year, the Robertsons came to believe that mission creep had turned into mission deflected, if not mission aborted. Princeton seemed committed to a course that their parents had not intended and would not have supported.

After years of disagreement and contentious meetings, the family filed suit in July 2002. In their complaint, the plaintiffs sought what their lawyers referred to as the "death penalty"—the transfer of the foundation's funds to other universities willing to carry out the Robertson mission. It is accurate to say that the lawsuit was filed and then pursued more in sorrow than in anger. Both of Charles and Marie's sons were themselves devoted Princeton alumni.

The university responded to the suit with a flurry of press attacks on the Robertsons—which I will not rehearse here—and launched a war of attrition designed to divide the family and exhaust its resources. And so the battle was joined . . .

Let me offer some observations on the winding course of this case that led to the settlement announced last month.

First, as Herman Kahn might have put it, a word about the correlation of forces. On the Robertson side, we had three first-class law firms—trial counsel in California, local counsel in New Jersey, settlement counsel in New York. We had two publicity offices. We had more than a dozen expert witnesses, each a brand-name specialist in some obscure corner of the nonprofit world. And we had a cadre of donors and would-be donors around the country that followed the case closely and provided sympathetic counsel. My own role fell under the category of litigation support, in which capacity I helped to give shape and direction to the case, while maintaining such coherence as we could between our twin campaigns, the one in the court of law and the other in the court of public opinion. (Yes, the great Irving Kristol was correct when he observed that the problem with contemporary society is that nobody can tell you what they do for a living in 25 words or less.) I had never been engaged in high-stakes litigation before, but I regarded our team as formidable, and likely to be irresistibly so. We had good people and plenty of them. That opinion was formed, alas, before the massed legions of Princeton University lumbered onto the field. In the conflict that followed, we might as well have been cast as the Tibetans, with Princeton as the Chinese army. What we discovered over the next six and one-half years is that if you walk down any corridor of New Jersey power—be it business, labor, law, media, finance, philanthropy or academia—you are likely to find ensconced in the corner office a chauvinistic Princetonian. You are virtually certain to find a person who hopes to send his or her children or grandchildren to Princeton. I have encountered such intensity of institutional allegiance only twice before. First at the U.S. Military Academy. During my White House Fellows days, I was surprised to find that Army officers, by then well established in their careers, still measured each other by how they had performed in classroom and PT contests waged 15 years earlier at West Point. Indeed, we know from their writings that even Eisenhower and MacArthur, well into late middle age, continued to eye each other through the prism of their performance as cadets. The other example is Yale. I returned to New Haven as a journalist in 2004, curious to learn why almost all of the stars of that political season had sprung from the same small college—George Bush, John Kerry, Howard Dean, Dick Cheney, Joe Lieberman. What I found at Yale was that curiosity ran elsewhere . . . to the question of how John Edwards had somehow managed to infiltrate their ranks. The point here is that Princeton was the home team and we were the visiting squad. Home court advantage was a factor from beginning to end, a reality that was punctuated by the hometown press coverage of the settlement itself. Readers of those stories could be forgiven for thinking that all of the issues had somehow been compromised away and that there had been no clear winner in the case.

Let me make a second point about the legal process. Watching big-time litigation up close should require parental consent. The process is nasty, brutish and long. Of the various motions filed by Princeton, none of them sought to sharpen the issue or resolve the case, all of them had the effect of delaying the proceedings, and not a few of them should have been memorialized on plaques in the Museum of Legal Nonsense. I am not a lawyer and I am thus not closely informed about the term "legal abuse," but to my untrained eye there was massive abuse of the system in this case. In her statement on the settlement last month, the president of Princeton opined that it was "tragic" that Princeton had been obliged to spend almost $40 million on legal fees—money that could have been better spent on education. I would observe, with due respect, that it was at the very core of Princeton's strategy to run up the legal bills and starve out the Robertsons. The Robertsons were ready—indeed, eager—for trial by 2004.

One result of a war of attrition is . . . attrition. On the family side, one of the original plaintiffs died. Members of the third generation grew to maturity and sought a voice in family councils. The original trial judge retired. His successor, swamped with administrative work, had to withdraw from the case. Her successor, a third judge, was called out of retirement to preside at trial. On the Princeton side, it should be conceded, there were signs of subtle improvement over the years, as the Wilson School seemed to tack back toward the original Robertson mission. I leave it to others to determine whether this late vocation was a matter of conviction or of case-related optics. Princeton even began a publicity campaign highlighting the contributions to public service made by its illustrious graduates. The results were mixed. One day I opened a document to find a glowing endorsement of the Wilson School from its distinguished alumnus, Eliot Spitzer. Shortly thereafter came the news that the governor had been conducting interstate commerce at the Mayflower Hotel. He was quickly replaced in the campaign by equally devoted Wilson alumnus Anthony Lake, about whom we have heard nothing but good things. And on the investment side, performance turned dramatically, from what had been notably good to what became alarmingly bad. Over the past year, the foundation fund, as a consequence of Princeton's huge bet on so-called alternative investments, has plunged precipitously. In its ill-fated attempt to out-Yale Yale in investment performance, Princeton had loaded up on private equity, hedge funds and other illiquid assets. My guesstimate is that at the time of the settlement the fund had declined to $585 million. (I should note that Princeton has disputed this figure, while declining to release supporting data.)

Let me comment, finally, on the settlement and what it means for the world of philanthropy. Just to remind you of the facts: Princeton paid $100 million to settle the Robertson lawsuit, the largest "donor intent" award in history.

One of the most heuristic documents produced during the discovery process was an audit of foundation spending. One of the Big Four accounting firms, PricewaterhouseCoopers, had been commissioned by the family to conduct a forensic audit of Robertson Foundation accounts. What PwC found was that large chunks of overhead had been misallocated, that professors and other personnel had been improperly billed to the foundation, that the construction of a building unrelated to the Robertson program—a building!—had been charged to the foundation. In total, according to PwC, more than $100 million of foundation funds had been misused by university officials.

Now, as it happened, the trial structure prescribed by the court would have begun with a presentation by the plaintiffs of the basic PwC findings. Day after day, a chronicle of Princeton's alleged misdeeds would have unfolded in the media capital of the world. Even at this distance, one can almost hear the taunts of the tabloids, the clucking of the *New York Times*. In my view—regardless of the verdict in the trial—Princeton's reputation would not have been stained: It would have been irreparably damaged. For Princeton to settle was a thoroughly rational decision.

The family had its own calculus of concerns. You've all heard the wisecrack, "If somebody says—'it's not the money, it's the principle of the thing'—you can bet it's the money." For the Robertson family it was, clearly, about the money *and* the principle. They wanted the money to carry out the original intentions of their parents to develop young talent for the Foreign Service and especially now, when a young and charismatic president has called on his fellow Americans to regenerate the soft power of diplomacy. The Robertsons also sought to uphold the lapidary principle that when a contribution is made for Purpose A, it cannot and should not be diverted to Purpose B. They sought to uphold that principle not only for their own family, but for donors and grantees everywhere. They succeeded. For donors, this case has brought a heartening example; for grantees, a sobering effect.

There were absolutists on both sides of the case—those who sought, on the one hand, a Mosaic reaffirmation of the Eighth Commandment or, on the other, a clarion declaration that donor rights should expire the moment the check clears. The absolutists were destined for disappointment at trial. In all likelihood, the verdict would have turned on an esoteric legal point, a conclusion fascinating to a few dozen lawyers and frustrating to a few million laymen. I sense no buyer's remorse on either side. The Robertsons reclaimed funds sufficient to the family task and secured at least for this generation the principle of donor rights. Princeton, for its part, was publicly embarrassed and financially penalized, but it managed to avoid the death penalty. Even before the legal contest was resolved, Princeton set up a new Office of Stewardship, whose responsibility it is to conform campus spending with donor intention. At this moment in time, the safest place on the planet for donor intent may well be Princeton, New Jersey.

At the risk of grandiosity, let me conclude by stating what I think this case means. At the heart of every charitable contribution is the concept of trust—trust by the donor that the grantee will do what he has agreed to do. If that trust is allowed to erode, if the donor can no longer rely on the grantee's assurance, then charitable contributions will decline and the civil society they sustain will decline along with them. If that were to happen—if the private, voluntary, civil society that Tocqueville first acclaimed, and that the Bradley Center still celebrates, were to wither away—America would abandon one of its defining national traits. Absent a vibrant civil society, only government would be left to fill the social vacuum and the America of tomorrow would come to look very much like the Europe of today.

As you work your way through your list of New Year's resolutions, please remember to thank the Robertson family. They have rendered a public service in the highest traditions of the Woodrow Wilson School.

PEOPLE:
APPRECIATIONS,
INTROS AND OBITS

National Review
April 19, 2011

THE INDOMITABLE SPIRIT

William A. Rusher, the indomitable spirit of the American Right, died on Saturday morning. From the early days in the shabby offices of *National Review* through the glittering days at the Reagan White House, Bill Rusher was the most impassioned and forceful presence in the modern conservative movement.

A few recollections:

• I met him when Bill and Pat Buckley invited me to dinner at their old townhouse on 69th Street, just across the street from an aromatic Chinese restaurant. A graduate of Princeton and Harvard Law School, Rusher had been a litigator with a top Wall Street firm and later, as a professional Communist-hunter, served as counsel to the Senate's famous (or infamous) Internal Security Subcommittee. He was prodigiously well-informed and sharply articulate—a man of hard commitments. My first impression of him was that, if you happened to be a Communist, you would be well advised not to let your scent find its way to his nostrils.

• When I got to *NR* in the early Sixties, Willi Schlamm had been expelled, Whittaker Chambers had died, and Russell Kirk's voice had become disembodied. The force fields were Buckley and Rusher, Burnham and Meyer, Bozell and Rickenbacker. The editorial meetings were occasions of high intensity. At that early stage, there was no operating manual for the conservative movement. We were making it up as we went along, issue by issue. At one pole was James Burnham, the "first neoconservative," a former Trotskyist, brilliant and intellectually playful. At the other was the voice of the emerging conservative orthodoxy, Bill Rusher, the grandson of a West Virginia socialist. These discussions, carefully moderated by Buckley, sometimes turned into debates and, somewhat less frequently, into ideological brawls. The moment that burns in memory occurred in the spring of 1964. Burnham had spun out an elaborate notion that, with Goldwater falling in the polls, *NR*, for exotic tactical reasons, should transfer its support to Nelson Rockefeller if he managed to beat Goldwater in the upcoming California primary. Burnham's bizarre pitch—*NR* wasn't just covering the Goldwater campaign; it *was* the Goldwater campaign—had its usual mesmerizing effect on Buckley, who seemed to be leaning toward Burnham's position. The meeting did not end well. Rusher stormed back to his office to draft his letter of resignation. (I, and perhaps others, did so as well.) In the event, Goldwater won the primary and the letters were dropped in the round file. A loss to history, I suspect. Rusher's letter, written in magnificent fury, would have singed eyebrows for miles around. Day in, day out, for 31 and a half years as publisher of *NR*, Bill Rusher was indispensable in hammering out what became the basic doctrine of conservative politics.

• Bill Rusher was the first conservative talk-radio star—not as a host, but as a guest. After a full day at the office and a fine meal—always a fine meal—Rusher would appear as the conservative token on late-night radio in New York City. Programs hosted by Long John Nebel and Barry Gray were regular stops: A liberal host and two or three liberal guests made the odds "just about right" for the scrappy, self-confident Rusher. Token, indeed. Well-prepared and bulldog-tenacious, he won a legion of new fans for his dog-bites-man politics. I later got him a gig on a PBS debate show called *The Advocates*, where each week he faced down a liberal opponent, a liberal audience, and, in the moderator's chair, an even-handed fellow by the name of Michael Dukakis. The debates were judged by viewers voting by postcard. Rusher became PBS's worst nightmare. He won week after week.

• Bill Rusher was a tireless recruiter and mentor for his cause and country. Thousands of us got letters of encouragement, hundreds a reference or an opened door, a few of us, the charmed inner circle, got the Rusher World Tour. No, not Paris and Rome. Taipei, Jo-burg, and other islands stretched out along the anti-Commie archipelago. How large did Bill Rusher bulk in these beleaguered capitals of political disfavor? True story:

In the early Seventies, I was in Tokyo on business and received an invitation to join Rusher for an official visit to Taiwan. I arrived early in the morning, rushed through a series of events, and then repaired to a government office for a briefing on the following day's schedule. The evening news was playing a series of clips on a television monitor—me at the airport, me disembarking from a limo, me at the Foreign Office, me at a reception at Madame Chiang's Grand Hotel. I became transfixed. This was not the sort of coverage that would have attended my arrival in, say, Cincinnati. I asked my government handler what the gist of the story was. He paused, pondered, and then said with a sweep of his hand, "Friend of Rusher arrives in Taipei."

National Review
May 16, 2011

WILLIAM RUSHER, PART TWO: DEBATER

T he young Bill Rusher took to debating pretty much as the circling shark takes to soft human tissue—with hungry purpose and to startling effect. Rusher received his basic training in the blood sport at Princeton's Whig-Clio society and then polished his skills as the feisty co-founder of the Young Republican Club at Harvard Law School. (For a sense of the correlation of forces in Cambridge, think of a School for Entrepreneurship at Moscow University along about the middle of the last century.) Rusher took his graduate debate work to Washington, chasing furtive Communist witnesses down dark testimonial holes for the Senate Internal Security Subcommittee. It was there, as a Senate investigator and quasi-prosecutor, that he developed the ultimate debate weapon: what we came to call The Rusher Question.

The Rusher Question never elicited, nor indeed expected, the courtesy of reply. It was in business for itself. In its basic form, it went something like this: "Mr. Smith, if you were not at the hotel on the night in question—despite the fact that, as their testimony will show, you were observed in the dining room by the maitre d', two waiters, three hotel guests, the sommelier, and the busboy—where exactly do you claim that you were that night?" The normal human response to such questions is some variation of: "Abba, dabba, dabba." As the witness fumbled through his memory files, Rusher would add helpfully, "I would remind you, Mr. Smith—if that is in fact your real name—that you are under oath."

Over the years, from the Senate to the college speaking circuit to the television studio, Bill Rusher became the premier debater on the American Right. Our own indigenous Mountie, he almost always got his man. Only a single exception sticks to the brainpan on this sad day. Rusher spent years, almost a decade, chasing Jacob Javits around the ideological block. Time and again, New York's über-liberal Republican would manage to skip past the snares set for him by Trapper Bill. In a 1968 book, Rusher finally conceded defeat. In a passage that deserves at least a footnote in the history of polemical writing, Rusher issued this verdict: "As for Jacob Javits, you pays your money and takes your choice. It is simply not possible to believe that his Communist contacts in 1945 and 1946 were all totally innocent. But was he a Communist sympathizer, as some of his critics believe? Or was he merely a garden-variety opportunist, as his more candid defenders contend?" That is a quintessentially Rusherian judgment, even if one doubts that Javits's defenders would ever so contend.

Bill Rusher could have written the book on debating and, in due course, he did. He published *How to Win Arguments* in 1981—explaining structure, pace, diversion, jujitsu moves, time-buying techniques, the whole bag of tricks. What's not in there is what Bill Rusher brought preeminently to the public arena: a competitive fire born of utter conviction. I can see him now—coiled forward in his chair, the klieg lights glinting off his no-nonsense glasses, measuring his opponent with gimlet eye, awaiting the opening that he knows will surely come. In wobbly moments, you could almost feel sorry for the poor bastard across the stage from him.

For an entire generation of American conservatives, Bill Rusher was our lawyer. We were all his pro bono clients, deeply grateful that he cared so much, and that he pressed our case so effectively.

National Review
April 16, 2012

MANAGING EDITORS

D
ear Priscilla Buckley. Yes, she had two first names and many of us used both of them.

I will have more to say on this tender subject in the weeks ahead, but two settled thoughts should be recorded immediately, one of them personal and the other corporate.

For me, she was a constant of the universe, from the day I stumbled in to *NR* in the 1960s and asked her to show me how to be an editor, until two weeks ago when she helped me resolve a sticky issue with the Buckley Program at Yale, on whose board she served, unquestioned, as the only non-Yalie director. She saved my bacon as a columnist. She saved my bacon in a dust-up with Frank Meyer, who was known to tear young ideological deviants limb from limb. She even saved my bacon with her little brother. For a decade, I served hazardous duty editing WFB's newspaper column. When on rare occasions we would reach an impasse over a point of fact or usage, we would appeal to the highest court in the land, Dear Priscilla, whose opinion carried the force of law.

Here's the larger thought. If you have loitered over the years in the hallowed precincts of *NR*—at dinners, book parties, cruises, and such-like—you will have heard the toasts and tributes to Priscilla. What a fine colleague she was, what an irenic office presence—that sort of thing. You probably took those encomia as grace notes, old-fashioned gallantries extended from old-fashioned men to an ornamental woman. That's not even close. Those old-fashioned men were stating a plainspoken truth: Priscilla *did* hold the magazine together, and by extension the conservative movement. Remember the cast of characters in the formative years: Willmoore Kendall, Willi Schlamm, Frank Meyer, Bill Rickenbacker, Brent Bozell, Bill Rusher—these were not all reliably clubbable gents. They were men of large ego and short fuse, bonded in the conceit that the future of civilization itself hung on their deliberations. Even Jim Burnham, behind his bowtie and avuncular countenance, enjoyed a good scrap now and again.

WFB, who had neither talent nor appetite for personal confrontation, would let the "spirited exchanges" play out. If they didn't subside in reasonable term, he would intervene with an ornate levity. That worked, sometimes, and the meeting would then proceed. When it didn't, and the debates rose to DEFCON 2 levels, we knew that it would soon be . . . Priscilla Time. Usually the only woman in the room and on occasion the only adult, Priscilla would gently scold the line-crossers, smooth a path for combatant retreat, and restore the meeting to anodyne sodality. It was a magical process, conducted by a real-life magician.

I recall only a single exception. In the late winter of 1964, Jim Burnham, feeling perhaps a bit pyromaniacal, offered one of his recondite theories on why the superior choice for *NR* would be Rockefeller rather than Goldwater. Bill Rusher, a Goldwaterite to the tips of his cordovans, reacted as all of us could have predicted: like Old Faithful, first fizzing, then burbling, and finally erupting in an explosive rant. It was too much even for Dear Priscilla. She quietly gathered her papers, made her excuses, and departed to attend to some urgent matter. John Paul II, he of the saintly patience, would have departed five minutes earlier.

For donkey's years, Priscilla carried the title of managing editor, and the job involved, among many other duties, the managing of editors. We miss you already, Dear Pitts.

The American Spectator
July 15, 2011

IN PRAISE OF M. STANTON EVANS

The following remarks were delivered at a celebration of Mr. Evans' distinguished career, held at the National Press Club in Washington, D.C. on July 12, 2011.

I have known Stan Evans for a long time, approximately ten years longer than he has known me.

When I arrived on campus as a college freshman, Stan's aura was very much present, even though he had graduated some years earlier. Just as it was assumed by us impressionable youth that a lanky prepster named George H.W. Bush might one day play a prominent role in public life, it was assumed, as well, that M. Stanton Evans would leave his mark on American journalism. And so it came to pass.

Stan will have forgotten this historic occasion, but I met him at an all-day meeting convened in Newark, New Jersey to contemplate the future of the Girl Scouts of America. In those hand-to-mouth days for us token conservatives, we would go almost anywhere for 200 bucks. I was late in arriving and took my seat at the long table of conferees, with the audience rising around us in serried ranks to the top of a modernistic amphitheatre. The ritual introductions were already in progress. They went something like this:

"Hello, I'm William Bigelow from the Committee for Racial Equality. If we do nothing else today, we must confront the racial oppression under which millions of Girl Scouts of color are suffering each and every day."

Murmurs of warm approval rippled through the audience.

Then: "Hello, I'm J. Somersworth Farnsby, co-founder of the Coalition for a Nuke-free America. I hope that we can all agree that the failure of the Girl Scouts to confront the overriding moral issue of our time—our government's stockpiling of nuclear weapons—is a national disgrace. That disgrace should end right here, right now."

There followed a sitting ovation for J. Somersworth.

And then: "Aloha. I'm Rev. Cindy Cistern from the Church for a Better Tomorrow! I'd certainly agree with Somersworth that we ought to rid the Girl Scouts of the badges, the uniforms and all the terrifying emblems of US militarism. And, as William says, racial injustice is clearly omnipresent in contemporary America. But the larger challenge for us is to throw open the doors for all young women to the full range of sexual possibility."

Thunderous applause for Sister Cistern.

Along about this point in the program, the calculation was hardening that I should have held out for 300 bucks. And then . . . rolling out of the American heartland, came a rich, reassuring baritone voice saying, "Good morning. I'm M. Stanton Evans, a nonpartisan observer of the public policy process." Tentative applause, much confusion, as a couple of hundred nervous Girl Scout officials strained to get a glimpse of the nonpartisan observer in their midst.

You will remember those Gahan Wilson cartoons in the *New Yorker*. Scenes of a movie audience watching a horror flick. People writhing in their seats, screaming, covering their eyes with their fingers. In the middle of the audience sits one weird, pudgy little kid, grinning wildly from ear to ear. That was me. With M. Stanton Evans in the house, I knew that we had them outnumbered. And so it came to pass. That conference proved to be a long day for the forces of peace and sexual possibility.

I learned that day about one of Stan's signal contributions to the public conversation: By the rigor of his thought, the clarity of his expression, and the sheer weight of his argument, he has leveled every playing field on which he has chosen to compete.

Another contribution—familiar to most of you here tonight—has been his rare gifts as a teacher. The first book I ever edited was a book written by Stan. In the front matter to that volume, Stan did the necessary, thanking his professional associates before making the conventional stipulation that any shortcomings were solely the responsibility of the author. That was a rare journalistic lapse on Stan's part and it should be corrected. For the next edition of his book, I have suggested the following language for the acknowledgment page: "I am grateful for any trace of wit, insight or erudition that managed to survive the clumsy interventions of my so-called editor, who if justice had prevailed would have been honing his dull editorial blade on some far distant whetstone."

It will come as no surprise to those of you who have benefited from his tutelage that Stan has been a pivotal professional influence for an entire generation of conservative writers and editors. He has been patient and nurturing in the early going, and then proud and puffing as we achieved some minor success. In recent years, Stan has taken on yet another role. In his magisterial book, *Blacklisted by History*, and in books still to come, he has kept the files, sorted the data, and inscribed the lists of those who betrayed the United States during the Cold War. It is lonely, widely unappreciated work and in doing it Stan has become the Elie Wiesel of the anti-Communist cause, the man who remembers everything.

Stan's influence now reaches deeply into the generations behind him. My own grandson Harry, aged five, found his admission to preschool slowed a bit when he was asked to identify his most enjoyable activity. The approved answer at this progressive institution is some form of "helping the disadvantaged." Instead, Harry announced his enthusiasm for "hunting rats." After an unnerving delay, Harry was finally accepted and began in his diligent way to prepare for his kindergarten interview a few months hence. I have suggested that—in tribute to his Uncle Stan—Harry should particularize his answer by announcing that he now enjoys "hunting Commie rats."

One of the most telling things ever said about Stan Evans was said by our dear friend Bill Rusher, who died this spring after serving for a half-century as the central gyroscope of the conservative movement. Bill said to me and, I'm sure, to others: "If anybody ever wants to know what ol' Rusher would have thought about something, and Rusher's not around, ask Evans." Well, some of us do want to know and we ask and we are never disappointed. Stan has become the indispensable man of our common enterprise, the wisest among us.

Let me give you just one example of that wisdom. Stan and I recently collaborated in an effort to reinvigorate a nonprofit institution. During the course of those deliberations, Stan gave me some advice that will henceforward guide all of my bureaucratic activity. Said Stan: "It's amazing how much credit you can take, if you don't care about accomplishing anything."

My remarks tonight have most assuredly *not* been a testimonial to Stan Evans. Such raw sentimentality would have no place in an occasion of this kind. It's merely an acknowledgement of my gratitude to Stan for being my mentor, my friend and our central gyroscope.

The American Spectator
August 20, 2009

BOB NOVAK, BOY REPORTER

T he news of Bob Novak's death recalled a line of Roy Blount's about a deceased friend: "I was shocked to learn of his death. It was so unlike him." So it was with Bob Novak. He was so relentless in pursuit of his boyhood dreams, so delighted to be the Joliet kid all grown up and still chasing big-deal Beltway stories, so alive. After working alongside him for a few years, I told him that I had finally discovered the secret of his success. "Novak, you're not all that smart. You just work harder than everybody else." He replied, "My secret is that, for me, it's not hard work." It is a great pleasure, unfortunately a rare pleasure, to run across somebody who knows *exactly* what he should be doing with his life. That was Bob Novak, boy reporter, dead this week at 78.

I was grateful to Bob Novak for many things, but especially so for three personal favors. (I'm assuming that anybody reading this page would know by now that Bob was not really a curmudgeon, that he just played one on TV.) My first encounter with him was back in the Sixties when I was dispatched to Washington to open a bureau for *National Review*. In terms of journalistic experience—that fingertip-savvy required to navigate one's way through a bureaucracy—I might as well have been dispatched to Ulan Bator. I was wet in front of the ears. The political climate was a bit chilly, as well. With LBJ and his Great Society liberalism running amok (and with many of its excesses covered sympathetically by then-moderate columnist Bob Novak, recently married to one of LBJ's pretty assistants), the idea of helping an indigent right-wing journal was not high on Bob's must-do list. But he was always a sucker for scrappy journalism and he lent a friendly hand. He found me some space that could pass for an office, invited me to press events (i.e., events with free food and drink) and, virtually alone among his peers, didn't seem embarrassed to be seen in public with *NR*'s callow correspondent. When my tour ended, Bob quickly took my successor in hand. It was a concierge service, I would later calculate, that he provided over the years to scores of young journalists.

Roughly 20 years later, with Bob by that time firmly established as a mega-pundit in multimedia, I, by that time a semi-established TV producer, was trying to persuade the ABC station to carry my new show, *MoneyPolitics*. I knew it would work, I just knew it would work, but of course TV executives spend all day talking to guys who just know their shows will work; almost all of those guys, the record will show, turn out to be wrong. There was no sale at ABC. What to do? It was time to call Bob Novak. I needed him, both as "talent" and as friend of the enterprise. He listened to my pitch, which we both recognized was canted several rungs beneath his station, almost insultingly so: "scale wages" (that's industry jargon for "peanuts"), no car service, no residuals and—best of all for a guy who owned a beloved beach house on Fenwick Island—we planned to shoot the show Friday nights. Only the last point provoked a question from Novak, a skeptical newsy's question: "You're going to tape Friday night for Sunday air?" I replied, trying to sound thoughtfully frugal, "Yes, we can split crew costs by using the hot studio between the 6 and 11 o'clock newscasts." To a pro like Bob Novak, a pillar of the talk-show punditocracy, this was the equivalent of Judy saying to Mickey: "We can borrow Mr. Wilson's barn and put on a show that will knock the socks off the whole town." Novak glowered at me for a long moment (he was a world-class glowerer) and said, "I'll do it." And he did. He helped sell ABC on the show and then, Friday after Friday, he showed up at the end of a long day at the end of a long week and knocked our socks off. The boy reporter would always arrive with a scoop for our viewers, our precious few viewers. Along about 10:30 at night, he would tool off to his beach house in a black Corvette, $367 richer.

Some years later, at a reunion of the *MoneyPolitics* crew, I noted that we all had gotten something out of the series. Several of our newbie talents had shot to the edge of stardom—Alan Murray, Larry Kudlow, Pat Choate and Jim Glassman, among others. TV can do that. Most of our production team had gone on to big-time network jobs. And I, of course, had gained street cred as a producer. (We frequently beat *Meet the Press* in the ratings.) All of us got something out of the show except Bob Novak, who had done us all a professional favor by agreeing to play Mr. Wilson's barn.

Then a few years ago, Bob brought out his autobiography, *The Prince of Darkness*. I have yet to meet a reader who was not simply stunned by that book. It wasn't that we didn't think Bob had it in him. It's that we didn't think he had it all in him: the patience, the fine judgments, the narrative skills and the sheer balls to pull it off. The book is a masterwork, capturing a time and place—late-century Washington, D.C.—as indelibly as Tom Wolfe captured Wall Street in *The Bonfire of the Vanities*. For the rest of time, whenever a student or an anthropologist or a cultural coroner wants to know just what it was like, that *fin de siècle* Beltway world, he has only to crack a copy of *Prince*. It's all there.

In the manner of all magisterial books, *Prince* can be read at several levels. For the citizen, it's a file from a clear-eyed foreign correspondent, reporting with an air of disbelief from a distant capital. For us recovering journalists, it's an operating manual. For every big story he covered, which was every story worth covering, Bob opens his files and tells us who told him what about whom. (His text settles the open question: Bob Novak, deadline Manichean, did indeed see the world as divided fundamentally between two opposing groups. No, not Righties and Lefties. But sources and targets. I suggested to him once that if he ever got around to founding the Novak School of Journalism, he should consider adopting the motto, "Leak, or be leaked upon.") Doris Lessing, feeling her years, once said: "The thing about getting old is the number of things you think you can't say aloud because it would be too shocking." In *Prince*, Bob Novak says all of those things, loudly.

Bob's autobiography also includes a few passages about himself, written, typically, with raw candor. He was too ambitious. He was too selfish. He drank too much. He was aloof in the Disraeli mode, never complaining, never explaining. Maybe. But he was nowhere near as tough as he pretended to be. He could feel pain, and never more sharply than when David Frum and *National Review* gang-punched him for being "unpatriotic." (His tense and moving account of this episode appears near the end of *Prince* and is worth a second reading.) But let's not let Bob Novak's candor bury our own lede. Even from his own unforgiving account, it's clear that he was all you could hope for in a friend, a journalist and a fellow citizen. He was honest in his work, humble in his quest for understanding, devoted to his country, faithful to his family and friends. A man in full.

Omni New Haven Hotel
New Haven, Connecticut
November 30, 2012

MITCH DANIELS

The following remarks were delivered at the dinner of the annual conference of the William F. Buckley, Jr. Program at Yale.

One of the objectives of the Buckley Program is to convey to students a sense of the political possibilities in American life. Some of those possibilities can be neglected on a campus where most of the students, the faculty and the administration seem to shuffle along to the same old drummer. The eponymous Mr. Buckley, as some of you will remember and others of you will have heard, was not much of a shuffler. It was Bill Buckley, in fact, who showed Yale and then the nation just how large the possibilities could be. When asked what he proposed to do with his young and financially malnourished magazine, Bill Buckley—no Burkean, he—would flash that lupine grin and say with theatrically false immodesty, "We propose to change the world."

Adults would laugh indulgently. Only young people seemed to understand that he meant exactly what he had said. Bill's boast was a kind of dog whistle, inaudible to many, a clarion call to some.

Our speaker tonight has sensed, engaged and realized many of the possibilities of political life. As a student at Princeton, he observed the gathering forces of reform. As a senatorial aide on Capitol Hill, he learned the mechanics of policy development. As political director in the Reagan White House, he began to shape the course of national affairs. He then became a senior executive in the pharmaceutical industry, where he mastered the subjects of cash flow, investment risk and capital return, subjects unaddressed, we can safely assume, by the curricula at Occidental, Columbia and Harvard Law School.

Our speaker then returned to Washington as budget director in the second Bush administration, where he attempted with passion and wit and intermittent success to restrain federal spending. I should note that he has been criticized for the profligate habits of the Bush years, but the record will show that, in the matter of budget deficits, the incumbent administration in its best year was three times worse than our speaker in his worst year.

By then roundly prepared for his dream job, our speaker moved back to Indiana and ran for governor. Elected in 2004 and then again in 2008, he has provided a model of frugal and imaginative governance. Compare him to his peers. When Governor Christie proposed minor labor reforms, the state of New Jersey shook with indignation. In New Jersey, as you know, indignation is rarely righteous. Just indignant. When Governor Walker proposed minor labor reforms, the state of Wisconsin burst into flames. It is instructive to recall, when tempted to fight fire with fire, that the Fire Department itself uses water. Our speaker tonight, dousing the flames with anodyne rhetoric, signed legislation this year making Indiana the first right-to-work state ever in the industrialized Midwest. What price did the governor pay for this effrontery? Riots in the streets? Recall elections? A lecture on public morals from Al Sharpton? As he retires from office in the next few weeks, our speaker carries with him approval ratings in the mid '60s, which, in Hoosier terms, is Larry Bird country. The governor's record, eight years in, bears the hallmark of commonsense conservatism—deep-going reform with no fuss and no feathers, the crystallization of what Bill Buckley used to celebrate as "the politics of reality."

A few months ago, our speaker was elected the new president of Purdue University, a position he will assume early next year. Those of us concerned about American education like to think that we now have a firewall: that academic fads, expensively incubated in laboratories at coastal universities, will now disappear in a series of unexplained accidents somewhere in the vicinity of Lafayette, Indiana. Purdue is well-known as a can-do kind of place, the alma mater of Gus Grissom, Neil Armstrong, Eugene Cernan and 19 other US astronauts. It will soon have a can-do president and we look to it for deep-going educational reform, with no fuss, no feathers.

Another hallmark of common-sense conservatism is the recognition that politics is and should be only one part of the well-lived life. You will thus not be surprised to learn that our speaker is a man of several parts, among them these:

• He is a four-tool second baseman in fantasy baseball camps.

• He is the leader of America's least menacing biker gang.

• And he is the man who calmed an anxious nation by pledging never to make Purdue the Princeton of the Midwest.

Ladies and gentlemen, the Honorable Mitchell E. Daniels, Jr.

National Review
February 5, 2014

AN AMERICAN STORY

The Triumphs and Struggles of Brent Bozell

The following is the Foreword for Living on Fire: The Life of L.
Brent Bozell Jr., *a biography of one of the conservative movement's most influential founders.*

Daniel Kelly, the author of the book you hold in your hands, was
a rare blessing to me—a good friend made late in life. When I
met him seven years ago, he was toying with the idea of writing
this book. I urged him to do it and, over the subsequent years, I pestered
him to finish it. He seemed for several reasons to be the right man for a
very challenging assignment.

Most importantly, Dan had seen the young Brent Bozell on a public
platform. When Dan was a graduate student at the University of Wisconsin,
Brent had come through Madison on a speaking tour. I asked Dan what he
thought of Brent's performance and Dan's one-word, decidedly unprofes-
sorial review was: "Wow." That settled the threshold question. Nobody
would have to persuade Dan Kelly that Brent had been an electric speaker,
a special forensic talent combining folksy, Midwestern affability with a
razor-sharp, legally trained mind. (As just one point of reference, Brent's
debate partner—some would say, junior partner—when Yale beat a previously undefeated Oxford team was a fellow named William F. Buckley Jr.)

Secondly, Dan had previously published a full-length biography of
James Burnham, the longtime senior editor of *National Review* magazine.
Jim Burnham was a man of the file, the comprehensive file, a habit born
of his early experience as a CIA analyst. If Dan had spent a few years immersed in Burnham's papers, one could be confident that Dan Kelly knew
the story of the conservative movement from the ground up. So that box
was checked, too.

Finally, Dan was a Catholic mensch. That a man named Daniel Kelly should have sprung from Catholic roots was not much of a surprise, but beyond any theological affinity with Brent, who was a convert to Catholicism, Dan was acutely aware of the vicissitudes of this earthly life. When I met him, Dan was still recovering from liver-transplant surgery. He soon developed a virulent cancer and, perhaps worst of all for a historian, a creeping diabetes that was stealing his eyesight. To borrow a phrase from this book, Dan was suffering from "a Homeric catalogue of infirmities." He succumbed to those infirmities in late 2012, but not before finishing the manuscript that would become this fine biography. (That Dan completed the book at all was an act of gallantry: In the dimming light of his own life, Dan told me that he couldn't bear to default on his promise to Brent's widow, the luminous Patricia Buckley Bozell, who had entrusted Dan with the unvarnished tale of her time with Brent.)

The subject of this book, L. Brent Bozell Jr., had been my predecessor as Washington correspondent for *National Review*. That gig was my dream job. But in 1964, after only a few months in grade, I resigned to join the Bozell-for-Congress campaign in Maryland. That was a rash career move, obviously, but it was not quite as crazy as it may have appeared. Those of us who worked on Brent's campaign felt privileged to be boarding the bullet train of contemporary politics. There was much chit-chat about John F. Kennedy's race for a Boston congressional seat back in the Forties. We Bozell-ites liked to think that we were on something of that same JFK trajectory. A couple of terms in the House, a U.S. Senate race, and soon after that, we fantasized, it would be off to the *Casa Blanca* for us. That was the raw expectation, anyway. I don't mean to suggest that we saw it as a slam dunk, Joe and Jack Kennedy-style, but neither did it appear to be a desperation three-ball. Brent was that good.

In Dan Kelly's sober judgment, that campaign became not the first rung on a ladder reaching to the sky, but, in the clear rendering of hindsight, the apogee of Brent's political career.

In this absorbing and moving account, Dan Kelly tells the full story of Brent Bozell, both the early triumphs and the heartbreaking stumbles.

By the time he had reached his late 30s, Brent was a man not just of youthful promise but of precocious achievement. Among his signal contributions, to my eye at least, were these: He launched the Goldwater movement, which triggered a seismic shift in American politics; he was one of a handful of men who salvaged the anti-Communist cause from the missteps of its boisterous champion, Senator Joseph McCarthy; and he was the lawyer–cum–policy wonk who framed the telling arguments against judicial activism—at the time, fresh and potent arguments—that reverberate to this very day in our national dialogue. (You will hear those arguments yet again when a candidate is nominated for the next vacancy on the Supreme Court.) Based on these early accomplishments, Brent Bozell must be reckoned, along with Buckley, Burnham, Frank Meyer, and Russell Kirk, as one of the founding fathers of the modern conservative movement.

The second half of Brent's life was not always pretty. After his early success, he turned from defending the country to defending his faith. From there, in stages, he became consumed by fervor, fanaticism, and, off at the end, delusion. His life became a protracted struggle in which a brilliant intellect fought valiantly against insidious maladies of the mind. Brent's downward drift became an agony not only for him but for those who loved him—his wife and ten children, his devoted friends, and his many distant admirers who had been exhilarated by his brief turn upon the public stage. Dan Kelly tells this part of the tale with candor and compassion and, in the last chapter of Brent's life, a story that was entirely new to me and, I suspect, to most of Brent's other friends. I won't ruin it for you here, but I can tell you this much—how Brent spent his last days was both astonishing and, ultimately, redeeming.

The story of Brent Bozell is an American story, a *big* American story, and one that should be more widely known. Thanks to Dan Kelly, it will be.

National Review
August 5, 1988

JUSTICE: LYN NOFZIGER

T his item just in on the ticker under a Fairbanks, Alaska, dateline: "Arnold Forbush today became the first person convicted under this city's harsh new anti-yo-yo statute. Forbush, 64, was apprehended last September 30 at 3:20 p.m., his string at full draw, twenty minutes past the municipal curfew. Hopwood Farnsworth, spokesman for Fairbanks' YoYo Patrol, commented, 'We intend to press for a jail term. This guy Forbush acts as if nothing much happened.'"

No, just kidding. Fairbanks is fine. But here in Washington, D.C, we're getting a bit jumpy, jurisprudentially speaking. The powers that be—and from the convicted man's point of view, they look mighty powerful—are contemplating a nice, long lesson-teaching jail term for Franklyn C. (Lyn) Nofziger. You remember him. He is the former White House aide who was accused of calling or writing three old friends in 1982, in each case asking for a favor for a business client. These favors did not involve wine, women, controlled substances, or Hawk missiles, but according to the Feds they were improperly sought. There is a law, it seems, that forbids people like Nofziger to ask for those favors until some months after they leave government service.

This law is called—and you'll be pleased to keep your face straight— the Ethics in Government Act. As it happens, its name is not only oxymoronic but misnomeric. For virtually everybody in government is exempted from it—all congresspeople of course (we noncongresspeople consider it something of a breakthrough that Congress has not exempted itself from the income tax), all judiciary-branch people, and almost all executive-branch people. Indeed, over the entire life of the Ethics in Government Act the Feds have found only one hide to nail under the statute: the aforesaid Franklyn C. (Lyn) Nofziger. And you thought Patrick Henry and Sam Adams had rid us of that legislative medievalism, the bill of attainder? (It's worse than that, actually. So murky was this statute that

Nofziger felt obliged to seek legal clarification before doing *anything* after he left the White House. His lawyer assured him that he was practicing safe commercial intercourse.)

When Nofziger finally went to trial in the winter of 1988 (that's right, 1988) he was thrust before a jury of his peers—as it happened, 12 peers from the District of Columbia, who if the law of averages means anything had voted against Ronald Reagan with aberrational intensity. The prosecution lost no opportunity to make the point that Nofziger and Reagan were politically indistinguishable. Nofziger had, after all, been one of Reagan's closest aides since the gubernatorial days in Sacramento. By the end of the five-week trial, jurors could have been forgiven for supposing that Nofziger had spent most of his year in the White House personally closing out welfare accounts. The jury voted solidly for Mondale and conviction. Even the working press, which does not shrink from the sight of a right-winger getting what's coming to him, felt that something other than justice had been done.

The flavor of the trial was captured best not by lawyers or reporters but by Nofziger's doggerel diary, *A Trial Is Not Necessarily a Tribulation* (rights to which, if Jim Wright's publisher shakes a leg, may still be available):

WHAT A BAD BOY AM I
I listen carefully to every charge
And wonder why I'm still at large.
No one as criminal as me
Should be permitted to roam free.

The other day I went round to see Nofziger in his 18th Street townhouse office. His business is a uniquely Washington establishment. He produces neither steel ingots nor handmade sweaters but influence, a business that has never won a place in public affection next to the family farm. When the going was good the business rolled ahead, not in the headlong style of Mike Deaver, but with enough dash and puff to excite some envy. Buzzing with high spirits a few years ago, the firm is now a quiet, barebones operation. But Nofziger keeps plugging; a few clients have stuck with him and, even more remarkably, 1,500 friends have contributed unasked to his legal-defense fund. Emotionally, Nofziger is on hold. The judge will decide this fall whether he goes to jail.

His secretary points me upstairs and into the presence of The Felon. My first impression is that the criminal type isn't what it used to be. He is 64, survivor of a stroke five years ago, tieless, fussing with that implausible goatee. His girth is slightly more ample than ample. ("I'm a nervous eater and I have a lot to be nervous about.") As he describes the crime, I consider the punishment. There *is* a democratic case for bringing the high and mighty low and feeble. And Nofziger is low if not feeble. His savings are depleted, his name stained, some of his good years chewed up by the big red, white, and blue legal machine. But sending him to jail, making an example of him, teaching him another lesson? Why? To whom? About what? Enough. Enough.

The American Spectator
March 23, 2009

STEVE ADAMS:
BULL'S-EYE PHILANTHROPIST

I knew Steve Adams in college. He didn't know me. He was a senior and I was a freshman and our relationship thus became frozen in time. When Steve is 105 years old and I am 102, he will still be the older, more mature presence, the wiser man.

Over the years I've watched Steve's career out of the corner of my eye. Following graduation, he went on to Stanford business school and then into private equity. This was 40 years ago, mind you, and well before private equity was cool. In those days, PE was a way to buy and build a business rather than a technique for stripping assets, or a hook from which to hang debt for the flipper's dividend. Think of Steve Adams as more Henry Ford than Henry Kravis.

Steve built himself a heck of a business. RV dealerships and equipment stores and magazines for the campers. If you've ever hit the open road in anything larger than an SUV, chances are that you've done business with Steve. And if you have, chances are even better that you returned as a satisfied customer to do business with him again. He's innovated constantly and improved the customer experience over and over. In his hands, recreational camping became an American obsession and, ultimately, a big business. Steve is generally regarded as one of the two superstars of his high-performing B-School class, the other being Phil Knight, the founder of Nike.

I may have given you the impression that Steve's some kind of trailer-park guy. If he sounds like a campground bumpkin, you should also know that he owns six chateaux in Bordeaux, including three in St. Emilion and one in Pomerol. Your correspondent can confirm, after extensive research, that Steve produces some of the biggest red wines in the world. He's a man of several parts, actually, and in his mid 50s he took up the piano. Not the way you and I might take up the piano, finger-fumbling our way through Cole Porter to Billy Joel. With characteristic diligence, Steve dug in and practiced until he became accomplished, until he could apprehend the almost-inaudible distinction between very good and great. He became very good. He preferred great.

In 1999 Steve gave $10 million to the Yale School of Music to bring its facilities up to international-class. The school's faculty, which was already good, improved further. Admissions to the school became more competitive and some of the students reached for greatness. Now and then, one of them broke through. Steve was thrilled.

And then puzzled. Why, he wondered, did so few of these high-potential student musicians go on to become career professionals? Why were young musicians with the kind of talent he could only dream of having—why were they quitting just when greatness seemed within their grasp? Steve worried the question some, turning it over like a business problem, and came up with the answer. Student loans, he surmised. When a Yale graduate tripped off to McKinsey & Co. or Morgan Stanley, he or she could pay off the loans with the first bonus check. No problem. For a young musician, those same loans proved to be a pile of bricks in the knapsack and, too often, they buckled the knees. In response to economic pressure, Steve concluded, potentially great musicians were turning into fungible management consultants. There was something wrong with that picture. So he went back to the School of Music with a suggestion. He offered to pay the tuition bills himself. For every student. Every year. In 2005, Steve Adams prepaid $100 million worth of student tuitions.

The results have been immediate and unsurprising. Admission standards have been elevated, the faculty has attracted new stars and the School of Music now offers a program fully competitive with the major conservatories—all of this with an Ivy League education thrown in as a side benefit. Yale may one day soon be celebrated more for its instrumental musicians than for its *a cappella* singing groups.

Stephen Adams. Of how many people can it be said that they enhanced the quality of music for audiences around the world?

I should note that Steve's not a horn-tooter. He made his gift anonymously. The only reason he's talking about it now is that, with his reunion coming up this spring, he'd like to encourage his classmates to think creatively. Perhaps he'll have that effect on others, as well.

National Review
September 6, 2016

A *FIRING LINE* CONVERSATION
WITH ANGELO CODEVILLA

I have been following the Trump camp in recent days, picking my way through rowdy campaign events and empty campaign offices, trying to sharpen my understanding not so much of the candidate, who has defeated understanding, but of his supporters who, having taken a summer-long blast from the media water cannon, are standing with him still.

On the basis of several dozen conversations with Trump supporters, these are my summary notes, served neat:

In every group of 1,000 Trump voters, there is one made-for-TV skinhead. With remarkable efficiency, the designated nut-job is identified and packaged for tele-journalists who in other circumstances might be expected to deplore the conflation of anecdote with datum.

Trump voters consider themselves to be the party of common sense. Honest.

They think it's "wrong" for an anatomically correct man to be in the girls' bathroom. They think it's even more wrong for the government to enforce his right to be there.

They think it's "stupid" to give more weight to a Muslim refugee's right to practice his religion than to an American citizen's right to protect his family.

They think it's "immoral" to suggest any moral equivalence between police officers and street protesters.

They think it's not just stupid but "insane" to tear down the inherited culture that has fortified the country for more than two centuries. They regard Obama as the principal malefactor in this assault, but of Paul Ryan-types, they ask this question, albeit in formulations more colloquial than this one: Is Ryanism a genuine alternative to Obamaism, or merely a stylistic mutation?

They consider Donald Trump to be undisciplined at best and cretinous at worst.

While they have no illusions about the quality of his candidacy, they revere Trump as one of the few national figures who in matters of cultural import is not willfully wrong, stupid, immoral, or insane.

They are contemptuous of NeverTrumpers and wonder when they will stop beating the dead horse of the flawed Trump candidacy and start supporting the values of the party of common sense.

To check these findings, and to project what they might mean for our political future, I engaged Angelo Codevilla, the longtime professor of international relations at Boston University and, before that, a powerful voice in Washington deliberations on national security. The author of 13 books, he is perhaps best known for an essay later turned into a book,

The Ruling Class, which called out the coastal elites that have dominated, and in Codevilla's view misdirected, our political culture for several decades past.

FREEMAN: Do any of these findings surprise you, or offend your sense of the current situation?

CODEVILLA: Your findings comport with mine.

Caricaturing Trump's supporters as skinheads is yet another instance of the ruling class's longstanding attitude toward America. To wit: America was born tainted by racism, sexism, greed, genocide against natives—a critique that is wrapped in both religious obscurantism and hypocritical promises of equality. This refrain from government, its clients in the media, the educational establishment, and major corporations has convinced millions to support whomever and whatever might disempower that class. Even Donald Trump.

Rejection of these caricatures is a unifying sentiment among his supporters. The accused's natural tendency is to think, "That's not who I am." And then, "Who the Hell do they think they are to say that of me?" Humans live by the sense of who they are and of what the world around them is. In short, by common sense. They rebel reflexively when confronted by assertions that run counter to it.

FREEMAN: And this reflexive rebellion carries the battle all the way into the bathroom?

CODEVILLA: What is the natural reaction to the assertion that someone with a penis can be a woman while someone else with a vagina can be a man? Is it not the same as that of Orwell's Winston Smith when first confronted with four fingers and the demand that he see five? In *1984*, it took all of society's pressure to force a prisoner to turn against his senses. It is unremarkable that Americans accustomed to freedom should resent the pressure that the ruling class is exerting.

FREEMAN: Tie in, if you would, the attitudes toward Muslims and street protesters.

CODEVILLA: Common sense recoils, as well, at the ruling class's peculiar protection of Muslims and Islam coupled with restrictions on, and denigrations of, Christians and Christianity, all in the name of morality.

The question imposes itself: *Which* morality? *Whose* morality? For most Americans, the answer is: not mine.

The same goes for the ruling class's tolerance if not promotion of mobs who ravage cities, loot, and attack police. Common sense says: Such people would do me harm if they could. Why are our rulers on the side of those who would harm us?

FREEMAN: And this is how, as implausible as it might have seemed, Donald Trump emerged as the candidate of common sense?

CODEVILLA: Nothing can so addle a good cause as a bad champion. One can wish for a better champion, as no doubt do most who will vote for him. But today—Trump himself and everything about him notwithstanding—his candidacy is the only alternative to the intensification of everything that the ruling class has done to the rest of us over the past half-century. His candidacy is the only shield, available now, against the ruling class's unconstrained expansion.

In short, the disdain that Trump's supporters feel for the ruling class has come to mirror that which the ruling class feels for them. This matters far beyond the coming election.

FREEMAN: How so?

CODEVILLA: The fact that the most politically active sectors of the population want unconstrained power over each other means that the very basis for sharing citizenship in a republic no longer exists. The culture of restraint, the sense of common citizenship so essential to republican life, is gone.

FREEMAN: That's a grim diagnosis and I want to get back to it. But let me ask you, first, about the correlation of forces. You wrote in *The Ruling Class* that "some two-thirds of Americans lack a vehicle for electoral politics . . . Sooner or later, well or badly, that majority's demand for representation will be filled." You wrote that, by the way, in 2010, not in the spring of 2016. Good call! How did you arrive at the rough calculation that two-thirds of Americans are, or feel they are, unrepresented?

CODEVILLA: Even back then, polls showed that three-fourths of Republican voters felt unrepresented by those whom they elected, as did a fourth of Democratic voters. Independents, by definition, are not represented by either party. That added up to at least two-thirds of the electorate. Since then, dissatisfaction has grown, meaning that the major parties now represent few voters outside their own apparatus and immediate clients.

FREEMAN: Let's cast you in the role of America's family metaphysician. Your dour view is shared by many people, millions of people. I ask you—patient to Doctor of Philosophy—what would you prescribe for the national condition? Among the more apocalyptic members of my own circle, the following options have been advanced and in some cases exercised: (1) we should build out the infrastructure of movement conservatism; (2) we should hug our books and sacred documents against the day when the culture revives; (3) we should prep as we've never prepped before; (4) we should ride the decline; (5) we should lay low for now but conspire to revolt against the ruling class. What have you prescribed for your own circle?

CODEVILLA: I answer with an educator's prejudice. Our troubles are rooted in the progressive monopoly of the graduate schools, where the teachers of the teachers are taught. Breaking it from the top is the work of Politics in the grand sense of the word. Breaking it from below is happening whenever a family opts for home schooling or a community either downsizes school districts or institutes charter schools. The infrastructure of movement conservatism is also important, especially if built around the "sacred books."

But such faith as I have rests on America's fundamental diversity. Ever since Roger Williams led his flock out of Massachusetts to found Rhode Island, Americans have dealt with cultural differences by *sorting themselves out into congenial groups*. Of course there is an element of secession in this. The good news is that if the good guys get up the guts to go their way, today's bad guys don't have the guts to stop them.

FREEMAN: Thanks, Angelo.

The American Spectator
April 25, 2015

YES, CARLY FIORINA WAS FIRED

We still have a week to go, but it's already clear that the Most Valuable Player of the Month will be Carly Fiorina. She wins the award because she has done what nobody else has thought to do or, more likely, had the nerve to do. She has said in a loud, clear voice that the Empress has no clothes.

Carly notes that, while the Empress Hillary went to fancy schools, ran expensive campaigns, held high political office, signed her name to multiple autobiographies, generated Kardashian levels of personal publicity and became Romney-rich while serving some never-quite-identified public interest, she hasn't actually accomplished anything. Carly has uttered an inconvenient truth, you might say.

For performing this public service, Carly got a taste of how the Clinton oppo-team responds to even unexceptionable criticism. It returns fire disproportionately. Just this morning, I found five hit pieces on the Internet, all of them noting with the predictability of a drill team that Carly Fiorina was fired from her last corporate job. The clear implication: Carly Fiorina's reputation as a successful businesswoman is a myth.

Perhaps this is a teachable moment.

Here's what happened. After graduating from college, Carly got a job as a receptionist in a small real estate office. Over the next 20 years, she worked hard, learned new skills, took risks, lost sleep and finally won herself a division-level job in big-time corporate America. How often does that happen? I don't know, but the answer is somewhere between never and not often.

But Carly wasn't finished, not by a long shot. In her division job, and later in a corporate sales job—at AT&T and its tech spinoff, Lucent—she found herself in a particularly unforgiving environment. In those kinds of jobs, you either "make your numbers" or the company finds somebody else who will. Carly made her numbers.

In 1999, she was tapped to be CEO of the struggling high-tech giant, Hewlett-Packard. It was a stunning appointment, one of the splashiest business stories of the year. Not just because Carly was a woman. And not just because she sprang from the secretarial pool rather than the management track. It was big news because the company involved was Hewlett-Packard, the iconic Fortune 20 company that for a generation had symbolized America's technological might to the nation and the world. (In Palo Alto, the garage where Stanford classmates Bill Hewlett and Dave Packard soldered their first HP gizmos is now an historic landmark. The little garage on Atherton Avenue is widely considered to be the birthplace of what became known as Silicon Valley.)

Carly was CEO for six years. She cut costs, tried to steady morale, and launched dozens of initiatives, some of them risky and many of them successful. But HP was in big trouble—strategically speaking, it had wandered into a box canyon—and she needed to take a big swing. Reviewing the available options, she decided to acquire a rival computer company, Compaq, to fill in what she and others perceived to be a gap in the HP line of product and service offerings. It was a big swing. The price came in at $25 billion.

Soon after the acquisition, it became painfully clear that Compaq was not the answer to HP's problems. It was not a good fit. The HP board of directors, a majority of whom had themselves voted in favor of the acquisition, reviewed the deal, concluded that it had been a mistake and moved to impose accountability. Carly Fiorina, the CEO, was fired. (It should be noted in fairness that, a decade later, HP, now under the leadership of the legendary Meg Whitman, has still not found a way out of its strategic bind.)

That's the way things work in the private economy. That's the way things should work. For a free society to flourish, success must be recognized and rewarded and failure must be recognized and punished.

Now compare Carly's story with the story of the Empress.

When Hillary Clinton failed to protect her employees in a U.S. consulate, and then evinced no apparent interest in finding out why they had been murdered—was she fired?

When, after long experience with government employment regulations, she systematically destroyed public records over a period of years—was she fired?

Or when, traveling overseas as our top diplomat to negotiate aid and security protocols, she accepted donations to her private foundation from those same foreign governments—was she fired?

No, unlike Carly Fiorina, Hillary Clinton was not fired from her last job. She served at the pleasure of the president, who seemed well pleased with her performance.

The American Spectator
November 12, 2012

TAKE A VICTORY LAP, ED FEULNER

These were the introductory remarks made when Heritage Foundation President Edwin J. Feulner was honored by the Maine Heritage Policy Center (MHPC).

Most of you are familiar with the seminal contributions made to conservatism by the late William F. Buckley, Jr. In the early years of conservative revival, Bill Buckley and his merry band were the movers and shakers of American politics—challenging the pervasive liberal pieties, building coalitions, calling our country back to the noble cause of ordered liberty. So commanding was his presence on the national scene that, for almost 30 years, conservatism was, roughly speaking, what Bill Buckley said it was. And what he said it was, on occasion, defied belief. I confess that the first time we heard Bill—at the time a recent convert to fusionism—contend that we could weave a durable political fabric from the wispy strands of libertarianism, traditionalism and a strong defense policy, I considered the fusionist notion to be preposterous. But under his brilliant cultivation and behind his charismatic leadership, conservatism became at first a coherent political philosophy and somewhat later, a compelling political proposition.

Some of you may not be as familiar with the contributions made by our speaker today. You should be. When Ed Feulner was named president of the Heritage Foundation in 1977, it was a tiny policy shop with implausibly large ambition, housed in a rabbit warren of offices that stood no better than a 50-50 chance of passing fire inspection. Ed Feulner has realized that large ambition. Today from its base in Washington—in fine buildings bestriding the U.S. Capitol—Heritage is the most important conservative organization in the country and the most influential think tank in the world. It is a 24/7 force for the good and the true and, when it comes to government, for the small and the modest.

Ed Feulner's ride at Heritage has been long and sweet, 35 years and counting, and was perhaps best described, if inadvertently, by our late friend, the essayist Christopher Hitchens. Early in his career, Hitchens was a man of the hard Left and he described the last sweet ride for international Leftism in the Seventies this way: "If you have never yourself had the experience of feeling that you are yoked to the great steam engine of history, then allow me to inform you that the conviction is a very intoxicating one." Well, Ed Feulner has experienced that feeling. It may be no more than historical coincidence, but the great steam engine of conservative reform began to rumble at just about the time Ed Feulner assumed command at Heritage.

Ed channeled that force Hitchens spoke of, that surging ideological momentum. Ed has refined it, amplified it and transmitted it to an entire generation of scholars, journalists, activists and intellectual entrepreneurs—in other words, to what has become under his leadership the contemporary conservative movement. Beginning with its indispensable support for Ronald Reagan and continuing into the present season with its withering critique of Barack Obama, conservatism over much of the past thirty years has been, roughly speaking, what Heritage and Ed Feulner say it is. All of us who push back against the insidious creep of statism, not to mention those among us who cling atavistically to guns and to God, are in Ed Feulner's debt.

As many of you know, a few months from now, Ed will be retiring from Heritage. He is doing our cause still another service by the graceful way in which he is departing. It was Ed Feulner who prodded the Heritage board to set up a formal succession process. It was Ed Feulner who pressed his colleagues to conduct a national search and to prepare for transition. We live in a time when too many of our leaders find excuses to stay too long: too many corporate executives, investment gurus, football coaches, senators from Nevada. Ed Feulner is leaving Heritage at the top of its form and at the top of his.

Admitting to only a trace of hyperbole, I have described the selection of Heritage's new CEO as the second-most important election in the country this year. We will know the name of the winner in just a few weeks. But we already know the name of the man who has made that job so prestigious, so powerful, so central to the future of our national enterprise.

Ladies and gentlemen, the Honorable Edwin J. Feulner.

The Harvard Club
New York, New York
October, 2016

DANIEL HENNINGER

These were the introductory remarks made at the Robert Novak Journalism Fellows Retreat.

My congratulations to those of you who have chosen a career in journalism. You have chosen shrewdly. Where else in American life can you depend on *other* people to pay for the satisfaction of *your* curiosity? In what other job would you have a middling chance to become rich and famous with no physical exertion beyond pulling a single piece of rolling luggage? In what other trade can you puff your friends, punish your enemies, change the law, topple a government? Indeed, in what other job would your professional behavior, however unseemly, be granted plenary indulgence by the nation's founding document?

Journalism can be so much fun that it's unsurprising to note that, in many parts of the world, it's illegal. As I say, congratulations to you all: Here in the land of the relatively free, journalism can be one long, sweet ride.

But along your way, remember always what the old economist said about the free lunch. For all its perks and powers, journalism does not come without cost. There will come into all of your professional lives a moment—a highly inconvenient moment—when the lunch tab will be presented and will have to be paid. There will come a moment when you learn that what "everybody" knows to be true is actually false.

Your predicament will not be new. Recall what Paul wrote in Second Timothy: "The time is coming when people will not endure sound doctrine, but they will accumulate for themselves teachers to suit their own desires and will turn away from listening to the truth, and wander away into myth."

Who knew that Republican animadversions against the mainstream media had been Scripturally based?

The novelist Alan Furst once explained how wars start: "Diplomats tell lies to journalists and then they believe what they read." Furst overstates the influence of both diplomats and journalists, of course. But his point survives. Journalists play an outsized role in all public controversy—in matters of war and peace abroad, in matters of power-grabbing here at home.

When you find yourselves in the vortex of public controversy—and you will—you will be obliged to stand with the truth and against the myth. Even when the drums of war are beating so loudly you can hardly hear yourself think. Which is, of course, the purpose of war drums, be they military, political, religious, or commercial.

It's a lonely business, standing against the crowd—a business that Bob Novak came to know well over the course of his long career. But you will be obliged to make your stand for the same reason Bob made his—to redeem the special privileges granted to journalism. That is your Constitutional compact.

Our speaker tonight writes the Wonder Land column each Thursday for the *Wall Street Journal*. You read him for the same reason I do. We can't help ourselves.

Why has he become a must-read? In my view, it's because he covers the American scene as if he were a foreign correspondent. And on occasion, not just as a correspondent from across the border, or across the sea. One Thursday in four, Dan Henninger arrives at the *Journal* as an interplanetary traveler, from a galaxy far away. In covering American politics, the tension in his writing builds from the fact that he has difficulty believing what he's seeing in this strange new land. He looks at Hillary. He looks at Trump. And you can almost hear him say to himself, with sonorous voice and beneath furrowed brow, "This is not the way things were in the ancestral village of Henningerville."

Dan is a graduate of St. Ignatius High School in Cleveland and Georgetown University in Washington, which is to say that he survived eight years of Jesuit education. He joined the *Journal* in 1977, and will thus celebrate next year his 40th anniversary with the same newspaper, a record that may stand for the rest of time.

In his various roles at the *Journal*, he has won the Gerald Loeb prize, the Walker Stone prize, the Thomas Phillips prize, and the Eric Breindel prize. (You know you're getting old when prizes are named for kids who used to work for you.) In 2002, Dan won the Pulitzer Prize as part of the paper's extraordinary team coverage of 9/11, tragic events that unfolded, some of them, across the street from his office here in Manhattan.

Dan is a man of several parts. Indeed, if you poke around long enough in search files, you'll come across this arresting question: "Is Dan Henninger's net worth greater than Queen Elizabeth's"? I clicked through to the answer, which, to the disappointment of all of us here tonight, appears to be, "Not bloody likely." Fellows will remember I said they had a "middling chance" to become rich and famous.

Ladies and gentlemen, it's my pleasure to introduce a must-read journalist, a warm friend of the Novak Program, and a man who even in moments of high inconvenience can be relied upon to seek and report the truth. Please welcome, Dan Henninger.

National Review
August 2, 2014

THE INDISPENSABLE BRENT BOZELL

These were the introductory remarks made when Media Research Center president L. Brent Bozell III addressed the annual Freedom & Opportunity Luncheon of the Maine Heritage Policy Center (MHPC).

Our speaker today needs an introduction. Not because you've never heard of him. You all know him as an omnipresence on Fox News. And if you have found your way onto his fundraising list, you have won a faithful correspondent for life. And perhaps beyond.

No, he needs an introduction because he is that rarest of creatures, the public figure who is better than he looks.

My first impression of Brent sticks with me. I was managing his father's campaign for Congress and observing strictly the Mayo Clinic's Official Campaign Worker's Diet, each of the five daily meals consisting of a pepperoni pizza, extra cheese, washed down with a Coke in the giant, Bloomberg-infuriating size. I had gained so much weight that my face disappeared behind a slab of pasty white flesh. Brent's mother, the sainted Patricia Buckley Bozell, took pity on me and invited me to join the family breakfast, where I rediscovered coffee, toast, and something called fruit.

Breakfast with Brent and his nine siblings was a lively affair. All of them sporting shocks of flaming red hair, all of them full of vinegar. One morning, laughter broke out around the table and I looked up to find ten Bozell children pointing at me. I then looked down to see two Cheerios spreading milk rings across my necktie. Brent's brother Johnny, a Rockwellian rascal, had mastered the mechanics of the spoon catapult.

Just as I was preparing a retaliatory strike, loading my spoon with bits of scrambled egg and hot sauce, Brent, aged eight, intervened. He dressed down Johnny, calmed his unruly siblings, and persuaded me, the putative adult in the room, to disarm. Thus began Brent's career in crisis management.

The crisis he has been managing these past 20-something years is the crisis of the American media. Thomas Jefferson once famously said, "Were it left to me to decide whether we should have a government without newspapers, or newspapers without a government, I should not hesitate a moment to prefer the latter." It is also recorded, of course, that Thomas Jefferson never visited Portland, Maine. As consumers of news media, we all sense when the *Press-Herald* is pursuing an agenda only distantly related to the people's right to know. We all sense when NBC News is bending a story. And for the handful of us who still read the *New York Times*, we have all found ourselves saying when reading one of those front-page trend stories, "Wow! What if that's *true?*"

But sensing and knowing are two different things. What Brent has done at the Media Research Center—which he founded as a bootstrap operation in 1987—is to identify and document and publicize egregious lapses by major media outlets. There are no shortcuts in this work. Brent and MRC have taken pains to build the record and to make the unassailable case.

I need not remind you that this is critically important work. A democracy can flourish only if its citizens are comprehensively informed. A democracy can flourish only if facts are regarded as sacred things, and only if there is a broad consensus to respect them.

In keeping the tablets these many years, Brent has become our own Bureau of Weights and Measures. In matters of media bias, his is the last word. And this singular stature has led, organically, to his role as one of the founding fathers of the new media—the alternative media to which people abandoned by the networks and the newspapers have turned in recent years. I refer, of course, not only to Fox News and talk radio, but also to the profusion of alternative websites, *The Maine Wire* very much among them, that accost the conventional wisdom.

Ladies and gentlemen, a thunderous Maine welcome, if you would, for the man who leads our fight to keep the media straight, the indispensable Brent Bozell.

National Review
October 17, 2016

A *FIRING LINE* CONVERSATION
WITH JAMES GRANT

F or the past 33 years, the estimable James Grant has published *Grant's Interest Rate Observer*, a newsletter covering in remarkable depth, as you might possibly have guessed, Jim Grant's observations on interest rates. If that doesn't sound like much of a business, you don't know niche publishing. *Grant's* commands an annual subscription price of $1,170 for its fortnightly letter, which compares with a subscription to the daily, home-delivered *New York Times*, for those of you still hungry for sexual-harassment news, of only $488. The *Grant's* renewal rate, I'm reliably informed, is considerably higher than that of the *Times*.

While an issue of *Grant's* is only twelve pages long, it's not a quick read. Readers don't flip through it before tossing it on the coffee table next to last April's issue of *House Beautiful*. They read it, ponder it, and, many of them, act on it by rearranging their financial affairs so as to bring them into alignment with Grant's expensive observations. Readers come for the information and stay for the insight, all of it delivered in a pellucid style that is rare in the murky world of monetary affairs.

Why all the fuss about interest rates? Here's Grant's unanswerable answer: "Interest rates are prices. They impart information. They tell a business person whether or not to undertake a certain capital investment. They measure financial risk. They translate the value of future cash flows into present-day dollars. Manipulate those prices—as central banks the world over compulsively do—and you distort information, therefore perception and judgment."

When he's not observing financial markets—and I can't imagine in what small hour that might be—Grant writes books, seven of them so far, including studies of Bernard Baruch and John Adams. Faithful to the governing criterion for these *Firing Line* Conversations—that the guest must be smarter than the host—I sought him out.

FREEMAN: This won't require much of an imaginative leap, Jim, but let's pretend that I'm underinformed about the appeal of negative interest rates. Why would I want to pay somebody to borrow money from me?

GRANT: Conservatives don't take naturally to negative interest rates: Today's are the first in at least 5,000 years. Nor do savers of any political stripe. A negative rate of interest means that the lender pays the borrower and it would seem to defy common sense. You can think of interest as the reward for waiting—for laying aside something for tomorrow. Alternatively, you can view negative interest as the cost of impetuousness. Negative rates penalize thrift and reward consumption.

FREEMAN: Peak Keynesianism?

GRANT: The Keynesian economists say we need less thrift, more "aggregate demand." Negative interest rates, imposed by central banks, are the means to the end of more impetuousness. The myth that we can spend and borrow our way to prosperity dies hard.

FREEMAN: In one estimate I saw, there is now $10 trillion of negative-rate debt sloshing around. If it's designed to be a demand-side incentive, how has it performed in the real world? Is it working?

GRANT: Sub-zero rates have unleashed no new wave of spending. Nor would they, once you think about it. Put yourself in the position of a Scandinavian saver or a Japanese businessman. Your central bank announces that it will drive nominal short-term rates where they have never been before. You think, "Something must be wrong. The economists must know something I don't know." Your second response might be, "Hold on a minute. My savings yielded little enough when deposit rates were zero. They're not going to be any more productive at minus 1 percent, or minus 2 percent. I've got to save more for retirement. Maybe we shouldn't go out to dinner tonight." The unintended consequences of economic policy are always more interesting than the intended ones.

FREEMAN: One of the consequences, intended or otherwise, is that we now have this massive debt sitting on the national balance sheet. Can we just let it sit there, rolling it over from time to time? Or is there a circumstance in which we'll be obliged to pay it off?

GRANT: You hear it said that "posterity will pay." Well, what are we if not someone's posterity? Yes, we pay the interest on the $14.2 trillion of federal debt—that's debt in the hands of the public, excluding the obligations held in various government trust funds. But we don't pay the principal because the world's investors don't want their money back. They continue to regard this country as a superior destination for money. In the twelve months through September 30, the U.S. government added $795.5 billion to its towering pile of IOUs—and refinanced $8.2 trillion of IOUs previously incurred.

FREEMAN: How long can that go on?

GRANT: Until the world comes to doubt the creditworthiness of the U.S., or the integrity of the U.S. dollar.

FREEMAN: Let's make the wild assumption that, under either a Clinton administration influenced by Bernie Sanders or a Trump administration influenced by Donald Trump, doubts might begin to creep in. We could then pay off the debt by debasing the currency, paying off dollars with dimes; or we could raise tax rates to pre-JFK levels; or we could default and stiff the creditors. Is there any other way to go?

GRANT: Why, yes. We could reduce taxes, reduce spending, reduce regulation, and institute sound money.

FREEMAN: Now you're talking. Leave aside the challenges of fiscal policy for a moment. Every politician in the country is talking elliptically about "Fed reform." If the next president turns to you for advice, what specific changes would you recommend in the monetary arena?

GRANT: Interest rates ought to be discovered in the market, not administered from on high. They can't do their essential work if someone, say a central bank, is muscling them around. Let's get the central banks out of the business of using interest rates—and stock prices and exchange rates, too—as instruments of national policy. Today, investors live in a hall of mirrors: They don't know which values are real and which are distorted by monetary manipulation. Market-determined rates will help restore clarity.

FREEMAN: And then?

GRANT: That chore out of the way, the next administration ought to open a debate on the nature of the dollar. As it is, the Fed materializes it on a computer keypad to pursue its macroeconomic agenda.

George Gilder correctly asks: Is money a measuring stick or a magic wand? The former is the correct answer.

FREEMAN: It is hereby stipulated that money is a measuring stick. Now, what is your recommendation on the fiscal side? Other than electing the next Thomas Jefferson, how might we "reduce taxes, reduce spending, reduce regulation," given the structural problems in Washington?

GRANT: Forgot to mention a prerequisite: civic virtue.

FREEMAN: Yes, there's not much civic virtue in evidence these days and we can agree, I hope, to put Rich Lowry on that case. But let's finish up here with your own threat assessment. As you look around world markets, what bubbles do you have on your watch list?

GRANT: If by "bubble," you mean a palpable distortion of value, I rank sovereign debt at the head of the class. A bond is a promise to pay money. Governments, which make the promises, also print the money. They are inherently conflicted, for which reason Comte de Mirabeau was known to say, "I would rather have a mortgage on a garden than a kingdom."

FREEMAN: Any specific counsel?

GRANT: I would advise the owners of ETFs to look inside the portfolios of their holdings to see what they really own.

FREEMAN: Thanks, Jim.

National Review
September 5, 1980

WELCOME HOME, GEORGE

Some of you may be old enough to remember the Ripon Society. A child of the Sixties, it served as an incubator for the ideas of an oxymoronic movement called liberal Republicanism. In the manner of like groups Left and Right, the Ripon Society claimed an influence far beyond its numbers. And if a microscopic membership could be said to validate that claim, the rolls provided ringing affirmation. To those of us observing from afar, in truth, Ripon appeared to have no more than two active members—a writer named George Gilder and a mimeograph operator who worked his crankhand to the bone keeping pace with Gilder's polemical output.

In the spirit of full disclosure, it should probably be said that some of us did more than observe from afar. There was a cultural edge here, you understand. These Ripon fellows made today's clean-fingernail Republicans look like Ralph Kramden. Nothing gave us more pleasure, in fact, than lobbing an occasional egg into the men's room of the Ripon Society. We took to calling it names, including, in the immortal phrase of T. J. Wheeler, the Capon Society.

And we blasted away at its position papers, each one of which seemed to cloak in bipartisanship a statist notion of Democratic origin. The tides of history were running with us and the Ripon Society soon drifted away. With the closing of the Great Society (and, as the cynics would say, with the closing of Nelson Rockefeller's checkbook), Ripon ascended to its place in that great mailing list in the sky.

For George Gilder, the honorable course was plainly evident: a note of abject apology would suffice, followed by a lifetime of silent service in a New England monastery. Alas, displaying the ornery streak for which he was by then well known, Gilder continued to write and to publish. And as he did so the Divine Plan was slowly, startlingly, made manifest. In a series of long and thoughtful books, Gilder undertook an examination of his earlier premises, found them empty and irrelevant and moved on to a sustained critique of modern liberalism. The body of work he produced through the Seventies (including a number of articles for *National Review*) was a major contribution to contemporary thought.

By the summer of 1980 George Gilder had traveled a long road. He had become for conservatives what he had been for liberal Republicans a decade and a half before—an idea-generator, a rhetorical scout, a leader.

One of our pleasanter chores this summer has been producing a cable-satellite television series for the Heritage Foundation, Washington's enterprising think tank. One of the programs in that series featured George Gilder confronting the redoubtable Ben Wattenberg on the topic, "Why I Am Not a Neoconservative." We can think of no better way to present the new and improved George Gilder than to record the following excerpts from his remarks on that occasion.

On neoconservatism: "I have come to believe that neoconservatism is to a great extent a strategy of evasion of the great truths and political imperatives that dwell just below the surface of neoconservative thought . . . It best resembles, if I may say so—with reference to the joke about the origins of the camel—conservatism designed by a committee."

On Moynihan: "I must regretfully say that Daniel Patrick Moynihan was a much more valuable asset for the Right at Harvard and at the United Nations than in Washington."

On Buckley: "Adding up all the writings of neoconservatives over the years—all endlessly sophisticated writings of America's most ingenious social analysts—I discover they constitute, in sum, after all is said and done, a body of conclusions, a distillation of wisdom and truth, rather less useful and timely than William F. Buckley's youthful insights in *God and Man at Yale.*"

On neoconservative methodology: "The neoconservative believes not chiefly in principles but in empirical techniques. He believes that through study and analysis of social questions one can arrive at reliable conclusions. This approach means that the neoconservative usually cannot tell you what is wrong with social programs until they have already been entrenched and done their damage. Then the neoconservative will tell you that these programs are part of the very fabric of our political culture and cannot be repealed. What use is that?"

On the War on Poverty: "What the War on Poverty in fact achieved was to halt in its tracks an ongoing improvement in the lives of the poor—particularly poor blacks—and create a wreckage of family breakdowns and demoralization far worse than the aftermath of slavery."

On capitalism: "Capitalist progress is based on risks that cannot be demonstrated to succeed in one lifetime. Thus it relies on faith in the future and in Providence. Capitalism depends not on greed but on giving, investment without a contracted return. The self-interest elaborated by Adam Smith leads not by an invisible hand to progress but to the dead hand of a growing welfare state. The workers under capitalism are motivated not by crude economic rewards but by love of family. The entrepreneurs succeed to the extent that they are sensitive to the needs of others, to the extent that others succeed. Altruism is the essence of the positive-sum game of capitalism."

On social issues: "Neoconservatives are afraid to fight on ERA, abortion, sex education, pornography, school prayer, and gay liberation. Once again, as in the case of poverty, they underrate the importance of stable families and moral values to a productive and creative society."

George, you're forgiven.

Amelia Island, Florida
April 9, 2016

MARK LEVIN

These were the introductory remarks made when Mark Levin addressed the Annual Leadership Conference of the Heritage Foundation.

My first job in the Reagan administration was in the Transition Office in late 1980. My colleagues spent long days recruiting the best and brightest for government service—the men and women with the most establishmentarian résumés and the most impressive paper credentials. I had a different assignment, given to me by a senior Reagan official who shall remain honored but nameless. My job was to stuff as many conservatives as possible into the incoming administration.

One of my charges was a voluble young attorney by the name of Mark Levin. Unfortunately for him, I was not able to find a plum assignment on Pennsylvania Avenue. Instead, he was sent to a third-tier job in a backwater agency, where he found himself surrounded by several hundred government bureaucrats, many of them dull-witted, most of them ideologically feral.

Young Levin did not fit in well. Over those first few weeks, I received phone calls complaining about him. He wouldn't mind his own business. He was too opinionated. (On its face, a baseless allegation.) Most damning of all, he wasn't a team player. To each complaint, I would respond hopefully, "Give it time. Levin has the right stuff. He'll be fine."

About six weeks into the Levin-as-bureaucrat experiment—talk about a low-percentage shot—I received a call from a top official at the agency. He was at the end of his rope: "Mr. Freeman, you've got to get Levin out of the building." "Why's that?" I asked. "This guy is even more Reaganite than Reagan." It seems that young Levin had been a team player all along. He was just not playing for the home team. He was playing for Team Reagan.

Mark Levin made of that dead-end job what he's made of every other opportunity in his extraordinary career. He worked hard, took chances, repaid loyalty, networked like crazy and made himself the obvious choice for bigger and more important jobs. Within a few short years, he had become Chief of Staff to the Attorney General of the United States, the legendary Ed Meese.

All of us who watched—and applauded—Mark's success in Washington knew that he was headed for bigger things. But I can't honestly say that those of us who'd swayed for years to the dulcet tones of Ronald Reagan predicted a big future for Mark in the radio business. Unlike his politics, Mark's voice could not fairly be described as Reaganite. The first time you heard him, you didn't say to yourself, "now, there's a soothing baritone from the heartland of America."

So how did Mark do it? How did he flout every convention of the radio industry and still rise to the very top? He did it by the usual Levin formula—that combination of hard work, commitment to principle, and confidence in his own abilities.

He is today, by any standard, one of the most successful broadcasters in the country. He is the author of five *New York Times* bestsellers. He is—as of this very week—the host of the new Levin TV series. Most importantly, he is a fast friend of freedom who reminds us each day of why we love this country and why we must rally to her defense, both today and tomorrow.

Ladies and gentlemen, Mark Levin.

York, Maine
October 2008

CALEB FOX

T ricia dear, thank you for giving all of us a chance to say goodbye to our pal Caleb.

As many of you know, we did not get off to a fast start, Caleb and I. As we confessed to each other a few years ago, he thought I was an uptight WASP. I thought he was a foppish trustifarian. Those first impressions began to change in the early-morning mists of Milldam Road. I would be leaving for a meeting, or making a run for Miss Jane on some labor of love, or obligation, and out of the Milldam fog would come huffing and clumping—Caleb F. Fox the Frigging Fourth, beet red, in the last mile of his jog, sweating like a pig but still managing to look like Mr. Just-Right. He would pause for a few minutes of banter and then move on. I marveled at the man's ability to insert into even the briefest conversation at least one crude anatomical reference. I began to time my morning departure to intersect with The Jogger.

As we got to know each other better, we found to our mutual disappointment that we were imperfect human beings. For his part, he found flaws in my tennis game and then my golf game and then my boating game. Basically, I was not much good at whatever we happened to be doing. For my part, I found myself fascinated by his religious views, which I came to regard as a kind of intellectual slum. I soon took on his theological rehabilitation as a personal urban-renewal project.

I would pose what I thought were clever and heuristic philosophical questions, which excited no response. I did better by appealing to his prudential side, suggesting that, given the actuarial realities, it might make sense for him to get right with God. Which at least momentarily arrested his attention. I pressed my advantage and asked him to join me at church that Sunday. My hook was that his friend Mark Hollingsworth would be preaching here at Trinity. Well, Caleb was perfectly willing to keep God waiting, but he would never disappoint a friend. At the appointed hour, he bounded in—blue blazer, crisp white slacks, looking as if he had just come from rehearsals for *Brigadoon*.

We sat on the left, about 25 rows back. His churchly habits were in a state of disrepair. When the congregation stood, Caleb knelt devoutly in prayer. When the congregation sat down, Caleb bobbed up, sore thumb-wise. Most memorably, when the congregation stood to sing Hymn 442, Caleb belted out the words to 224. It was a long, long service. But we muddled through to Communion, at which time I took him firmly by the elbow and guided him toward the altar. As it happened, we took our places at the railing with Lou Baker, Carol Hollingsworth and other members of Mark's family. I received the Host and then rose to leave, making way for the next cohort. I turned back to see that Caleb had not moved. He was still kneeling at the altar, motionless. (Perhaps he thought there was another course? A fruit compote, perhaps?) I went back to tap him on the shoulder and saw that this strong, athletic man, this man's man, was weeping uncontrollably. He had been overcome by the emotional beauty of the moment, the sight of Mark serving Communion to his mother, to his sister. It's not often in life that you know the exact moment when an acquaintance becomes a friend.

I should add a word of context, lest you think that I will soon be knocking at your door and thrusting pamphlets at you. Like most of our neighbors Downeast, I'm a flinty New Englander who keeps his religion to himself. At my home church in north Florida, I have great difficulty getting with the testimonial program. I've never proselytized anybody in my life. Why then, you might reasonably ask, would I hound your poor husband? What lit my missionary fire in his particular case? I have given that question some thought these last few days and have concluded that Caleb was the most fully formed Christian man I've ever met. The essence of his character was generosity. Not in the material sense, though we were all the beneficiaries of his lavish hospitality. But a generosity of the spirit. I think of almost any encounter with him. He wanted you to know how pleased he was to be in your company, although the pleasure was always more yours than his. He wanted you to know how delighted he was by the triumphs in your life, however small they might be. He wanted, most of all, to communicate his deep satisfaction that you had chosen to join the circle of his friendship, although it was of course he who had done the choosing.

We all knew how lucky we were to have been admitted to membership in The Caleb Fox Pals' Club. It's why we have been so sad these last few days and why we will be sad for many more. We all know that life will never be quite as much fun again. Which is why I take some comfort—and hope that you can find a way to do likewise—in returning to the Christian syllogism: If you believe in God; if you believe that He calls his children home to a place something like Heaven; then you can be secure in the belief that celestial outings, now under the direction of Captain Caleb F. Fox IV, will be one long, sweet ride.

FOR THE GOOD
OF THE ORDER

The American Spectator
September 26, 2010

THE FAIRNESS INITIATIVE

Kudos to *USA Today*, that most mainstream of all major media, for reminding us who "we" are. In an enterprising and courageous story published in August, the paper reported that the average U.S. private-sector worker receives $65,051 in compensation while the average U.S. government worker receives $129,049. I say "enterprising" because that latter figure, The Number we've all been looking for, has been a closely guarded secret for decades, more effectively guarded, manifestly, than most of the nation's military secrets. To tease The Number out of data designed to obscure it was a remarkable piece of journalism, an old-school, First Amendment-justifying "talking story." And I say "courageous" because the paper was predictably attacked by agents of the bureaucracy, who variously alleged error, irresponsibility, base motivation and bad manners. Even in the media doldrums of late summer, the constituency for big government recognized a mortal threat and lumbered on to the field to combat it.

Let's look first at the nature of the threat and then at the campaign to defuse it. For most of our history, the reigning metaphor for government employment has been "public service." Embedded deep in the national imagination is the notion that a government job is the kind of work to which a responsible citizen is occasionally called, usually on a temporary basis, and for which he is expected to sacrifice not only creature comfort but also family time and the disruption of professional development. Although it is sometimes an adventure, that is, government work has traditionally been perceived as more duty than job, with Cincinnatus arrived reluctantly in town but still glancing longingly back at the plow. (In my own short stints in government, I was told by recruiters to expect sharp cuts in my paycheck and, on this particular commitment at least, the government delivered in full. That was a political generation ago, however, before the Bushes and Clinton managed to rebrand the old liberalism as big-government conservatism.) Most Americans, despite accumulating evidence to the contrary, have liked to believe that our public servants are high-minded sorts willing to serve the community at some economic cost to themselves; the kind of people who went into government, we liked to think, were in some ways like pastors or nurses or those nice people down at Goodwill Industries, most of whom seemed to be answering to spiritual vocation rather than material incentive. What *USA Today* did with the publication of The Number was to explode the central myth of democratic governance: namely, that taxpayers are the masters and bureaucrats the servants. What became sunrise-clear as The Number was passed from barber shop to lunch counter to factory floor to yoga class was that our public servants are paying themselves twice as much as we have managed to keep for ourselves . . . after paying them. Without our notice, it has now been universally noticed, our public servants have been giving themselves quiet raises all these years, tweaking benefits, fattening pensions. Without our notice, they have been adding hundreds of thousands of new employees to their own ranks even as we taxpayers faced layoffs and cuts and freezes and closings: As we tightened our belts, they loosened theirs. The question has now re-formed itself in the national imagination: who, exactly, is working for whom?

In the aftershock of The Number, then, just who are "we?" We are the people who got snookered by the myth of public service, that much is clear. Confessedly, we are also the people who let the bureaucracy run wild. But we remain the people who have the power to redress this new and unacceptable situation. It says so right there in the Constitution, doesn't it? (I checked. There's nothing in there about bureaucrats being spared discomfort in an economic downturn.) That's what it says all right, but the pertinent questions for this historical moment are not so much formal as procedural. Do enough of us still live and work beyond the reach of the bureaucracy? Do we citizen-taxpayers still have the raw numbers to survive a democratic showdown with the governing class and its political arm, the dependency class? And even if our numbers are sufficient to the task, can we muster the will to resist the encircling and stifling forces of statism? Read any blog, listen to any talk show and you know that many of our fellow citizens sense that we are approaching a Gladwellian tipping point, the point beyond which we would be incapable of reclaiming a vigorously free society. Just where are we on that graph—are we still on the near side of the tipping point, the side from which we could still recoil and recover? Or have we just passed over to the far side, the side from which we would have no choice but to slog numbly toward the fading light of the American day?

Return for a moment to the attack on The Number itself. The most widely sprayed rhetorical pesticide was this: The Number misinterprets statistical reality by ignoring the fact that government workers are, on average, considerably older than private-sector workers: It would be only natural for older workers, with greater seniority, to earn more than younger workers. That's axiomatic, of course, but it's tautological as well. One of the reasons that government workers are older is that government work is the kind of work that older workers can do. (Shuffling papers from an ergonomic chair, it's been reliably reported, puts little strain on the lower back.) The other reason that government workers are so much older than the rest of us is that they are a static workforce, happily cemented in their privileged positions. They are rarely hired away, they are almost never fired, they are rewarded for immobility by steadily escalating compensation and, off at the end, they elide into a pension system so rich that many of them will ultimately make more for staying home in retirement than they made back at the office. Indeed, now that these "defined-benefit," income-for-life pensions have all but disappeared from the private sector, public-employee pensions have become an open scandal. Let's be clear about what's happened: *After* it became clear that taxpayers could no longer afford to pay for their own pensions, they were compelled to pay for government pensions. That would seem to settle the question of who is working for whom.

The other argument launched frequently against The Number is that *USA Today*'s analysis was simple-minded, almost risibly so, in that it compared apples not even to oranges but to nectarines. Government jobs, the experts assure us, are not fungible with private-sector jobs and valid comparisons are thus impossible to draw. To which the answer from outside the Beltway echo chamber would be: "No problem. We'll handle it." No two jobs are identical in the private sector, either, but every HR director at every private company is obliged to make defensible comparisons. That's what HR people do in the real world. They develop benchmarks and comparables, which is to say that they define with some precision the relationships among apples, oranges and nectarines. And if they happen upon a particularly novel or recondite question, they call in one of a dozen world-class management consulting firms, any one of which would be delighted to provide the same service to government. What *is* risible is the idea that our government considers the task of evaluating its employees so analytically daunting that, just to be safe, it has resolved to overpay all but the senior-most executives. It should be understood that men and women with significant HR experience share a presumption that government employment data do not in fact defy analysis, and the further presumption that, once that data is comprehensively analyzed, it is highly unlikely that the average government worker will be demonstrated to have been twice as productive as the average private-sector worker.

For a brief shining moment in late August, the big-government noise machine floated a third argument in rebuttal to The Number. It was snatched back so quickly that we barely caught a glimpse of it, but the gist of the argument was—"we deserve it." The rationale for the compensation premium advanced in that moment of unguarded candor was that because the government worker is a) older, b) better educated, and c) engaged in more difficult work than the average citizen—because he's a member of the clerisy, if you will—he *should* be paid twice as much. Adult PR supervision was soon imposed (it's considered bad form just before a contentious election for bureaucrats to be caught chanting at voters, "we're better than you are") and so the argument was never allowed to take full form. Its brief appearance, however, revealed still another dimension of the problem with our governing class. Because of the high pay, rich benefits and scandalous pension payouts—*because government employment is now so financially attractive*—government is becoming in these bleak economic times an employer of first resort. As such, it is beginning to attract, if not yet the best and the brightest, many people who could have succeeded in the private sector and would have elected to do so in more economically secure times. The result on a macro-economic level is that our government is beginning to outbid the private sector for the scarce resources of brains and talent. That development is unwelcome in *any* form of market-based economy.

A still-larger presumption upon which HR professionals would agree is that the government workforce is "thick in the middle." Here's a translation of the jargon. You will have noticed the almost daily "earnings surprises" reported in the business press over the summer, those blurbs on quarterly earnings results that "exceed analysts' expectations." Virtually none of those upside surprises was the result of sharply increasing revenues. Across the board, sales are flat to weak. Almost all of the earnings gains reflect, rather, cost-cutting initiatives and improved productivity. Granted, it seems counterintuitive: sagging sales and booming profits. How have American companies managed to perform so well, at least on the bottom line? Companies both public and private, slowly at first and then in hurry-up mode following the 2008 crash, have innovated in many ways but *primarily* by embracing the digital revolution to thin the ranks of middle management. Corporate America is now lean and mean, thin in the middle, with a few real decision-makers at the top directing the real workers who produce the product or provide the service on the front lines. Middle management has simply gone away and the resulting savings have fallen to the bottom line. (Maybe you've noticed: Nobody admits to being a middle manager any longer. It can be hazardous to your corporate health.)

Government, as we have seen, responded differently to hard times. It ignored them. It continued to swell its ranks, continued to ratchet up its wage scales, continued to leave the digital opportunity largely unrealized and continued to send bigger and bigger bills to the taxpayers. Now that the winds of digital change have blown through almost all of corporate America and much of nonprofit America, the government stands as the last refuge of the middle manager, the kind of "executive" whose job description is speckled with one or more of the telltale slacker nouns: liaison, outreach, coordination, review, interface, feedback, schedule, assistance, oversight and the like—i.e., the functions most taxpayers perform in their spare time on a PC.

The hour is late. Both time and trend work against the citizen-taxpayer. Day after day, the governing class expands incrementally, inexorably, uncontestedly. They control the data, set the budgets, publish the timetables and enforce the rules. If there's any smart money still around, it would have to like the chances of the governing class over against what remains of the freedom class; the former steadily gains strength even as the latter watches its own leech away. All of which, in my view, argues for an early division of the house, an early headcount of just how many of our fellow citizens will stand with the freedom class. All of which argues for a citizen initiative that would declare straightforwardly: *It shall be the policy of government at every level to cap public-sector wages and benefits at private-sector comparables.* This new policy would restore a measure of balance to the relationship between the citizen and his government; when the economy heads into choppy waters, we would all be in the same boat. It would establish the principle in equity that taxpayers and the people who work for them should receive equal pay for equal work. It would free up critical resources for the private sector to restock the national economy. And it could be set in motion without delay. Senior government officials—mayors, county executives, governors, even the president—could in many cases start the process by executive order. We could begin the transition period immediately. We could call this new policy the Fairness Initiative.

The legendary British marketing guru Maurice Saatchi remarked some years ago that "America's one-word (brand) equity is 'freedom.'" In a language with 750,000 words, he noted, that's a priceless asset. How much is it worth today?

National Review
October 3, 1980

ANYONE FOR URDU?

J ust when you think your flabber has been terminally gasted, those little bureaucratic beavers come forward with yet another so-called solution to yet another so-called problem. Today's problem, says the Department of Education, is that many American schoolchildren do not speak English. The solution, you ask? Something called bilingual education.

If you haven't heard about bilingual education, hang on for a few weeks, you will. It will be reflected in several ways: first in an increased level of rancor at school-board meetings, then in higher taxes, then in broken lives and embittered families, then in national discord, and, finally, too late, in a general understanding that the program was fundamentally ill-conceived. But we're getting ahead of ourselves . . .

Bilingual education is, on the surface at least, just what it sounds like. It is a program designed to teach basic education subjects such as math, science, and history in the language in which the student is most comfortable. The idea is that the foreign student can keep up with his peers in the standard subjects while he is learning English on the side. When he masters English, he merges with his native-born classmates in an all-English curriculum and lives happily ever after in the dominant culture.

There are so many things wrong with this scheme that even the Department of Education has anticipated a pocket of resistance here and there. It has therefore proposed that the program be made compulsory for every school system in which there are 25 or more students speaking the same native tongue. (The compulsion-stick is that schools that fail to comply with the rule would be denied federal funds.)

If the rule sounds reasonable, consider the practical effects of application. In our own home county of Fairfax, Virginia, based on 1979 student data, the local school system will be obliged to offer bilingual programs in the following languages: Arabic, Cambodian, Chinese, Hindi, Japanese, Korean, Laotian, Persian, Portuguese, Spanish, Thai, Urdu, and Vietnamese. There are world-famous universities, of course, whose linguistic resources do not stretch that far, so let us hasten to concede that Fairfax is not the Peoria of American counties. It has an extraordinarily large population of international business and diplomatic personnel. Elsewhere, in more settled communities, the curriculum changes would be less drastic. Most school systems would have to offer a single course only, usually Spanish. Nationally, however, we are talking about massive numbers and especially about massive numbers of new teachers.

This brings us to the central question about any bureaucratic scam, *cui bono*? And when we are talking about the Department of Education, Jimmy Carter's election-year gift to the National Education Association, the answer is easily discovered. The principal beneficiary of bilingual education will be the teacher unions; for every course, be it math or music, will now require two teachers, one speaking English, one Spanish. One can extrapolate with confidence to the day not far off when the program will also require two sets of administrative staff. *Then two of everything.* Then three. Then four. Thanks to the new rules issued last month, bilingual education is now a growth industry. According to the *Wall Street Journal* for September 2, "Many schools reopening this week lack enough bilingual teachers to handle the recent influx of Cuban, Vietnamese, and Russian refugees." When demand outraces supply, a price increase is never far behind.

Well, what about those Spanish-speaking, and Urdu-speaking, kids? What are we going to do about them? One incident from a neighbor county, Arlington, is edifying. Arlington has an exceptionally high incidence of foreign-born students, close to 15 percent, and the county school system had established a bilingual program for Koreans even before federal rules required them to do so. Showing more sense than the bureaucrats, however, the Koreans stayed away in droves, and the program has been cancelled due to "lack of interest." The Korean students, far from trying to create a Little Korea in suburban Washington, are trying to escape from Little Korea and join the greater America that surrounds them. (One can almost hear the Orwellian shoe-drop: Attendance at bilingual classes will become mandatory, after which the burning social question will make its way slowly and expensively to the Supreme Court: Just what is a Korean, anyway?)

Perhaps the billions of dollars paid to teachers will be the least expensive part of the bilingual education program. The cost in productive services lost will be virtually incalculable. One of the wellsprings of American progress for 200 years and more has been the steady infusion of energy and confidence from the freshly assimilated. Our public schools have succeeded more often than not with the traditional prescription— intensive English courses, followed by integration into the general curriculum and the mainstream culture. Bilingual education represents a long stride to the rear, into a society in which the outsider is institutionalized first as a student and then, in the aggregate, as a special interest.

One senses a tragedy in the making when one reads statements from Hispanic groups supporting bilingualism on the grounds that it will "preserve the heritage" of Spanish-speaking students. There are many tasks with which our public schools can and should be entrusted, but surely this is not one of them. Quite the contrary. If we wish to keep the flame flickering under the melting pot, if we wish to redeem the promise of America, if we wish to avoid our own Quebec, or worse, we must teach our young people the lessons of America in the language of America.

The Weekly Standard
August 25, 1996

PEER REVIEW AND ITS DISCONTENTS

T he most terrifying moment in journalism occurs when two scientific studies thump on your desk simultaneously. One study, from Ph.D. Smith, says, roughly, that the sky is falling. The other study, by Ph.D. Jones, says, roughly, that the sky is just fine. In fact, the sky may be *rising*. These studies can be about the air we breathe or the water we drink or the food we eat or the drugs we take. The anxiety attack is quick and sure.

What to do, as the clock on the wall ticks toward deadline? Most journalists (including those of us who produce science television) face such moments armed only with a semester or two of hard science. The practical options reduce to these: 1) Read the studies and try to make sense of them. This never happens. 2) Yield to the natural instinct and fire off a slightly hedged version of "the sky is falling." This happens only occasionally, but still too often: Journalistic careers are not built, after all, on thick files of "the sky is just fine" stories. 3) Search for an authoritative source, a credible third party on which to hang the story. This is the option of choice—and the source of serious problems now emerging in the scientific community.

What a journalist needs in these anxious moments is protective cover, and he finds it in these magic words: "peer review." It's a marvelously reassuring phrase, summoning images of avuncular mentors looking over the shoulders of researchers at the bench, double-checking data, approving methodology. And in some cases, the images are reasonably close to reality. If you want to see your tax dollars effectively at work, check out a peer-review hearing at the Food and Drug Administration. The agency invites top experts in the field—FDA staff, academics, practicing physicians. They sit around a horseshoe table in the middle of which stands a bare microphone. In the audience are professional rivals, investigators from related studies, corporate reps, Naderites, kibitzers of all sorts. The atmosphere is polite but tightly structured. The author of the study introduces his thesis and the group then has at it. For eight hours or more. Peer review at this level is full-contact intellectual roller derby, and only the rigorous survive.

But there's peer review, and then there's peer review. Take the case of magazines invariably referred to as "leading medical journals"—the *Journal of the American Medical Association* (JAMA) and the *New England Journal of Medicine*, to name the two most prestigious. The fact that they are peer-reviewed casts the same tranquilizing spell over journalists as does an open FDA hearing. When JAMA comes out with a big story, it jumps the editorial queue and appears immaculately on the evening news. How many times have you heard Tom Brokaw or Peter Jennings speak the ominous words, "The prestigious *Journal of the American Medical Association* reported today that . . ."

Note the verb: Leading medical journals *report*. The pope doesn't report. The dean of Yale doesn't report. Even Colin Powell doesn't report. The president of the United States is lucky if he *announces*. More often these days, he *charges*, or if he's having a bad verb day, he *denies* or *shrugs off*. The poor Speaker of the House *claims*, which is the journalistic equivalent of an FDA warning label. *Report* is a heavy word, and one is hard-pressed to think of another institution routinely entitled to use it.

Which begs this question: Just how reliable is the peer-review process upon which this extraordinary authority is based? Here's how *JAMA* subjects an article submitted for publication to peer review. First, the study is sent out to as many as ten peers with credentials in the field. So far, so good—but then the exceptions begin to creep in.

For starters, there are times when only three, two, or even one reviewer actually participates—for all kinds of reasons. And there is no rule that reviewers must recommend unanimously that a study be published. Indeed, there is no *JAMA* rule that a study must command even a *majority* of reviewers. (The distinguished British journal *Lancet* uses only two reviewers, but will not publish if both of them review negatively. "It wouldn't be right," says staff editor Clair Thompson. The *New England Journal of Medicine*, which also uses two reviewers, will print studies panned by both reviewers. "It's rare," says editor Jerome Kassirer, "but we do it.") One scientist who publishes frequently (but not in *JAMA*) treasures a note from a journal editor clipped to a file of negative reviews: "F— it, I like it and we're going to publish." *JAMA* does not feel obliged to inform its readers when reviewers recommend against publication.

And then there's the policy that reviewers are never identified with a particular study. JAMA explains that anonymity secures a higher level of objectivity while insuring reviewers against professional reprisal. (A curious response, at least to the journalistic ear. The reporter's experience has long been that, in most circumstances, a source willing to go on the record is more credible than a source who requests anonymity. And of course it's the rare lawyer who assumes anonymous allegations to be intrinsically more credible than charges made in open court.)

What we have, in the case of *JAMA*, is a peer-reviewed journal that publishes articles selected by an editor after he has consulted with unidentified reviewers who may or may not have deemed the article worthy of publication. In other words, peer review does not mean peer approval. For the editor, this comes pretty close to absolute power, and we all know what absolute power can do.

Fortunately, *JAMA*'s incumbent editor is a man of distinguished background and, by all accounts, high character. George Lundberg is himself a medical doctor and an editor with 14 years' experience at the magazine. But if *JAMA* is published with integrity, it's because of Lundberg's sterling conduct: There is not much of a system, a process, on which other, lesser beings can rely. *JAMA* is practicing "trust-me" journalism, the scientific equivalent of Bob Woodward's deathbed interviews. Woodward gets away with it because he's Woodward, and Lundberg gets away with it because he's running *JAMA*, which appears to speak for most American doctors. The history of the human race is clear on this point: Free societies do better when power is restrained by rules and conventions rather than by the unfettered judgments of individual men, however high-minded. (Another scientist, generally an admirer of Lundberg's, told me that all editors play favorites and researchers must game the system to avoid reviews "by people who hate me.")

Just as peer review tends to take idiosyncratic shape in the eye of the beholder, so do the adjectives Velcroed to medical journals. They all seem to be "prestigious" or "authoritative." Take the case of a journal much in the news lately, the *American Journal of Hypertension*. It is a relatively new publication, eight years old, and serves a readership of less than 4,000. It is not generally considered a first-tier journal, but it is one of the industry's most energetic practitioners of science by press release, in which a study's findings are summarized, and hyped, for media distribution.

Follow the likely chain of evidence and you'll see the problem. The researcher, an expert in a narrow specialty, reports to the editor, who is perforce a generalist. The editor then explains the study to his publicist, who then explains the story to a network-news producer. The producer's natural query is, "How far can we go?" The publicist wants to be cooperative. The producer then explains the story to the broadcast's managing editor/anchorman, whose first question is, "What's the headline here?" The anchorman then takes 22 seconds to explain it to the rest of us. Anybody who played Telephone in second grade will be able to calculate the odds that the researcher's nuance survived this journey. In *Hypertension*'s case, one of its own officials complained in an internal document that a recent press release was "as inflammatory a statement as can be imagined." That inflammatory statement, of course, made the network news intact.

Hypertension is the beneficiary of a happy confluence of motives between journal staffers and the news outlets they flak: The staffers wish to elevate themselves to "prestige" status for all the obvious reasons, and the media types seek to hang their sky-is-falling stories on "prestige" sources. Thus is a prestigious publication born. The press traditionally sees its role as questioning authority, but in this circumstance the press is vesting authority. Reporters who wouldn't think of taking handouts from, say, the Pentagon, snatch them from obscure medical journals.

When dealing with peer-reviewed science—the point at which even skeptics and ideological opponents must be prepared to say as a society that the jury is now in and the truth is now out—laymen have a right to expect solid fact and sound process. We have a right to expect transparency—the traditional scientific approach in which the researcher's work is open to inspection, the reviewers stand by their critiques, the debate is joined, and the community works toward consensus. The public has placed great trust in our scientific institutions—in many cases, the trust to make life-and-death decisions for the rest of us. It's time for the peer-reviewed journals to undergo some rigorous peer review.

National Review
October 31, 1980

THE CARTER CENSUS

Y ou are all familiar with the Chicago School of Political Science. That distinguished body of opinion holds that no American should be denied his civil rights on the basis of race, creed, color, or pulse rate. If a man has been a loyal American citizen throughout his life, it is maintained, there is no cause in justice to cut off his right to vote simply because some meddling bureaucrat has certified him deceased. Fair is fair.

Over the years the Chicago School has operated with singular efficiency. Its political favorites, John Kennedy and Lyndon Johnson among them, have won startling come-from-behind victories. Its political opponents, those upon whom the school did not smile, have fallen victim to campaign blunders; in several cases, their strategists failed to allow for the possibility that voter turnout would exceed registration figures. Ah, those simple mistakes. Beginning in the mid '60s, however, after JFK and LBJ had pulled the ladder up after them, the Chicago School began to attract a bad press. Boy Scouts dressed up as editorial-page editors began to goo-goo them onto the defensive and, with the death of Richard Daley and the enervation of Carmine De Sapio, the Chicago School fell into disrepute and, with a few exceptions, desuetude.

It may come as something of a surprise, then, to learn that the Chicago School is making a comeback this year. Not in the clubhouses of Cook County, you understand, or Tammany or Duval, not in the back rooms of spaghetti restaurants, not in the storefronts with metal desks, not behind the plate-glass windows with the "Law Office—Insurance—Real Estate" lettering, but in the middle of the busiest street in town at high noon. In 1980, as in every decennial year since the founding of the Republic, the national administration has discharged its constitutional duty to enumerate the citizenry. Now the real count begins.

We have written about the Census before and we conclude from the thundering silence that we were not addressing one of your white-hot concerns. Before you shove this issue all the way off your list, however, consider for a moment the stakes involved. The Census numbers are the very *premises* of the '80s. When we arrive at the final figures, we agree to be bound by them, much in the same way attorneys accept stipulations at trial. We accept a statistical definition of who we are and what we have become. When the president accepts the data from the Bureau of the Census on December 31, there will be no appeal from subsequent bureaucratic formulations. Both the distribution of federal funds and the structure of political representation, in the Congress and the Electoral College, will be set in something more unshakable than cement. They will be set in computer programs.

Like the making of sausage and legislation, the enumeration of the citizenry is not much fun to watch. (Congressman Jim Leach of Iowa, who has followed the process closely, calls it "statistical gerrymandering.") There are three stages. First comes the enumeration: 275,000 election-year patronage appointees fan out across the country counting eeny-meeny-minee-moe. Now, given the high incidence of Chicago School graduates among the appointees, we can assume that certain subtotals are not inflated: the middle class, whites, professionals, suburbanites, and so on. On the other hand, slum apartments, junkie alleys, and transient hotels have been known to escape close personal inspection by skittish enumerators. A modest amount of extrapolation has probably saved a life here and there. If there is a systemic weakness in the counting process, it resides in the Southwest, where even Bureau officials will admit there may be mass undercounting of Hispanic immigrants to Arizona, New Mexico, and southern California. Even so, the figures are not bent grotesquely out of shape, and for the first 19 enumerations the process stopped there—with the Bureau count. In 1980, however, Jimmy Carter gave local officials the right to "review" the data before official submission. In most cases, the review process featured a Democratic patronage appointee confronting a local Democratic pol. Understandably, these were not knock-down drag-out adversary procedures. If the review process resulted anywhere in a downward adjustment of local population figures, that fact has not been made public.

To recap. Stage 1 is an enumeration administered by patronage appointees, Stage 2 is a local review and adjustment process conducted predominantly by Democratic officials. Those "safeguards" ought to satisfy even the legendary Mr. Richard J. Daley. But no: They are unable to roll back the tides of demography, and the data continue to show that the 25 congressional districts suffering the heaviest population losses since 1970 are all in core urban centers. Make that core Democratic centers. (New York City alone could lose four seats in the House.) And thus we come to Stage 3. The urban centers are going to court, which in most cases means that Democratic mayors are pleading before Democratic judges. Detroit, Chicago, Philadelphia, New York, and other cities claiming an undercount are asking the courts for a new type of federal aid. They seek an award of what amounts to a phantom population—invisible but assumed to be present. (On September 25, a U.S. District Court judge ruled in favor of Detroit, barring the Bureau from releasing data until adjustments are made. A week later, New York won a similar ruling.) You see, the greater the population, the higher the revenue-sharing check. The principle here seems to be that if a gravestone is entitled to vote it ought to have the right to go on welfare. Fair is fair.

National Review
October 17, 1980

COLONIAL AMERICA

W e are indebted to Philip Dunne, of all people, for his insight into the nature of our current leadership. A longtime writer and producer and on the side a Hollywood political activist, as the euphemism still has it, Dunne records a synecdochic incident in his recently published memoirs, *Take Two: A Life in Movies and Politics*. The scene is a plush Tinseltown studio, a story conference is in progress, and the atmosphere is charged with—well, what else? Electricity! Darryl Zanuck—the irrepressible, autocratic Zanuck—takes command. Swinging the polo mallet that was his trademark prop, Zanuck cruises the room, talking, reaching, creating. "And now, and *now*, her love turns to hate," Zanuck intones. The group of screen writers absorbs this wisdom silently. Then a lone voice pipes up, "Why, Mr. Zanuck? Why does her love turn to hate?" Zanuck pauses, then leaves the room. A few moments later a flushing toilet can be heard. Then Zanuck strides back into the room, points the mallet at the questioner, and says, "All right, her love *doesn't* turn to hate."

That, my friends, is leadership in the Carter mode.

Consider our position in the world today. It has become the rhetorical twitch not only of our elected officials but also of the public declaimers to describe our role in imperial terms. Our military bases are far-flung. Our economic penetration is deep. Our cultural presence is ubiquitous. We are a Superpower, of which there are no more than two. The rhetoric is high-blown, but it does in fact reflect how most of us feel most of the time. The pertinent question, however, is this: Do these words describe the actuality of the American role in the world today? Do they capture the essence of the current situation? Suppose, for the purposes of argument, that our mindset is not imperial but rather colonial. What symbols and images would we employ to describe our condition?

Take our military bases. To be sure, in the geographical sense they are far-flung. Year-end editions of pretentious newspapers still run maps with forests of pins representing planes and ships. Those pins stretch from one border of the map to the other. But what is the *function* of those far-flung bases? Are they entrusted with an imperial mission? The enforcement of moral-legal codes? Collecting taxes? Consolidating gains won on the fields of military or economic battle? Or could it be said that they are protecting, and *in extremis* fighting for, the Germans, the Japanese, and the genuinely strong economies of the world? Are they, in a word, serving as colonial troops, fighting wars in which the indigenous peoples prefer to remain uninvolved? Is the apposite metaphor a nuclear umbrella or a Hessian troop?

Or take a look at the structure of economic relationships. It is the bias of our educational system, and fundamental to the hierarchy of civilizational beliefs, that the American economy is the best in the world. We carried the Industrial Revolution to its glistening conclusion; we honored the entrepreneurial spirit; we went multinational with a vengeance. The business of America *was* business. But a quick trip through the financial section of the paper confirms that veritable sea-changes have set in. We now find our currency manipulated by forces beyond our own borders. The dollar, the Godalmighty dollar, can be yanked around by a few guys wearing sheets in a Vienna hotel lobby. Our central manufacturing enterprises—those firms whose corporate names are synonymous with American economic might—go begging to the government for protection against foreign dumping, never risking to inquire how Panasonic and VW and Michelin can sell their products below cost and still make a handsome profit. (The mini-managers of Detroit would no doubt answer: They make it up on volume.) The only entry that begins to balance our national checkbook is raw materials, which in classic colonial style we trade for the lower-priced, higher-quality manufactured goods we now import. (Scanning the stats for hopeful signs, the business press has invested great promise in another emerging export industry. *Textiles!*)

Liberate yourself from imperial rhetoric and you can see something of the same pattern in the developing problem of immigration. Traditionally, it has been a source of national pride that foreigners seek America as a new home. They come here, we like to believe, because they have recognized the superiority of American life, the siren opportunity of the free society. What has happened in recent months, however, is sharply at variance with the sampler-philosophy. Castro is not letting the best and the brightest of Cuban society slip through his fingers to south Florida. He is sending us, instead, his old, his infirm, and, in especially generous amounts, his criminal elements. As the rash of hijackings has made clear, these are not your budding capitalists yearning to be free. These are social undesirables who are being sent to the great penal colony to the north. Shipped out from the home country, as it were, to the remote outpost from which return passage is a forlorn, desperate hope. Next stop: Devil's Island.

It was with some of these notions in mind that we wrote in this space about bilingual education. That pernicious program is very much of a piece with the progressive colonialization of America. When a foreign power first stakes its claim to a new territory, the agenda can take many forms but it always begins with a single item: The waxing power imposes its own language on the waning, subjected peoples. (And taxes them, of course, for the privilege of diluting their own culture.)

It goes without saying, but perhaps shouldn't, that we are not arguing here for a new American imperialism. In the present circumstance, such an argument would be irrelevant. We have neither the will nor the force of arms to restore the *status quo ante*. But we think it is neither too much nor too late to ask of our national leadership that they conduct our affairs with a semblance of pride, with prudence, and with a decent respect for the greatness that was America.

National Review
January 23, 1981

THE MIDDLE OF AN ERA

T he lessons for today are drawn from Fibonacci, Kondratieff, and Schacter. Your first guess, alas, is incorrect. This threesome did not make up the GOP ticket in New York's 1965 municipal elections. They were, rather, three of the more asseverative students of the human condition, each of whom made a durable if unintended contribution to political understanding.

Leonardo Fibonacci, a 13th-century Italian scholar, is best known for his study of the Great Pyramid at Giza. During the course of his research, he concluded that Egyptian architects had employed in their design a fixed progression of numbers: 1-1-2-3-5-8-13-21-34-55-89 and so on. In this series, as will be seen, the ratio of successive numbers comes asymptotically to 1.618. These numbers, cannily promoted and widely remarked, came to be known as the Fibonacci series.

Now it is a signal honor to have a series of numbers carry your name. As well as an irresistible temptation. Impressionable bystanders began to see Sr. Fibonacci's numbers everywhere, a phenomenon known to psychologists as "illusionary correlation." Indeed, as the centuries passed, the Fibonacci series was perceived to be the underlying pattern in all manner of developmental functions—the rings on elephant tusks, the blips on a pineapple, the curls on a seashell, and suchlike. There are even botanists who will swear that the number of branches on a tree increases each year exactly by the Fibonacci increment.

Following Richard Clopton's dictum that for every credibility gap there is a gullibility fill, the Fibonacci series was soon assigned to explain the inexplicable, including, perhaps inevitably, the stock market. Using the 1.618 formula, security analysts found that they could "project" almost any data with felicitous precision. It was only momentarily troubling to discover that other analysts, equally devoted to the power of the Fibonacci numbers, were predicting altogether different outcomes.

It was all a matter of interpretation, it seemed, with each analyst reading into the great Rorschach blob whatever patterns he was predisposed to discern.

Nikolai Kondratieff's experience was somewhat different, and somewhat the same. As a young economist in the early days of the Soviet revolution, Kondratieff studied Western economic statistics and concluded that capitalist societies move in cycles, each lasting approximately 50 years. That there is an ebb and flow to life, a few ups and a few downs, seems to be less than a heart-stopping revelation. But Kondratieff's pronouncements were heard as thunderclaps. *Of course*, said his admirers. *Reactionary*, cried his critics. (No doubt Kondratieff's reputation was enhanced by the official disfavor his studies encountered in Leninist Moscow. Manifestly, he had wandered from the true socialist path. A progressive analysis would have revealed that the cycles of capitalist society can be traced in a precipitate southward plunge, ending abruptly at the point at which capitalism dashes upon the rocks of history.)

The theory of the Kondratieff wave was embraced by economists in many countries and maintains today a firm grip on a small but outspoken band of devotees. Its basic attraction is that it explains everything. If you can draw squiggly lines on a piece of paper, you can insulate yourself against information overload and achieve *fundamental understanding*. Just as a stopped clock is right twice a day, a squiggly line on a sheet of graph paper will occasionally intersect with reality. On such occasions, the Kondratieff wave tightens its grip still further on the true believers and adds, at least for the nonce, a circle of new adherents.

A little bit later in the century, after Kondratieff had perished in a Stalinist prison for his effronteries, a laboratory scientist by the name of S. Schacter gave us another insight into how we receive information and how we act on it. He injected a number of volunteers with the drug epinephrine, which induces temporary heart palpitations and other symptoms of anxiety. Schacter told his volunteers that the drug was a vitamin. He then placed the volunteers in cells with dummy patients who had not received epinephrine. In one cell, the dummy was antic and lighthearted, in another he was frowning and angry. The question Schacter sought to answer was this: How would his volunteers act? In the large majority of cases Schacter's volunteers acted the way the dummies did. In other words, when all about them people are losing their heads, most people will lose their own.

We adduce the examples of Fibonacci, Kondratieff, and Schacter for short-term therapeutic purposes. Over the next 90 days it will be important to immunize oneself against cycles, waves, and crowd reactions as well as against eras, charts, sunspots, and tea leaves. Every time one picks up a paper or a newsweekly, one will be struck with a big-picture piece that, from whatever point of ideological departure, concludes that we are at a) The End of an Era; b) The Beginning of an Era; or c) Both of the Above. We are here today to introduce the humble notion that we may be at None of the Above. As difficult as it may be for all of us to admit, we may have come no further than the very middle of an era. For as Paul Anderson once put it: "I have yet to see any problem, however complicated, which, when you looked at it the right way, did not become still more complicated."

National Review
February 20, 1980

THE NEO-NAZI OLYMPICS

T he political memory is notoriously convenient, and nowhere more so than in this town of professional frontrunners. To believe the dinner-party chatter here is to believe that Richard Nixon was shut out in 1968. *Nobody* voted for him. Détente, we have learned only in recent weeks, has been the object of universal skepticism these many years. And we now understand that the SALT II treaty, despite wildly inaccurate press reports to the contrary, never commanded a single firm, publicly identifiable vote in the U.S. Senate. All quite remarkable. The phenomenon runs so far that we find it difficult to locate anybody who opposed an Olympic boycott . . . in 1936.

In defiance of what we gather was the opposition of right-thinking men everywhere, those 1936 games did go off as scheduled—the summer games in Berlin and the winter games in Garmisch-Partenkirchen, it being the custom in those days for a single nation to host both halves of the Olympiad. As they say, it was the first time in modern Olympic history that the games were held in a totalitarian environment, and the experience was rich with historical lessons. The best summary of those lessons can be found in Richard Mandell's tough-minded book *The Nazi Olympics*. Written in 1971, before the games were awarded to Moscow, Mandell's book offers a number of resonant passages.

1. "*. . . much of the success of the 1936 Olympics was due to the pursuit by the National Socialists of supremacy in mass pageantry. Hitler's success as a whole is inconceivable without the application of the contrived festivity that enveloped Nazism from beginning to end.*" Change a date here and a word there and you have a preview of the Moscow "games."

2. "*After the first day of the Berlin Olympics, American track and field athletes, many of the best of whom were Negroes, made a haul of medals. The Nazi leaders were fiercely embarrassed. They scrambled to devise some sort of scoring system that could hide the size of the American lead. One candidate would have discarded all medals won by Negroes, whom the Nazis considered subhumans. Then, as the days went on, Germans, in events ranging from gymnastics to marksmanship and yachting, won more gold, silver, and bronze medals than the athletes from any other nation, thus emerging victorious.*" Moscow may be different in one conspicuous respect, in that the Soviets consider all peoples subhuman regardless of race, color, or creed, but in major ways it will be identical. The Soviets in their methodical way have completed their scrambling and have devised a scoring system that will properly reflect socialist glory. Take basketball, for instance. The American squad, twelve strong, will be favored to win the gold medal. Their accomplishment, great as it is, will be dwarfed statistically by a single Soviet gymnast who because of "medal inflation" will be favored to win as many as a half-dozen golds. Or take weightlifting. The Soviets and their socialist brethren have proved to be especially proficient at pumping iron, a sport in which, perhaps not coincidentally, phar-

macological assistance can be of decisive value. So exhilarating have been the triumphs of Soviet sportsmen that Eastern officials have demanded more of them. Responsive as always to socialist logic, international Olympic officials have obliged by slicing the weight classes more finely, with the result that Moscow will award 33 medals in weightlifting, up from a total of 21 at the 1952 games. Under the current scoring system, then, weightlifting is eleven times more important than basketball. Only reactionary elements would contend otherwise, of course.

3. *"The hundreds of foreign journalists, businessmen, and diplomats invited to the 1936 Games had their judgment skewed (a predictable consequence of festivity) by what they experienced there. Even as the thousands of athletes struggled before hundreds of onlookers and happy millions more reveled in the massed parades, flapping banners, and staged solemnities, there was ample evidence that the masters of Germany had charted that nation on a collision course. In August of 1936 Hitler was meddling purposefully in the Spanish revolution and becoming more ambitious in his plans for Austria and Czechoslovakia. The generous congratulations he and his lieutenants received for their Olympic successes were both emboldening to them and deceiving to their opponents."* For the press, a Soviet Olympiad will be a two-week tour of the Potemkin village; for the businessmen, a tempting opportunity; for the diplomats, a distraction from unpleasant geopolitical realities. For the Soviets, if their success proves to be "emboldening," it would carry only the force of redundancy.

4. *". . . all the athletes who competed at Garmisch-Partenkirchen and at Berlin were made to feel that they were the corporeal manifestation of intellectual and political forces let loose to compete in other spheres later in that troubled decade."* One's heart aches for the American athletes, many of whom honestly believe that the world of sports is wholly separate from the world of politics. One day they will see clearly and painfully that Moscow's interest in the games is *exclusively* political.

5. *"The world drew lessons from the Berlin Olympics . . . Athletes from totalitarian nations performed best of all."* Form charts suggest that the Soviet Union will finish first at Moscow, with East Germany a close second. Cuba will lead the Third World.

6. ". . . *the end result was tragic, because the new Germans were al-most universally viewed as not only powerful and stable, but respectable as well.*" Respectability for an illegitimate regime—the greatest triumph of all.

For the moment, try to forget Vietnam and Angola and Ethiopia and the Yemens and even Afghanistan. Was there *ever* an argument in support of the Moscow games? Should we *ever* participate in an Olympiad run by totalitarians?

National Review
June 13, 1980

KEEPING THE FAITH

The great man holds these dinners once each month, on Fridays at eight o'clock. Punctuality is appreciated. Latecomers are admitted, of course, there being no civilized way to deny them, but the regulation-issue libation, a weak highball, must be sacrificed to the demands of the schedule. At 8:45 the company moves briskly to the dining room and, under the firm hand of the hostess, arranges itself in the prescribed pattern around the brilliantly polished table. There are 24 of us, as always.

The great man makes a few remarks before we turn to the exquisite meal. Everything seems to remind him of something else; seemingly unrelated events and personalities are cobwebbed with recollections of the '30s and the '50s, and especially of the '40s. These are dangerous times for America, he says in so many words, employing the elegant circumlocution where a flat-out cliché would do just as nicely. His remarks are compellingly interesting, not so much for their intrinsic cogency as for their barometric significance. The great man has served at the elbow of three presidents. He has lived through dangerous times and not-so-dangerous times and he knows the difference.

His remarks concluded, and a respectful pause observed, we fall to the meal with a gusto quite inappropriate to the surroundings. All of us are at least 30 years the great man's junior and, in the manner of workaholic Washingtonians, we have not seen a morsel of food since the ham sandwich at noon. Most of the wives work, too, and they have had nothing since breakfast but a gallon of coffee. The table talk is perfunctory; waiters hover nearby awaiting the great man's signal to clear the table.

With the arrival of coffee and cigars, the great man resumes his remarks. Within the space of three syllables, the table's attention is undivided. His tone suggests that tonight's conversation will depart from custom. He is not so much interested in our views—keeping his mind open to the opinions of young people has become almost an obsession in late years—as he is interested in our actions. He wants to know what we have done for our country, what investment we have made in the American enterprise. He wants to know if the conduct of our lives can be said to be in conformity with the conclusions of our analysis. Specifically, he wants to know what each of us has accomplished over the last year of which we are truly proud. There is more than curiosity in his question. Accusation lurks close by.

Twenty-two pairs of eyes study the grain of the tabletop. A rare tabletop it is. But the great man is not about to lighten the burden of his question. "Let's start with you, Peter," he says, pointing a cigar at a 36-year-old government official. Groping for a handhold, Peter stumbles off into a lengthy recitation of how he has reorganized his agency to ensure faster response to congressional inquiries. The new procedures he has installed will make it possible for cases to be identified, extracted from file, and reviewed within eight days, whereas under his predecessor the normal case cycle would run to two weeks and more. He searches the great man's face for benign response and, finding none, accelerates the pace of his narrative to the very edge of the sound barrier: We are sitting barely ten feet from the poor man and we cannot understand a single word he is saying.

And so it goes around the table.

Jennifer is going to law school. This year has been her Turning Point. Daycare centers are wonderful.

Chuck, an attorney, has won a case against a Major Corporation for his regulatory agency.

Arlene, on the basis of important research, has secured a grant from the National Institutes of Health to study plant life in Southwest Asia. Arlene's voice is quavering so badly it's almost a yodel.

William, a graduate of special courses, has gotten in touch with his feelings and has become a better person. He knows that sounds silly, but he now feels capable of realizing his full potential, which is much greater than he had suspected.

Topsy is working for the hottest shop in town, the EEOC, and is on the verge of "busting things open" for women in all forms of governmental employment.

John has just landed his own radio talk show on one of the best stations in town. With his column and lecture deals, he is "putting it all together."

Millie has finally learned the most important thing in life, which is that she is a competent human being. She is leaving home to work for the head of a think tank in the area. It's the beginning of her "second life."

As the conversational ball rolls inexorably to our place, we glance at the door. Alas, the messenger from the Nobel Committee fails to burst through in time. We are on our own. In what has become a heavy and unpleasant atmosphere, we attempt a high-risk levity. We inform the great man that we are most proud of coaching the Screaming Eagles from last place to first in the Vienna, Virginia Boys Soccer League. Silence, then a ripple of strained but grateful laughter, followed a beat later by a modest chuckle from the head of the table. Given time and a second brandy, he just may forgive us. He seems to have the answer he has been looking for. Now he can stop scolding and get back to the lesson at hand.

National Review
February 20, 1981

AN ALMOST GOLDEN AGE

We were leaving a meeting at the International Center in Reston, Virginia when a fellow con-fabulist turned to us and said through clenched teeth, "You know what you've done, don't you? You've just destroyed the networks." The year was 1973, and the gentleman with the gift for hyperbole was referring to a decision by the Corporation for Public Broadcasting to adopt the technology of satellite transmission.

It was the gentleman's contention, widely repeated in the trade press in those years, that if public broadcasting broke ranks with the commercial networks, and with the monopoly transmission facility of Ma Bell, there would follow as the night the day an era of chaos in the communications industry. Every local television station in the land would be free to run out and purchase its own "dish" and pick up its own signals. Every local television station would be free to program its own schedule, snatching from thin air the shows it liked and discarding the rest, even if it came down the network pipeline. New program suppliers would be emboldened to offer alternative fare. New technologies, including what was then known as community antenna television and later became known as "cable," would exploit the political weaknesses of the traditional broadcasters and, riding on the R&D nickel of the public broadcasting industry, prove out the dazzling economies of satellite transmission. What could happen, we were told, is that the national umbilical cord running from the West Side of Manhattan to the local "affiliates" across the nation could be severed. Permanently.

Dropping down a few decibels into the confessional voice, we will admit that this prospect did not fill us with fear and loathing. As a father, as a conservative, and as an average citizen with an IQ in three digits, we were never persuaded that the commercial networks had earned a prior claim on our national gratitude; nothing on, say, the order of national defense or the public library. Not even on the order of that other extra-constitutional stolen base, the two-party system. At the same time, the notion of entrepreneurial diversity in communications did not so much frighten as titillate us. We could at least conceive the possibility of a fourth network, a fifth network, a 20th. If *The Dukes of Hazzard* should dip below a 30 share, well, we were prepared to live with that.

Remember, though, that this was 1973. It was a boom year for conspiracy theories, most of which relied for their narrative drive on the menacing character of Richard M. Nixon. (The sun never rose at all in those arctic months, children. The streets were cold and deserted, except for the roving bands of disease-carrying rats.) It was a given of civilized discussion in those days that any change in the media environment was a) bad and b) the result of Nixonian manipulation. The early '70s were, in other words, the heyday of communication monopoly. Network television and the telephone company could do pretty much as they liked.

The technological revolution, which can never be resisted, was thus slowed. In the twisted world of media politics, those of us who were for change, for free expression, became the agents of repression. *Nixon appointees*. In the code word of contemporary *Washington Post* coverage, we became known as the "hardliners," which in practical terms meant that we did not approve the funding procedures then well-established in public broadcasting. (These amounted, roughly speaking, to hurling vaultsful of tax money at every self-described producer waving a four-page treatment titled, *The Rosenberg Case: A Reappraisal*.) It was a difficult passage, tiptoeing between the Scylla of the media establishment and the Charybdis of the political establishment. Not without a few scrapes, and not without a few hundred meetings, public broadcasting finally entered the satellite era. It had to. The economic arguments were overpowering.

Soon, as a result more of free-market forces than of innovations on the part of public broadcasting, technology had its way across the communications spectrum. Cable television was liberated by the Federal Communications Commission and began to wire the nation with a vengeance. Video-cassette recorders began the market transition from class to mass. And even as we write, the videodisc is preparing to enter the home-video sweepstakes under the powerful auspices of RCA. Inevitably, with each technological advance, the network share of the television audience was sliced still thinner. By the end of this decade, according to Wall Street analysts, the network share could fall by between 25 and 40 percent. (Concomitantly, the other mass medium—the general-circulation newspaper—is redesigning its own product to appeal to the special-interest reader. Many of the industry leaders are now test-marketing information-retrieval systems for the home with which the reader can, in effect, become his own editor.)

The result of all this change will be enhanced freedom of choice for the information consumer. In our view, that is an end eagerly to be sought. A society without free access to available information is a society only partially free. But before we celebrate unreservedly the coming of the golden age of communications, let us pause to consider the price we shall be asked to pay, for in every economic advance there lurks a social trade-off. That trade-off, it seems to us, may be reflected in a loss of social cohesion, in a diminution of the shared information pool and thus in the shared premises of 220 million Americans. As simplistic, as distorted as the mass-media account of human affairs may have been, we were all aware of it. That account gave us a place to start the national conversation. It gave us a framework within which to draw up the national agenda. In the new electronic supermarket, however, each consumer will gain the right to define his own informational needs. There will perforce be 220 million different definitions. And we may one day in the not too distant future hear ourselves start to say: Bring back Walter.

National Review
September 18, 1981

RICH FOLKS

The rich is happy in the plenty giv'n,
The poor contents him with the care of Heav'n.
—Alexander Pope

S ay what you will about Alexander Pope, he was no supply-sider. If he were serving today as poet laureate of the GOP, and why bloody not, he would probably be most comfortable nestled in among the Rockefellers and Scrantons, the Heinzes and Weickers—men made more or less happy by the plenty giv'n. Ronald Reagan, it seems reasonable to suppose, would make him nervous. Very nervous.

It is the contention from this soapbox that Reagan's principal achievement to date can be seen in the new contours of our national self-image. In the brief span of his incumbency, we have inched away from an egalitarian society in the direction of a merit society. Note the evolving language of the Reagan era. The unassuming word "incentive" now carries the force of a paralyzing dart; and the word "redistributionism" brings groans from the highly informed. (At last, our own code words!) The entrepreneur has reclaimed his place in the national imagination, and economic growth has been accorded the presumption of innocence. It may be no more than a flirtation with the truly free society, and then again it may be the beginning of a real change in American life. That we have come even this far, however, is evidence of the particular contribution of Ronald Reagan. He was poor and God-fearing, but he did not content himself with the care of Heav'n. He preferred to be rich and God-fearing, and his subsequent witness to the supply-side faith is more compelling than a billion Rockefeller benefactions.

Paradoxically, it is precisely this association with the rich that the press knights say will push Reagan into political hot water. They recall the inauguration as a metaphor for conspicuous consumption, and, in truth, it did seem to offer a bizarre competition in baubles, bangles, and beads. They point to the family friends, many of whom did in fact ride one California trend or another to flashy wealth. And they note the fiscal patterns of the first 200 days—tax cuts for the rich, budget cuts for the poor. It adds up, they say, to a political problem. The public opinion surveys seem to concur: Reagan's *for* the rich and *against* the poor.

What the press knights are overlooking is the difference between envy and resentment. The point is nicely illustrated by a story Herman Kahn used to tell about a visit to the Rockefeller estate. As Kahn was driven around the estate, one of the Rockefeller brothers pointed out the riding trails, the airstrip, the tennis courts, the sundry mansions, the not-so-tiny village constructed for the help, the seven-figure bric-a-brac. Turning reflective for a moment, the Rockefeller brother opined, with more than a hint of anxiety, that passersby must resent bitterly his family's wealth. It was left to Kahn to explain that the average American spends less than five seconds per year grinding his teeth over Rockefeller wealth. The average American, said Kahn, is inflamed by the desire to add $10,000 to his annual income, not $10 million. Quite so. There is much envy of the Rockefellers, but little resentment. Their example provides an economic spur, not a source of social unrest.

But if Americans at large *envy* the Rockefellers, they *resent* the source of much of their wealth—Exxon. Indeed, all of big business has earned the deep-seated suspicions of the public. The distinction between free enterprise and big business, frequently blurred in administration policy, is perfectly clear to the general public. They know intuitively that while big business continues to pay its debt to free-enterprise rhetoric, in the quiet moments before dawn it wants nothing more than to be AT&T.

Entrepreneurial capitalism, by contrast, is enjoying both a boom and a vogue. It is creating most of the new jobs and most of the genuinely innovative products in our economy. It thus represents the central hope of Reagan's economic recovery plan. If supply-side economics is to work, it will have to work, well, on the supply side.

Against this background, the political problem the administration is creating for itself can be seen clearly. Take the matter of accelerated depreciation schedules, for which Reagan has plumped enthusiastically.

They are of use only to those who already have capital to invest—i.e., big business. Then take the related matter of interest rates. Even at rates of 18-plus, IBM has no problem raising money. The government of the City of New York has no problem. But how about the entrepreneur? How about the small public company? In a word that does no justice to their plight, they have a problem.

Which leads us to the bankruptcy rate. During the first six months of this year, bankruptcies increased by 21 percent over the previous year, business reorganizations by 36 percent. Those bankruptcies and reorganizations were small businesses, little guys squeezed out of the market. Those were the same guys who voted for Ronald Reagan and upon whom he is relying to re-energize the economy. Denied their daily bread, they stare sullenly at the circus: a corporate stampede for Conoco, in which the ripoff for legal fees alone is said to have run to $20 million.

We suspect that economic understanding in this country would be instantaneously elevated if all rich people would just report to the U.S. Treasury one Monday morning, there to apply every last dime they had to the liquidation of the national debt. It would be a cathartic democratic scene: Mellons, du Ponts, Perots, and Paoluccis all jostling in a bureaucratic queue with blond newspersons asking impertinent questions. The point would be quickly grasped that, as a matter of statistical reality, the rich are irrelevant in our middle-class economy. We would learn also in that moment how much we wish to preserve the *right* to be rich. And our national leadership would learn that the disabling political indiscretion lies not in favoring the would-be rich over the hopeless poor, but in favoring the large over the small.

National Review
December 9, 1988

OLD PEOPLE'S POWER

—Washington, D.C.

I love old people and you love old people, but let's face it, they're killing us.

In the season of political piety just past, a sea change in American politics was recognized and affirmed: The old are the most powerful political constituency in the country, indeed the only constituency whose claims on the commonwealth have been placed beyond democratic debate. Politicians of both parties and of all ages now believe, at the operational margin, that it is safer to play with inflation, safer to cut back on housing programs and food assistance, *safer even to cut the budget for the nation's defense*, than it is to restrain the transfer of wealth to the old. From the evidence of Election Day 1988, one concludes that the process of intimidation is complete.

How did it happen, this political coup? One of the answers is organizational. Along Washington's power alley, the K Street lawyer/lobby zone, old people built the biggest and best organizational machine. The American Association of Retired Persons has signed up 30 million members, twice as many as the AFL-CIO and second as a "membership group" only to the Roman Catholic Church. The AARP has a paid staff of 1,300 and annual revenues from several businesses, as well as dues of $235 million. Its magazine, *Modern Maturity*, has now passed *TV Guide* and *Reader's Digest* to become the nation's largest. On Capitol Hill, congresspeople say to the AARP's army of lobbyists, "Thy will be done."

What has been done, on the Hill and down the street at the White House, is a series of federal fixes that tilted the generational playing field. The old were helped and the young were hurt. As benefits to the old ratcheted up, taxes on the young shot ahead. In 1958, the maximum Social Security payroll tax was $95 per annum; this year it will be $3,380. For more than half of all U.S. workers, Social Security taxes are now higher

231

than federal income taxes. Medicare benefits moved ahead even more smartly, with the result that during the current year almost $300 billion will be paid out to elderly beneficiaries of Social Security and Medicare. Forget for a moment that old people benefit from all universal government programs. From these two programs alone, old people, accounting for 12 percent of the population, consume 27 percent of all federal spending.

To justify these intergenerational transfers, one could point with alarm at the plight of the elderly poor. A heartbreaking sight, to be sure. One could point with alarm, that is, until the numbers began to shift a half-generation ago. Now they point in a very different direction. Consider these generational wealth figures and how they have moved over time.

NET WORTH		
AGE	**1973**	**1983**
65-69	$169,366	$321,562
25-34	$59,624	$49,046

In other words, the old get richer and the young get poorer.

One is obliged to remark here that federal transfer programs have not been the only engine of wealth-creation for the old. The other major contributor has been the escalation in residential real-estate values. The old owned the houses and the young did not, in part because the generational tax made it impossible to save a down-payment and carry costs. So what has the incumbent policy, whatever its intentions, actually wrought? We are taxing the producing citizens to protect the assets of the non-producing citizens—assets that were put aside precisely to finance retirement!

By 1988 we as a nation have recorded an historic accomplishment. We have virtually eradicated poverty among the old. Responsible authorities, much to the chagrin of the old folks' lobbyists, have put the figure as low as 5 percent (compared with 20 percent for children). Good for us, and let's hope that we can eliminate it altogether. But let's pause to look at the price tag and kick the tires and cut through the spiel of the guy in the window-pane-checked sports jacket. When the subject gets around to Social Security, let's go through the numbers and point out that the benefits are not simply a return on weekly payroll deductions of the past. The average beneficiary receives almost four times what he put in after adjustment for the interest he would have earned on private investments. He receives, on average, a full payback of contributions and interest within 21 months. After that, he's not on his own, a prudent retiree who saved for his golden years. He's on us. He's on welfare. Which is fine with the rest of us if he really needs it. If he's part of the 5 percent. Otherwise, he's asking us to fund an asset-protection program by overtaxing workers in their middle years and by denying benefits to the voiceless young.

National Review
August 19, 1988

IT'S KEMP!

B y the time you read this, George Bush may have named Alan Simpson, Peter Ueberroth, or Darryl Strawberry to run with him this fall. Such are the hazards of long magazine lead times . . . and presidential nominees with too much time on their hands. But if there's any political horse-sense resident in Kennebunkport, it's Kemp!

First, let's separate the women from the girls (this being an equal-opportunity journal). With the nomination bestowed in mid-August and the campaign in full swing by Labor Day, there is simply no time to prepare an amateur to deal with the full range of issues, foreign and domestic. Not even Evelyn Wood could get up to speed. So let's forget about the talk of Rudolph Giuliani (suggested by Mark Shields), Sandra Day O'Connor (Melvin Laird), Colin Powell (Robert Strauss), Peter Ueberroth (George Will), Jeane Kirkpatrick (okay, me, in weak moments). Voters demand that veep candidates be prepared to be president starting

January 21. These amateurs, however gifted, are not so perceived.

Then turn to the pros, the people who on a daily basis have been grappling with national issues, taking stands, calculating consequences. These prospects bear surface credibility and could persuade the electorate to suspend its disbelief for a week or two. Put in this group Senators Simpson and Nancy Kassebaum and (but for his recent health problems) Representative Dick Cheney. Three winning personalities, to be sure, but all unknown and untested in national campaigns and—the decisive point— incapable of giving the ticket a regional lift. (We pause to note the disproportionate contribution to national virtue of the Wyoming congressional delegation—Simpson, Cheney, and Malcolm Wallop. But three electoral votes are still three electoral votes.)

Turn finally to the governors, who might balance the mighty Bush résumé with front-line executive experience. Here the prospects include Governor James Thompson of Illinois and Thomas Kean of New Jersey. The killer argument against Thompson is that he would not be a dead lock to carry Illinois for Bush. *Adios*. And the knock on Kean, in my view, is that no ticket should have more than one candidate who is in the line of succession for the British crown.

Which brings us, as Richard Nixon told us all along, to the real candidates: Bob Dole, George Deukmejian, and Jack Kemp. All three have survived the ordeal by perception: They have handled themselves well in big-time, big-stakes politics. The question then becomes, which would be most effective against Dukakis and Bentsen?

Take Bentsen first, a sad story in the making. He will spend the next three months—and, if he's "successful" in the fall, the rest of his political life —explaining how he can live with the dismantling of SDI, how he's taking a fresh look at right-to-work laws, how he's going to compromise with Dukakis on abortion, why the next tax increase will be no more than a marginal adjustment to his supply-side prescription. It won't be pleasant for a proud man, but he will have done his duty for the party: He will have wrested Texas from George Bush.

Well, that's the premise. But remember that the Boston-Austin axis of 1960 worked so well, in part, because Nixon made the mistake of invading Kennedy's home turf with Henry Cabot Lodge. I find it hard to believe that the legendary Lone Star dealmakers, given a choice between president and vice president, between Mr. Big and What's-his-name, will belly up to the electoral counter and say, "Son, give me some of them small potatoes." I find it hard to believe that on election night Houston's finest hotels will rock to the chant of "We're Number Two! We're Number Two!" I find it hard to believe, that is, if George Bush offers a bit of ideological excitement. If he persuades the folks that this election is about real differences.

Now take a look at Dukakis. The definitive comment on him was made recently by Bill Rusher, the publisher of this journal. Rusher worked long, hard hours with Dukakis on a public-television series called *The Advocates*, during which, as Rusher put it, "you get to know a colleague fairly well." His settled memory of Dukakis? "The curious fact is that I cannot recall . . . a single anecdote about Mike Dukakis. He was—how to put it?—utterly bland." (Others will be somewhat more impressed with this account than your correspondent. As it happened, I also worked on that same series and was struck by Rusher's power of total concentration. I'm not sure that he would have recalled Mitzi Gaynor dancing on the conference table.) Dukakis is steady, relentless, mistake-free. He is plodding toward the political middle and Bush—not his running mate—will have to meet him there.

The task for Bush, QED, is to avoid the routine, one-dimensional choice (Deukmejian) and the Beltway smart-money choice (Dole) and reach for the *missing* ingredients of youth, vim, and ideas.

It's Kemp!

National Review
October 28, 1988

WIMP THRASHES NERD

The best seat in the house from which to watch a presidential debate is the one next to Anthony R. Dolan, chief speechwriter for the president. Dolan has been, these last eight years, the principal composer for the best oratorical instrument of our time. He knows how words move people around, and he knows how people move words around. His comments on the first debate, synthesized here, lead me to predict with confidence that George Bush will win the second debate going away.

The rules of engagement with Dolan require me to state clearly when he is speaking and when, as is almost always the case, I am twisting his words into harsh and censorious distortion. With fannies thus covered, let's go to the videotape.

The first mistake. These were Dolan's words a beat after Michael Dukakis's first sentence, which was, "I agree with Mr. Bush." If he agrees with Mr. Bush, what's all the fuss about, ask Joe Sixpack and Joseph Perrier in unison. Dolan is reminded of Nixon's mistakes of ingratiation against Kennedy, those Heepish, lawyerly locutions designed to give the devil his due. As customary as they may be on the floor of Congress or before an academic audience, they have no place in a debate where differences are to be sharpened, not resolved. Any candidate will do best when he opens with, "Here's where I disagree with my opponent."

The gambit misfired. As predicted here, Sasso the Magnificent tried a daring, rhythm-breaking gambit in the opening minutes of the first debate. He had Dukakis turn to the camera and say with a steel-teeth grin that Bush was becoming the "Joe Isuzu of American politics." The intended effect was to incite a stammering, squeaky-voiced Bush to respond, "Are you calling me a liar?" Instead, Bush shrugged off the insult (in my own view, because Bush is one of the seven people left in America who have no idea who Joe Isuzu is). Sasso must have been astounded that his ice pick drew so little blood. But he will be back at it next time.

Bush's long ball. In Dolan's view, there was gold in the ACLU hills. "The election may have been decided." Americans don't want their grandchildren appearing in X-rated movies, they don't want to shut off tax exemptions for the Catholic Church, and they don't want an elitist organization of lawyers telling them any different. Case closed.

The nerd vote is a lock. It takes a fine taxonomic touch to separate your nerds on the one hand from your wimps on the other. Bush seems to have blown the wimp vote in recent weeks by being an open, likable guy who is rising to meet his moment. One saw what we are coming to think of as the real Bush in a moment of spontaneity in the first debate: When Jim Lehrer got the clock bollixed, George Bush broke out of the format corral and showed a winning good humor. In that same moment, Dukakis tightened almost to the point of paralysis, timid to venture beyond the conversational zone marked "Issues." He is, it appears, just about what he was in first grade—the smartest little guy in the class—and you find yourself liking him now just about as much as you liked him then. (It is stipulated that senior White House official Dolan did not call Dukakis a nerd.)

Surprise. Dukakis wanted the campaign to be about competence rather than ideology. What else would you expect from a candidate who, when pressed about his apparent lack of passion, responds finally that he "cares deeply" about "people all over this country who in some cases are living from paycheck to paycheck?" The stunner is that Bush in the course of a single debate hit every ideological hot button of the last generation: Vietnam, the death penalty, ACLU, abortion, drugs, and the media. Bush is trying to drive the last nail into '60s liberalism.

The omissions. Remarkable by their (relative) absence were references to: the Massachusetts miracle (Bush missed a bet by not slamming it, in Dolan's view); Dan Quayle (Dolan assumes that Dukakis will jack up the anti-Quayle rhetoric in round two); Jesse Jackson (*nobody* knows how to handle Jesse); the sleaze factor (Deaver had just been sentenced).

Curious inclusions. Time after time, Dukakis found his way back to Noriega, prompting Dolan to ask, "Is there any juice in that issue? They must have numbers that suggest that there is." Neither of us can believe that they do. The other curiosity is Bush undergirding his economic position by listing endorsements from worthies Boskin, Feldstein, and Tsongas. Dolan asks the television screen in disbelief, "Who told you to say that?" Conspiracy theories abound.

The bottom line (mine). In our times, most Americans experience presidential leadership only through the medium of television. The presidency is, in that sense, the series that cannot be canceled. And while Americans may not take their politics very seriously, may not even stir their stumps to get out and vote, they take their television very seriously indeed. The average Home Using Television (HUT) in this country watches more than seven hours each and every day. That kind of exposure generates all manners of side effects, but one of them is that American viewers have become very demanding consumers of television images. My firm impressions are that, in a close election with no overriding issues, televised debates may well make the difference . . . and that the Nielsen family will not vote to give Michael Dukakis his own show.

National Review
June 24, 2004

BULLDOG BROTHERS

Yale used to cultivate leadership.

I t's not absolutely required that you attend Yale before running for president, but it's strongly recommended. Over the past three decades, Yale graduates have occupied the Oval Office for 18 years, thanks to Gerald Ford (1941L), George H.W. Bush (1948), Bill Clinton (1973L) and George W. Bush (1968). And of course that streak is certain to continue for the next four years after President Bush faces off in November against John Kerry (1966).

But the trend runs deeper still. While it's not widely known, Vice President Dick Cheney is also a Yalie and, paired with Bush, will comprise an all-Yale GOP ticket this fall. I picked up this obscure datum from a highly reliable source: Dick Cheney. One night at a Washington dinner, the table talk turned to college impressions and 'round we went, talkshow style, each of us giving a bite-sized bio. When it was Cheney's turn, he said, "I was in Neal's class at Yale." Cheney added amiably, "I flunked out." A ripple of expectant laughter went around the table, but it was immediately clear that Cheney was not setting up a punchline. He was merely reporting a fact. It was a moment so thoroughly extra-Beltwayish as to be what we've learned to call Reaganesque.

Look elsewhere in the administration and, despite the twanging from the West Wing, you'll find a lot more New Haven than Odessa. At Justice is hard-nosed John Ashcroft (1964). On his way to the United Nations is the righteous John Danforth (1963D). In Baghdad is the courageous Paul Bremer (1962). When he needs economic advice, the president can turn either to supply-siding Arthur Laffer (1962) or to his classmate from the other side of the political aisle, Nobelist George Akerlof (1962). Scott McClellan seems to be settling in as White House spokesman, but if Bush ever needs backup, who better than presidential mouthpiece David Gergen (1963).

Lest you think there is partisan bias at work here, consider that the greatest single moment for Yale Democrats occurred last fall. The primary contest turned out to be all Yale, all the time. Howard Dean (1971) had moved smartly to the front but John Kerry (1966) was building momentum, and Joseph Lieberman (1964) seemed poised to make a move if the frontrunners stumbled. Then, with the nomination finally settled, Old Blues started thinking the unthinkable—was it possible that nominee Kerry would turn to one of his fallen brothers, Dean or Lieberman, as his running mate? Could we be looking at an historic (and for the public at large, insufferable) Yale sweep? For tactical campaign reasons, probably not. But then again, let's not rule out Hillary Clinton (1973L).

Well, you get the point. A small school—a fifth or sixth of the size of a state university—has produced for our generation a wildly disproportionate percentage of national leadership. What's the deal–who was passing out the political steroids? Is this a trend that will continue? The answers are, respectively, "the campus culture" and "no."

Before the zeitgeist of the '60s blew it away, Yale's culture taught its sons—daughters would come later—that they should prepare to lead. Not to cope, not to interface, not to relate, but to lead. Yale was directionally agnostic. The leadership obligation could be discharged in politics, in business, in things academic, diplomatic, or philanthropic. But the terms of the transaction were clear: Yale would deliver the education, the credential, and the network, and would hold an IOU against the day when its sons could report faithfully, "We did our best." This culture was, of course, overtly and unsustainably elitist. But it explains the implausible political drama now unfolding on the national stage. Why it won't continue is also clear. The campus culture has changed, and the students have now joined the rest of the human race.

I'll close with a pop quiz: Of all those young men who quick-stepped through Yale beginning in the late '50s and up through the early '70s, who was considered *by his peers* as most likely to become president of the United States? I have not seen a poll on this question, but I have no doubt as to the answer: It was John Heinz (1960). He seemed destined to go all the way.

The American Spectator
February 15, 2010

GENTLEMEN, START YOUR ENGINES—QUICKLY!

—Daytona Beach, Fla.

I was trapped in conversation this week with a candidate for high public office who, anticipating my rude question, blurted out that she was "running to restore people's trust in government." All I could think to say in return was, "Why would you want to do that?"

You will already have surmised that the nice lady was not quoting from the platform of the Tea Party. No, she is the leading candidate, in a medium-red state, of the Republican Party and that's the message she will carry to the voters this year with a high-church sense of GOP purpose.

You see our problem.

Here we are, stuck in a political cycle where almost nothing has gone right. We have taken a beating on politics, on economics, on culture. It's tough out there for everybody without federal fix or favor. The only ray of sunshine is this healthy skepticism of government that's been rekindled among the citizenry—and now, here comes our well-coiffed candidate with the straight seams determined to stamp out all the sparks before personal freedom breaks out in unplanned ways. I'm kicking myself. I should have cajoled her into joining me for the race down here and then introduced her to the crowd. There's nothing like the sound of 195,000 constituents booing to sharpen a politician's sense of direction.

Truth be told, there are few places in the world like the Daytona International Speedway when it comes to spritzing lighter fluid all over that rekindling process. Remember that scrawny little C-SPAN wonkenanny they held over in Nashville the other day? They called it the Tea Party Convention, but it served up little more than tourist samples of see-through herbal tea. Here at the Daytona 500 we are mustered up at the Southern Command, surrounded by the fully caffeinated, double-shot foot soldiers of the national Tea Party movement. Most of these folks can't even remember when they lost their trust in government and they wouldn't spend much time in lamentation if they did. The very heritage of stock car racing, we are reminded, is swaddled in the myth of the moonshiners, the backcountry boozers who, sensing the approach of the revenoors, revved up their '57 Chevys and trusted their wheels to be somewhat hotter than the government's. My candidate would have rooted for the revenooers. But she's a quick study, give her that. It would have taken her about ten minutes to figure out that, while some of these folks have evidently been looking for love in the wrong places, not a one of them has been looking for much trust in government.

What she also would have noticed is that these small-t tea partiers are intensely political. They plaster wit and wisdom all over their T-shirts, none of it reflecting the 46 percent of the country that, Mr. Gallup insists, support the president. Unlike a baseball crowd, or a Philly crowd, they actually cheer for the good guys. They like Tim McGraw's songs. They like the preacher who prays for a good race "in the name of Jesus." They like the F-15's aerial turns and the waterskier's tricks. They like Harry Connick Jr.'s old-school rendition of the national anthem. But most conspicuously, their affection for Sarah Palin is uninflected. After the shortest political speech in history, they like her for Grand Marshall or President or Best Female Recording Artist or Whatever That Gal Wants. They just plain like her, almost as much as they like giving the digital salute to David Brooks, David Gergen and various other pairs of fancy pants.

The point is that, as wired as they are just now by the politics of the day, they care a lot more about their families. And their communities. And their churches. And lots of other things that never pop up in the box slugged "Today's Events" in the *Washington Post*. Today, for instance, they like cars. I claim no expertise in things NASCAR. I'm just dipping into the bucket list and traipsing after Miss Sarah, but I think I get it. Fans from across a ten-state region hustle over here three hours before the flag drops to steep themselves in a uniquely American experience. Handsome young men strapping themselves into high-performance machines, performing unnatural acts of skill and courage. This isn't curling or poker. These drivers are great athletes. And it helps, I'm told, if you have a bit of the crazy in you. To win the "great American race," you have to average—*average*—140-some miles per hour around a tightly banked track that's only 40 feet wide and 2.5 miles long. That's like trying to gun a motorcycle around your living room. Tough enough to do if you're out there all alone, a damn-sight tougher if you're banging fenders with 42 other crazies, most of whom would probably prefer that you survive the afternoon but have no strong feelings on the question. And here's the kicker: You have to keep up this suicidal pace for more than three hours and 500 miles, which of course would be 804 kilometers for those of you seeking to restore trust in government. What I'm saying is that these folks are real Americans, which means that they have better things to do than mess with politics. They're making a one-time offer to the rest of us and the expiration date is fast approaching.

It's my clear sense that we're at an inflection point in the Tea Party movement. We know what they're against: the sad and widely unremarked fact that Obama is conducting what looks to many people very much like a third Bush term—bailouts, stimulus, entitlement expansion, war escalation, wall-to-wall Tenth Amendment overreach from the school to the hospital to the bank to the gas station. Over the last few years, alarmingly, we seem to be getting all the government we're paying for.

It's not nearly as clear what the Tea Partiers are for. Now that they've busted up the incumbent paradigms, where will they turn next? As I count them, it could be any one of three ways. First and most likely, they could go home. They don't fancy politics, most of them, and they could easily slide back into apathy and disgust, back there with the normal people. Second, they could stumble toward a "third way" and nominate their own hard-case candidates, many of them unelectable in the fall but most of them capable of inflicting damage on incrementalist Republicans. The third possibility is that they could be wooed and won by a reinvigorated GOP and provide the winning margin for conservatives in 2010 and beyond. A reinvigorated GOP, did I say? Okay, that may be asking too much. How about a GOP that can add and subtract?

My advice to Republicans is to take yes for an answer. Slick down your hair, dash across town and make your best pitch . . . *now.*

If exhortation doesn't do the trick, let me try an analogy. For 35 years, beginning in 1945, the United States, eyeball-to-eyeball with implacable enemies in the Soviet Union, followed a strategy first advanced by George Kennan and generally identified by the shorthand term, "containment." Over the course of those years, we more or less succeeded, blunting the thrust of Soviet expansion here and there while keeping the nuclear peace for several decades. But in the 1980s, we phased out "containment" and replaced it with the more aggressive approach, first promoted by James Burnham and later adopted by Ronald Reagan, described as the "liberation" strategy. By directly confronting an overstuffed and unstable regime, the U.S. managed to liberate the captive peoples of the Soviet empire. Before the decade was out, the Soviet empire had receded, withered and died. Question: Is it possible that we stand at a comparable moment today, as we struggle here at home with the pervasive power of the administrative state? Is it possible that, with the infused energies of the Tea Party movement, we could muster the resources, moral and political, to replace our current strategy of "containment" with a strategy of rolling back the intrusive powers of central government? Is it possible that we have before us an opportunity, both unexpected and unearned, to rebalance the relationship between the citizen and the state? Is it possible, in other words, that the Tea Partiers are making us an offer that we not only can't refuse, but shouldn't?

A final thought for D.C. Republicans: When you get across town and knock on that Tea Party door, not to worry. If you find yourself fumbling for words on the front porch, feel free to crib from my own ten-plank platform for 2010:

- Cap government employee pay and benefits at private-sector comparables.
- Rescind the Bush drug benefit for everybody under 60.
- Pressure Bernanke to drain the monetary swamp by selling $1 trillion worth of bonds over the next 18 months.
- Pick a war and win it. Close down the other one.
- Admit a mistake. Abolish the Department of Education.
- For all agencies other than Defense, freeze budgets for two years.
- Raise the retirement age to 70 for all senior benefits.
- Dump Obamacare now. Take a fresh look at health care in 2011.
- Extract pledges from 2012 candidates that they will veto any bill with earmarks or budget overages.
- *Then*, go ahead and set up that deficit commission.

The American Spectator
May 4, 2015

THERE WILL BE NO PROBLEM WITH MONEY IN POLITICS THIS YEAR

There will be no problem with money in politics this year. Such problems arise only when Republicans have more money than Democrats.

Hillary Clinton has let it get about that she will be spending $2.5 billion this time. If that number is even roughly accurate, it means that she will spend far more than all of her Republican opponents combined.

Hillary will portray the $2.5 billion as (a) a way to get her message out, (b) a way to make the process more inclusive and (c) a way to fight back against the scourges of Wichita, the Koch brothers. Somebody, somewhere will buy her story.

You could say that if the Koch brothers didn't exist the Democrats would have to invent them. You could say that, but you would be wrong. The Democrats *did* invent the Koch brothers. Over the past six years, the Koch fundraising circle, as estimable as it is, has never been even remotely competitive with the Obama money machine. Over the next two, it won't be even remotely competitive with the Clinton machine. The Koch brothers, alas, rarely dominate elections. They just play political villains on TV.

There's a qualitative difference, too, between the Kochs and the Clintons. While the entrepreneurs who fund alongside the Kochs no doubt hope that regulatory agencies will lighten up and that the Ex-Im Bank will go away, Clinton donors represent a swarm of rent-seekers. As we learned back in the '90s when the Clintons were auctioning off the Lincoln Bedroom, and as we were reminded last year when Hillary was shaking down foreign governments for her foundation, all Clinton fundraising is transactional.

Think about that. Hillary's $2.5 billion would represent a very thick stack of IOUs. It could take even the Clintons a long time to pay them off. Who knows, she may be thinking she needs two terms.

Imagine if, say, Ted Cruz were to spend $2.5 billion. I'm just guessing here, but the press might see that as a problem—perhaps as a dark, corrupting and (yes!) obscene new force in American politics. Just guessing.

Obama shattered all previous records by raising $1 billion last time around. To hit the big $2.5, Hillary will have to be not just shameless but innovative. It says here that she will be. Who else would have thought to "monetize the incumbency" at the State Department? Who else would have turned the office once held by Thomas Jefferson into a dialing-for-dollars shop?

Think about that one, too. Would Dean Rusk have sluiced foreign government funds to a private venture? Warren Christopher? Cy Vance? Even John Kerry? (And those are just Democrats. If anybody had made the suggestion to George Shultz, he would have had them perp-walked out of Foggy Bottom the same day.)

Campaign fundraising comes in two sizes. Too large and too small. As a conservative, of course, I am familiar only with the latter. But over the years I have observed one or two of the former—campaigns, that is, with more money than useful purpose. What happens, especially in the last few weeks of a campaign, can be unsightly. Aides with check-signing authority start throwing money at ill-defined but vaguely defensible targets. The objective is to finish the campaign with a zero bank balance, so that nobody can say the candidate didn't need every single penny raised. (Funny thing. That late spending flurry can have the collateral benefit of leaving an aide's future nest well-feathered.)

Tip to media covering the Clinton campaign: Some of you will be fascinated by the quid pro quo deals made to bring in the money. A nubile story, to be sure, and one that should be pursued doggedly. A few of you, though, would be well advised to watch how the money is spent. Those last few hundred millions won't be needed for any legitimate campaign purpose.

Jeb Bush huddled here in Florida the previous weekend with his top donors and the vibes were all but giddy. Bush is required to report his fundraising results by July, but he may leak the number earlier. It will be large. (His aides haven't bothered to push back against rumors that it will top $100 million.) The Bush number, reported or leaked, will be intended to intimidate his GOP rivals. It won't.

We should end this dreary review on an upbeat note. One of the happy and I suspect unintended consequences of *Citizens United* is that insurgent candidates now have a chance to make their case against the establishment favorite. On the Republican side, at least, there will be no "inevitable" candidate. It's now clear that Ted Cruz, Rand Paul, Marco Rubio, Scott Walker and quite possibly others will have the resources to make a credible run against Bush.

The American Spectator
August 18, 2011

NEOCONSERVATISM INTERRUPTED

You will remember the Obama campaign of 2008. His was a fresh and pleasingly multicultural face and his candidacy, although unexamined by an incurious national media, took pains to present a foreign policy sharply different from either the meliorism of Hillary Clinton or the jingoism of John McCain. Barack Obama was unambiguously the peace candidate and it was on that basis that he became our president.

That was then. Once in office, Obama established Ms. Clinton as his Secretary of State, listened long and mindfully to Sen. McCain, and then proceeded to outreach both of them in an intermittently coherent but unmistakably neoconservative assault on the Middle East (however horrified the anti-Israeli Obama would be to know he's acting neoconservatively). Obama amped up the war in Afghanistan, started another one in Libya, helped to topple a staunch U.S. ally in Egypt, and launched "kinetic military actions" against Somalia and Yemen that, to the locals, looked very much like war. All of these initiatives were undertaken in the name of Western democratic values and, unlike the Bush wars, could not be said to have been contaminated by either a thirst for Arab oil or a hunger for Israeli favor. Obama's policy was manifestly propelled by neoconservative impulse, most brightly illuminated in the *putsch* against Mubarak. In that instance, the U.S. made it clear that it would support *any* successor regime. Our strategic judgment, ultimately arrived at, was this: Better the street mob, any street mob, than the aging autocrat, even a reliably pro-American autocrat. That judgment represented neoconservatism in its distilled form.

The reaction here at home to Obama's neocon tropism has been both predictable and disappointing. From the peace movement, predictably, there has been protest so restrained as to be almost inaudible. It appears that only Republican wars summon "the movement" to principled dissent and ideological flash mob. Democratic wars are different somehow and must be examined closely for nuance overlooked and consequence unintended. As of this writing, that examination continues. (Sanders? Waters? Anyone? Anyone?) Within the broader base of the Democratic Party, out beyond the anti-war fringe, there has congealed what appears to be a resigned and perplexed acquiescence. If Obama will just get on with the central business of income redistribution, the party activists seem to be saying, he is free to spray Western values around the Middle East even if he chooses to do so at the tips of missiles.

The disappointing response has come from the Republicans. On Capitol Hill, we now have reports of "conservative congressmen" mobilizing against the skin-deep cuts proposed for the defense budget (even before the specific reductions are particularized by the so-called Super Committee). I don't pretend to have interviewed these Pentagon hawks in depth, but a quick scan suggests that the operative word here is much more likely to be "congressmen" than "conservative." It is hard to find a conservative anywhere, either sitting in Congress or fretting at home, who thinks that the U.S. should continue to spend more on defense than all of the other almost-200 hundred countries of the world combined. (The minor cuts suggested—what the Pentagon lobby describes as "gutting the military"—would impose a reduction in the rate of increase.) Do Republicans support a strong national defense? Absolutely. And they have no trouble whatsoever in separating Obama's wars from our heroic warriors: Virtually all conservatives and most libertarians support American servicemen and women without reservation. But . . . legions of democracy imposing "Western values" on Muslims at the point of a bayonet? Trust me. There are reservations.

My sense of the Capitol Hill hawks, in other words, is that they are acting very much like congressmen and not at all like conservatives. They want to keep the juice flowing to the military base back in the district, as also the grants to the research outfits, the contracts to the suppliers, and the fees to the lobbyists who keep the process running agreeably for all concerned. (For all of those directly concerned, to put it more carefully.) If any of these congressmen are zealots fired by the neocon incubus, I haven't spotted them. They seem to be nothing more than politicians doing what politicians do, which should be cause more for ongoing dismay than proximate alarm.

The response from the GOP's presidential candidates has been more disappointing still. With the usual exception of Ron Paul—a phrase that, in a more perfect world, political reporters could type with a single keystroke—all of the candidates are flipping through the old neocon songbook about legitimate aspirations and democratic structures and the blessings of modernity, all of which will soon be attainable if we will just exercise patience and sign the check and embrace the wisdom of, uh, wait a sec, here it is—Plan F. Each time the GOP candidates debauch from the time capsule and strut out onto the 2011 debate platform, it is as if the last decade never really happened. It is as if we were still back in 2001 and, with our troops marching off to Afghanistan to deliver a much-deserved, swift, and punitive blow, the commander had crossed out the original orders at the last minute and scribbled in, "Oh, and while you're there, replace their ancient society with one like ours. No hurry—and spare no expense."

What's that old wives' tale about nature abhorring a vacuum? Not in contemporary politics, it doesn't. Nature this year is put off by the vacuum and buffered by the consensus. All of the GOP candidates, *pace* Mr. Paul, are clustered around the conventional wisdom that we must back our troops—as if these missions were of *their* design—and continue to stare into the blackness of the abyss. Wouldn't you think that Providence or raw political calculation or even a Hail Mary pass from a single-digit outrider would offer up some alternative possibility, some shifting of the exhausted paradigm? (Gingrich? Johnson? Anyone? Anyone?)

Actually, you *would* think that if you had spent the summer as I have done. Eager to learn how regime change might possibly be configured next year, I have been out talking to people with skills and passions and long lists of digital contacts. (I have too much respect for the Broders and Novaks of journalistic legend to call these wanderings shoe-leather reporting. It's more of a Yogi Berra thing, where I have attempted to see things by looking around.) What I have found, or tripped over, is what I predict the major media will find, and view with alarm, before the snow flies. Namely, that there's a potent new force in American politics and that it is coming together crisply with strength and purpose. Call it the extended military family. It includes not just active-duty spouses and retired military personnel, and not just their families, friends and base-neighbors. It includes also a vast number of Americans who love the military, honor them and see in them a unique restorative capability in a society gone soft and common sense-less. For the first time in my reporting experience, this extended military family has become fully engaged in the political process: You see them at gatherings everywhere, from Republican and Tea Party to independent and goo-goo. And they're no longer sitting in the back taking notes. They are moving up front and taking leadership roles. My assessment, for what it's worth, is that these are not summer soldiers: In the early rounds of the 2012 battle, including Wisconsin and Iowa, there's been no quit in them.

What are the members of this uniquely American family saying to each other and to those who will listen sympathetically? A few general themes emerge from a few dozen in-depth conversations:

• There is not a trace of cockiness among today's best and brightest, but something much closer to wariness. With the U.S. military scaled to fight two wars, they feel acutely the strain of fighting two-and-a-half wars simultaneously. They worry about the possibility—no more than that just now—that there could be breakdowns and that they could let their country down. They will do whatever they are asked to do, that is, but they may have been asked to do too much.

• They are primed and poised to defend this country. We are in very good hands on that score. But they are made uneasy by a mission creepiness that casts them as the paramilitary arm of the international welfare state or, even less comfortably, as the enforcement division of D.C. think tanks.

• Military families, better than most, understand the basics of forward planning—budgets, priorities, discipline. While they brush off the mindless charges of "isolationism," they wonder quietly if the Fulda Gap might better be defended by Germans, the 38th parallel by South Koreans. Most of them think that foreign nations should be built by other, non-American people and preferably by the people who live there. In sum, they are utterly loyal to civilian authority, but they are more measured and considerably less grandiose.

The story of the extended military family will play out over the months ahead, first as breathless Exclusive! and then as pensive thumbsucker. But one thing the extended military family knows for sure (and, in this, they are miles ahead of both the press and the politicians of both parties). When it comes to neoconservatism's global agenda, the question is now closed. We can't afford it.

The American Spectator
May 23, 2014

THE GOP NEEDS REAL HEROES

A Speech to the Philadelphia Society.

The media reports these days make conservatives look like a fractious bunch—as indeed we sometimes are. I am deeply informed about grumpy conservatives and paranoid libertarians, bellicose neocons and navel-gazing paleocons. What I know as a matter of basic political arithmetic, however, is that we will need all of these groups—and more—if we are to restore some semblance of conservative governance. The path to that convergence, if not all the way to civility, is not only rhetorical but doctrinal. We should start with the latter challenge, which lies, most consequentially, in the field of international affairs.

When it comes to defense and foreign policy, we, the leadership of the conservative movement, have done a very unconservative thing: We have spent down our intellectual inheritance. We have blown through the fusionist bequest passed down to us by Frank Meyer and Brent Bozell. Their fusionism, which conjoined Meyer's freedom and Bozell's virtue, was a fine piece of ideological cabinet-making. It stood handsomely in our front hall for a half-century, a welcoming introduction to our conservative worldview. But even the finest piece of tongue-and-groove carpentry must be maintained or, over the years, it will begin to loosen, then crack at the joints, and then splinter into pieces and panels. That's where we are now.

We have only the two side panels—one represented by Rand Paul's demobilization, the other by Marco Rubio's interventionism. Both of those themes echo honorably down through conservative history. Paul recalls Meyer's freedom; Marco Rubio echoes Bozell's virtue. But they do not, either Paul's views or Rubio's, represent in themselves a coherent or widely acceptable policy alternative, any more than Meyer or Bozell, standing alone, did in their day.

Our proximate political problem is that almost all Americans—upward of 80 percent, the polls suggest—agree with neither Paul nor Rubio. They find themselves somewhere in between, thus rendering our intramural debate, in which we shout at each other across a vast chasm, all but incomprehensible. What we need is some hard, doctrinal work to fashion a new foreign policy pertinent to these times, a foreign policy in which military power serves national purpose and not ideological abstraction. What we need, I'm suggesting to our friends in academe, the think tanks, and the media, is some fine, fusionist cabinet-making.

But we first need to rediscover a rhetorical path to civility. Conservative rhetoric has lapsed into a state of disrepair. It is intended to rouse and unify, and today it does neither.

The magnitude of the problem was manifest most recently at the Conservative Political Action Conference in Washington, D.C., last month. I diagrammed a few of those speeches. They were constructed along these lines: Step one: Call your opponent names. I gather from CPAC, in fact, that contemporary liberalism is just about equally divided between two rival factions—the idiots and the morons. Step two: Assert your moral superiority. To win a sitting ovation, it is recommended that you do so at the top of your lungs. Step three: Chant the following phrases with the rhythm of incantation: limited government, free enterprise, individual responsibility. Step four: Exit to a standing ovation.

These speeches begged—and answered—this question: To whom were the speakers speaking? To the national television audience? Or to themselves?

Amid the several blessings of talk radio and internet bloggery, we have created for ourselves one very large rhetorical problem. We have learned to savor the many satisfactions of talking to ourselves, while forgetting how to talk to people who do not yet agree with us. That is a luxury that Bill Buckley and the founding brethren never enjoyed. Separated from the public by what were then the monopoly media, Buckley could not get away with condemning and asserting. He would have had the impact of a B-B bouncing off the hull of an incoming drone. Rather, he was obliged to beguile and persuade—obliged, first, to beguile the monopoly media into granting him access to their audience, and then to persuade the audience to entertain what seemed to be his eccentric views.

If we hope to win national elections now and then, we must acknowledge that "condemn and assert" won't cut it. We will have to learn once again how to "beguile and persuade." And those incantatory phrases: limited government, free enterprise, individual responsibility? We conservatives love them. We can dance to them. But nobody outside this room has any idea what they mean. They are limp and lifeless. All the juice has been sucked out of them by mindless repetition.

Hard as it may be to believe, we—the descendants of the Great Communicator himself—have been losing the rhetorical war. How could that possibly be? How have we managed to make sodden and tedious the most exciting story in recorded history, that of human freedom? Why in our public discourse have we substituted Beltway wonkery for the plain and powerful speech of Main Street—the power of the concrete over the abstract, the particular over the general? The power, most refulgently, of the role model?

I think it's because we have spent far too much time looking for the next Ronald Reagan—a fool's errand, in my view—and far too little time remembering what he taught us. And at the heart of what he taught us about political communication was this: To revive the culture of opportunity, we must bypass the bogus claims of group politics and instead celebrate the heroism of individual accomplishment.

We all know who Obama's heroes are. He displays them as if in a trophy case in the First Lady's box at the State of the Union. There's the witness to the venality of corporate America. There's the pioneer in some exotic form of separatism. There's the victim whose plight could have been averted by higher government spending. And there's the rich guy who thinks he isn't taxed enough. I am tempted to say, that's the Obama coalition—the resentful, the aggrieved, the dependent, and the guilt-stricken.

That wasn't Reagan's coalition. No, his heroes were ordinary men and women growing into their roles as free American citizens—the greatest role one could play upon the human stage, in Reagan's view. His heroes were us, and for seeing us that way, we loved him. Today Reagan would see heroes all around us, even if we have trouble picking them out through the thickening socialist haze. Unlike the Obama coalition, our heroes make no claims upon our attention, much less our resources.

But they're out there. Take the political realm, where we seem to have a new hero popping up each week. Kevin Faulconer, the new mayor of San Diego, has set California on a path to becoming a two-party state. Bob Corker stopped the UAW from organizing the Volkswagen plant in Tennessee, and thereby derailed the union's plans to do for Mercedes in Alabama, Nissan in Mississippi, and BMW in South Carolina what it had already done for GM in Michigan. And there's Tom Coburn, who, if there is any justice, will soon be recognized as the first great senator of the 21st century.

Why haven't these heroes been celebrated for their good and replicable deeds? They should be. But they are not classic Reagan heroes. Reagan had the quaint notion that politicians were public servants and he thus saw little heroism involved when politicians served the public.

Remember Julia from the 2012 campaign—the welfare-maximizing, benefit-gaming single mom featured in that Democratic ad? She was an authentic Obama role model, making her way, with the help of omnipresent navigators, onto multiple platforms of public assistance.

But she shouldn't be confused with *our* hero, who we'll call Julie. She's the single mom who runs the bakery in the middle of town. She has a tough battle on her hands, and not just against the onslaught from Safeway and Walmart. There used to be two jobs at Julie's Bakery: the guy who baked the cakes and the guy who sold the cakes. Now there's a third guy. He observes, tests, records, and second-guesses the cakes. He's from the government and he's there to help. Every time there's a staff meeting at OSHA, EPA, FEMA, FDA, IRS, DOJ, or the Labor Department, a new directive flutters down on the desk Julie keeps in the back of her shop. Her government is conducting an experiment. It wants to know *exactly* which straw will break Julie's back.

Much of Julie's heroism lies in the fact that, despite all obstacles, she is creating economic value, out of which she pays herself, supports the families of her employees, and subsidizes, at progressively higher rates, that third guy at the bakery.

Compare her economic life to that of her tormentor, Barack Obama, who is said to be a role model for young Americans and especially minorities. Over the course of his career, he has moved seamlessly from subsidized schooling to the tax-exempt Left to government work. He will soon move seamlessly to a lifetime pension paid for by Julie and her peers after—*after!*—it has been determined that they can no longer afford to pay for their own. A pension for the government worker, a 401K for Julie. Because bureaucratic life is so . . . hazardous?

After what we all hope will be many years of pension payouts, Barack Obama will have spent a long life without ever once making direct contact with the real economy. A role model, indeed. In Obama's America, perhaps every child can grow up to be economically unproductive.

The government worker may have the power. But it is Julie who should have not only our admiration, but our support. Can't you see Ronald Reagan beaming that million-dollar grin at her up in the balcony at the State of the Union?

What I'm suggesting is that our heroes should be the men and women who are emblematic of *our* aspirations and symbolic of *our* values. It is up to us to identify them and celebrate them—or we will be trapped, inevitably, in the Left's rhetoric of class, creed, race, sexual preference, and whatever corrosive division comes next.

Our heroes are all around us. Our job is to pick them out, lift them up and install them as the first citizens of our shining city on a hill. Just the other day I came across a new hero, Leonard Smith. I never met ol' Leonard, but I think I would have liked him. Here's his obituary from the local paper:

> *Leonard Mason Smith, 86, a veteran of World War II and Korea and longtime resident of Pine Island, Florida, passed away this week. Leonard Smith hated pointless bureaucracy, thoughtless inefficiency, and bad ideas born of good intentions. He loved his wife, admired and respected his children, and liked just about every dog he ever met. He will be greatly missed by those who loved him. In lieu of flowers, the family asks that you cancel your subscription to the* New York Times.

The American Spectator
June 19, 2015

INCOME INEQUALITY, BELTWAY STYLE

I had to be in Washington the other day, so I squirreled away an hour to drive by my old house in northern Virginia. My wife Jane and I had bought it when we went to Washington with Reagan. Heady days, those. We were young and idealistic and determined to help the Gipper beat the Soviets in the Cold War, free up the American economy, and put a halt to the spreading bureaucracy of central government. In time, we came around to the idea that two out of three ain't bad.

It was a great house to raise a family—a graceful Cape Cod-style clapboard with a big yard. Shade trees with swings for the kids. A garden for Jane, a library for me. First thing in the morning, and then again after school, you'd see a pride of pigtailed riders trotting their horses down the trail behind the house. Teenaged girls and horses—I don't pretend to understand it, but there's some kind of magic going on there. Roadside stands were the place to buy your corn, cukes, and tomatoes, all farm fresh. Good schools, safe streets. Demographers would have called our life exurban, I suppose. We called it just about right.

The neighbors were good people, if not especially welcoming in the small-town ways we had come to expect. Harry Truman was slightly off the mark when he remarked that if you want a friend in Washington, get a dog. But he had a point. Almost all of our neighbors had come to town from somewhere else, some place they continued to call "back home." They were just passing through Washington and assumed that everybody else was doing so, as well.

I'll give them this. They all worked like beavers, leaving before the sun was up and returning to their bosky dells long after the day had died. It took me awhile to figure out what they did for a living. They didn't make stuff or sell stuff or provide a service in what we still thought of as the real economy. Many of them had unusual-sounding jobs. They worked for the American Pickle Council or the Committee to Combat Discrimination Against Left-handed Dentists or the Plastic Flower Institute or Seniors United Against New Technology or the Friends of Chechnya—a bewildering variety of narrow-gauge groups all doing exactly the same thing: They lobbied the central government to take money from the people "back home" and give it to their narrow-gauged group.

They were pretty good at it. By 2004, with our kids up and out of the nest, and with Washington in the grip of an oxymoronic Big Government Republicanism, Jane and I looked for greener pastures and put the house up for sale. It sold in four days. For a ridiculously high price.

What had happened was that, while the house remained resolutely on its original foundation, our bucolic exurb had been transformed by the kudzu-like growth of the lobby culture into a suburb of Washington, D.C. To our amazement, the real estate agent advertised the house as "within easy commuting range of D.C." (That may have been technically correct, as long as you left for work no later than 4:45.) To our further surprise, the agent said in her closing argument to the buyer: "With room for additional parking, this house would be perfect for fund-raisers." (That may have been correct, too. Jane and I were just child-raisers.) The exurbs, it seemed, had been moved out close to West Virginia.

I didn't know what to expect when I drove by the old house, but I certainly didn't expect to find a mock-Tudor McMansion replete with distressed beams, stained brick, and heraldic flourishes. The new owners had managed at great expense to transform a handsome house with clean lines into a dark and forbidding manse suitable for the shooting of horror flicks. It was a bit of a mess, frankly, but what a parking lot! A broad swath of the yard had been covered in rich, black asphalt, with individual spaces striped off for the arrival of BMWs, Infinitis, and all manner of expense-account lobbywagons.

The house itself was up for sale again. At more than twice the price we had sold it for.

Which brings me around to the issue of income inequality. In the grand scheme of things—perhaps I should apologize to the *New York Times* here—it's not an issue that keeps me up at night. As my old friend John Roche might have phrased it, income inequality comes in at Number 98 on my list of things to worry about, just after my fear of being eaten by piranhas.

Put it this way. If Elizabeth Warren or her surrogate, Hillary Clinton, were to look me in the eye and say, "Do you realize that the head of Acme Widget Company makes a hundred times more than the man who waxes his office floor?" I wouldn't be able to manage much more than a shrug and a "So what?" Those arrangements were arrived at freely between consenting adults. If both the boss and the cleaner are gainfully and willingly employed, why should their income be at the top of anybody's list of things to worry about? Especially a government official's, who neither runs a company nor cleans an office but lives off the labors of those who do.

But that's the free economy, or at least what's left of it. In Washington, and marbled throughout its pricey suburbs, there's income inequality of a different sort. The richest counties in the country—Fairfax, Montgomery, Loudon, and the rest—are now clustered in the metro Washington area. They're rich not because D.C. has just emerged as the Silicon Valley of the East or the North Dakota of the South. The D.C. region produces few new products, few new services, but it is rolling in boomtown money, nonetheless. Its faux prosperity is generated the old-fashioned way: by state coercion. The central government takes money from the folks "back home" and spreads it around the lobby culture, creating a fix-and-favor economy so prosperous that it outstrips all—literally, all—of the productive communities "back home."

This situation can't be politically hygienic.

So let me ask both of you, Senator Warren and candidate Clinton: Do you realize that lobbyists make a hundred times more than millions of taxpayers who, neither willing nor witting, are taxed to pay for them?

National Review
June 6, 2005

NAVASKY'S LULLABY

Review of *A Matter of Opinion* by Victor S. Navasky

I n this absorbing account of his long stewardship of *The Nation*, Victor Navasky provides unimpeachable testimony that in matters of national consequence he and his magazine have been—what's the word we're looking for here?—wrong. Yes, that's it: Wrong on the Stalinists. Wrong on terrorism. Wrong on the nuclear freeze. Wrong on socialism. Wrong on welfare reform. Wrong on educational choice. Wrong on tax incentives. Wrong on the culture of life. And of course wrong on people, from Reagan to Vidal to Castro to Thatcher to Hiss. (Navasky carried the torch for Alger Hiss even after the last flame had flickered dead from oxygen deprivation. One can almost hear Hiss crying from some dark smoke-hole, "I love you, Vic, but let it go, man, let it go.") For his misperceptions and misprescriptions we didn't really need a book-length recitation. A handwritten note of apology, terse and abject, might have struck the right tone.

But this book, lodged as it is in the dictatorship of relativism, isn't really about right and wrong. It's the story of a guy who falls head over heels for a little magazine, a real bodice-ripper, and for that we forgive him almost everything. Don't look here for media trivia about power, fame, and money. If Navasky had fallen for a big magazine, or a cable channel, there would have been no romance here, no boy-meets-magazine lullaby. No, with the career recounted in this book Navasky takes his place in that distinguished line of peace-disturbing editors who kept the democratic conversation going: men like Addison and Steele, with *The Spectator* and *The Tatler*. Walter Bagehot was a little-magazine guy, at *The Economist*, as were Albert Jay Nock at *The Freeman* and Carey McWilliams at *The Nation*. In our own day, we have an editor named Buckley at *National Review* and Martin Peretz at *The New Republic*. Victor Navasky, arriving later but asserting his claim every bit as forcefully, is in their company.

As distinctive, even singular, as their voices have been, these little-magazine guys have much in common. Most conspicuous is their Archimedean conceit. While most human beings trudge to the office to perform a job and pick up a paycheck, the little-magazine guy dashes down to the office to *move the world*. The world is not so much his oyster as a hod to be carried, an object to be levered from where it is and obviously shouldn't be to somewhere else where, properly positioned, it will produce a *better world*. This is heady work, bordering on the delusional, which may explain why little-magazine staff dynamics sometimes resemble those of Jack Nicholson's wardmates in *One Flew Over the Cuckoo's Nest*. It's a tough job, this world-moving business. Results differ, we can see, depending on the angle of leverage and the rhetorical force applied. One sees clearly for instance that, in Buckley's case, with a nudge here and a shove there, he managed to turn the world upside down. Navasky, for his part, could only watch in pain as the world rolled back over his exposed toes. But who's counting wins and losses here, it's how you play the game. Or to sound less like a loser: It's important that the game be played, that the debate be intelligent and protracted, that every idea get its chance and that none gain uncritical acceptance.

Little magazines are thus concerned always and everywhere with the principle of the thing. As payday approaches, however, the principle may be put to one side as the boss concentrates on the money of the thing. Or lack of it. For it is the dirty little secret of journals right, left, and center that their persistence rebukes capitalism's assumption about economic decisions being driven by profit motive. To my knowledge, and more conclusively, to Navasky's, nobody has ever invested in a little magazine with the expectation of financial profit. Psychic rewards abound, of course. Nothing sets you up in the morning like a good earth-moving edition of your little magazine. But the economics of the little magazine simply don't work (which is why, naming no names, some little magazines have become cruise lines that publish magazines on the side). Navasky recounts in fine detail and with high hilarity, some of it intentional, the money chase he's run to keep *The Nation* going. He's protean. He's Sisyphean. Hell, he's Odyssean. He's also something of a whiner.

My own take is that harsh conditions tend to bring out the best in little magazines: They must hold their readers close; they must cultivate a defensible space in the literary supermarket; and they must find and nurture new writers. New writers tend, happily, to be cheap writers, but little magazines can create an alternative universe in which brand-name writers like Calvin Trillin, under Navasky's editorial spell, work for fees in the "high two figures." The economics of little magazines may not work but they are in some circumstances workable, nonetheless. *NR* has proved as much. Under the great Ed Capano and the underrated Wick Allison, it has flirted with commercial viability.

Another common thread winding through the history of little magazines, a thread dyed an arresting shade of red, is legal bills. For tiny enterprises little magazines seem to run up very large legal bills. Why? It's usually the principle of the thing. That's not the principle that all available funds ought to be siphoned off by law firms lest they corrode Spartan office habits; the principle, rather, that words are important artifacts, the sacred relics of democratic process, and must be defended. Even unto the courthouse steps, so help you God.

Navasky recounts here at impressive length his own legal battles, fascinating I'm sure to those directly involved in the disputes. What is striking to the noncombatant is the difference between Navasky's (and, occasionally, Buckley's and Peretz's) response to the actionable offense and, say, the average businessman's. When the latter is accosted by Eliot Spitzer about the missing $100 million, the businessman asks, "How much do you want?" and, as the saying goes, tries to put the matter behind him. The little-magazine guy, inflamed by an offhanded insult, says, "I'll see you in court for the rest of our natural-born lives." As we were suggesting earlier, little magazines are not for people hung up on issues of mental health.

Through it all, through the deadlines and lawsuits and volcanic eruptions of staff distemper, the little magazine perdures, struggling issue by issue to make its case perfectly, always failing, always advancing. Its role in the life of the free society was perhaps best described by James Curran, former editor of *New Socialist*: "We perform a knitting function, bringing together groups with very different ideas." That's exactly how it was when long ago I first walked the corridors of *NR*, dodging redwoods named Burnham and Kendall and Meyer, as issue by issue Buckley and his band of brothers knitted together what came to be known as the conservative movement. The question was always, How can we edge closer to the bull's eye? How can we nick the combustible core of an issue so as to explode it into public concern? It was neither an original concern nor a new question and it was usually reduced to proxy discussion of editorial technique.

In the early 1800s, *The Edinburgh Review* considered the relative merits of bylined pieces, which tended toward obscurantism, over against unsigned editorials that could be off-puttingly oracular: "It was true that anonymity made possible the monstrous charlatanry of the 'editorial we.' Equally it enabled a vain editor to rewrite reviewer's copy with impunity. Yet on the other hand the reviewer who has signed his name was apt to turn into a mere performer; a crowd pleaser who wrote only what was expected of him." Pick your poison, little magazine, but answer the question. How can you make your point so compellingly as to move the world?

National Review
April 30, 2010

CHARLIE CRIST: A PARTY OF ONE

—Jacksonville, Fla.

I n his mad, careerist dash through Florida politics, Charlie Crist has always listened to an urgent voice calling him to high purpose and vast design. While that voice has never been audible to those nearby, he has been quick to amplify it for the hearing-impaired. Usually, he has confided, it is "the people of Florida" who, with their basic goodness and plainspoken common sense, are urging him to do the right thing—which, happily, seems always to coincide with his own momentary whim. Occasionally, it is "our children," or, when working a backwoods locale, "the kids," for whom he feels obliged to sacrifice his current, much-loved job in quest of the next. More recently, across the Bible Belt, he has taken to pausing portentously midspeech before reminding the devout that his very name, in its original Greek form, means "disciple of Christ." Yea, verily, it must have been His will that Crist desert the Republican party and seek salvation in the green uplands of independence.

This afternoon in St. Petersburg, 40 minutes late to his own party, Charlie Crist announced that he is leaving the GOP, the party that had handed him a state Senate seat, anointed him attorney general, and then elected him governor. He is turning his back on the party, he explained, because . . . because . . . well, he never quite explained, did he? The dispositive answer to why he defected, to those who watch him closely, is that he saw no better alternative for the people of Florida or the kids—or indeed, but quite incidentally, for himself—than to pursue a campaign as an outsider, appalled by what's been happening in Tallahassee lately. Let's check off the list. Marco Rubio was pulling away in the Senate primary. Kendrick Meek, the presumptive Democratic candidate, did not blink. The Obama people preferred to let Crist stew in his own juice. The university offer would have to wait until December, as would the several law-firm deals. So let's be reasonable here. What did we expect Charlie Crist to do for the next eight months? Sit around all day being governor?

The proximate question is what effect his decision will have on the Senate race. The answer, from the Republican perspective, is nothing good. Charlie Crist has assembled over the past few years an odd coalition, including, as principal building blocks, the party base, tort lawyers, and gun owners. The party base is now gone. They liked Rubio better from the jump, and they are now in a white-hot rage at the lover who left them. (One of Crist's campaign tropes is to startle casual supporters by telling them he "loves" them.)

The tort lawyers seem to be sticking. Crist made a devil's deal with the tort bar back when he was attorney general, and he reconsummated the relationship as recently as this week by signing a "tort-reform bill" that will have the intended consequence of raising awards to tort lawyers. Crist already has $7.6 million (as of March 31) in his campaign account—more than Rubio and Meek put together, and not required by law to be returned—and the tort lawyers will provide whatever else Crist needs. Money should not be a problem. Then there are the gun owners, a critical constituency in this huntin' and home-protectin' state. The NRA and other gun groups have been solid for Crist for several cycles and, while they are now under intense pressure to back away, they have an otherwise admirable record of sticking with their friends when the going gets tough. Well, the going just got tough. Watch that space.

The key to Crist's possible success will be whether he can somehow replicate the party base, with its filigree of county committees, volunteer platoons, and turnout machinery. In some parts of the state, conspicuously including the Tallahassee-Jacksonville corridor, the GOP organization is formidable, even intimidatingly so. Crist's bet seems to be that he can replace the party apparatus with a statewide effort by his new best friends, the teachers' unions. (Crist's veto of the GOP's merit-pay bill two weeks ago was widely seen as the presentation of a gaudy political engagement ring.) The unions have lots of members and lots of money and a visible presence in every county. They are particularly potent in the southern part of the state, where Republicans have traditionally been stretched thin. So, while it's possible that the unions could put together a sturdy campaign structure, there's a problem. Just as the NRA will get pressure from its right to move away from Crist, the teachers' unions will encounter pushback from the Democrats if they edge toward Crist. Watch that space, too.

The bottom line on the election is that, despite polls showing him highly competitive in a three-way race, we're not likely to be greeting a new Senator Crist (Me, Fla.) this November. The historical record is reassuring on this point. The last third-party winner in Florida was "the Cracker Messiah," Sidney Catts, elected governor on an anti-booze platform in 1916. (The electorate soon recovered its senses.) More recent history argues a similar conclusion. Florida's only other widely popular political figure, former governor Jeb Bush, is now all in for Rubio after observing a decorous distance from the Senate campaign for the past year. Crist's repudiation of the GOP is a repudiation of his predecessor as well, and Bush is reliably reported to be ready to rumble. So, while it's self-evidently true that "things change," as Crist explains his bizarre wanderings, his independent campaign looks like a loser. It may even have peaked today. But can he damage Rubio's chances and improve Meek's? Absolutely.

What we know for sure is that, when it comes to Charlie Crist, it's never over even when it's over. If Charlie slips to a deep third place over the next few months, you can bet that he'll be hearing those voices again.

National Review
January 8, 2013

'Swonderful: Charlie Crist's New BFFs

His new cohorts grin and bear him.

C harlie Crist has changed parties, and this time he means it. It's now official. Just before the holidays, the tanned Florida politician enrolled as a Democrat, and his new party could not be more delighted. No, really, it is a wonderful surprise.

Democrats across the state have welcomed the former governor with all the enthusiasm reserved for the news that your mother-in-law has just arrived, not for supper but for a nice long visit. There she is on the front stoop, not clutching a bouquet for the dining table but flanked on both sides by bulging suitcases. There's nothing to be done but to force a grin and holler over your shoulder, "Honey, tell the boys to clean out their room and take the sleeping bags up to the attic—Mama's here."

State senator Nan Rich is sticking to the script. Already testing the waters for the Democratic nomination for governor, she has a ready reply when asked what she thinks of Crist's arrival. 'Swonderful, says Rich. She's lying, of course. A saucy liberal who has paid her party dues and then some, Rich has to be saying to herself as she eye-frisks Crist, *I didn't know they could pile it that high.*

Well, what about Alex Sink, the former CFO who lost the 2010 gubernatorial race to Republican Rick Scott by a false eyelash—what's her take on Crist as Democrat? 'Swonderful, says Sink. She's lying, too. She has to be thinking, *I've got an unpopular incumbent on the run and now this? Who invited Mr. Perma-Tan?*

Let's not forget Florida's own Debbie Wasserman Schultz, who plays a recurring role on MSNBC as a poodle-haired, fact-challenged partisan. What's her take? 'Swonderful, says Wasserman Schultz. Is she lying, too?

Hard to tell. She may be the first public figure since Bill Clinton who can look down the barrel of a camera and say things that aren't necessarily so, without betraying the slightest voice break, facial tic, or runaway eyebrow. It's a neat party trick. And, with nobody able to tell when she's telling the truth, the default assumption in most circumstances is that she's not.

But even in the Democratic party, by now fully data mined and Obamacized, not everyone gets the memo. Here's the reaction to Crist's enrollment from Barbara Effman, the leader of a powerful Democratic club in Broward County (which, with almost 2 million residents, is the 18th most populous county in the nation): "A lot of people don't trust him. He didn't want to be a Republican, and then he didn't want to be an independent, and now that he's been a Democrat for a few days, he thinks he can be governor?" Oops. It sounds as if Ms. Effman might have skipped out on reeducation camp last summer. There she goes, gaffe-ward, sounding as unprogrammed as a real human being.

On the basis of a dozen sotto voce conversations, I can report that Ms. Effman is saying what many and perhaps most party workers are thinking. Hard-core Democrats have campaigned against Charlie Crist for state senate, for education commissioner, for attorney general, for governor, and for U.S. Senate; some of them have 20 years in the trenches against him. They have gotten to know him well, and they've learned that to know him well is not necessarily to regard him as a man of unshakable integrity.

Charlie Crist himself, refusing to be swayed by reports from his lying eyes and ears, has described his reception by Democrats as "overwhelmingly positive." Not even close, Charlie. The current political forecast for him would be more accurately described as somewhere between "chilly" and "chance of overnight freeze." (I allow for the possibility that Crist is simply confused, temporarily disoriented by the pace of his own political evolution. He's been a "proud" Republican, a "proud" independent, and a "proud" Democrat, all in the space of three years. That's a lot of pride, placed and replaced.)

I have been talking to Republicans who are planning their agenda for 2013. They don't seem to be confused at all. *Their* response to Crist's defection has been, to borrow the phrase, "overwhelmingly positive." From the Georgia border to the Keys and from the Atlantic seashore to the Gulf

Coast, Republicans are savoring a rare moment of unity. In their view, Crist committed one of the few political sins still generally regarded as unforgiveable in post-Clinton America: He raised money as a Reagan conservative and spent it as an Obama liberal in the same political cycle. Many of the GOP loyalists here in Orlando fell for Crist's bait-and-switch move, and they are mad at him; and, yes, they are mad at themselves. They relish the possibility that Crist will now do unto Democrats pretty much as he did unto them.

The presumption on both sides of the aisle is that Crist will run for governor next year against Rick Scott, a presumption fortified by a recent poll showing Crist up 48–45 in a trial heat. That's certainly possible. But that wouldn't really be Crist-like, would it, a path forward in which purpose and effort are aligned so conventionally? Let's take an imaginative leap and suppose that Crist is looking at the situation from a consumingly selfish perspective.

Here's what we know. First, when Crist held the office himself, just two years ago, he was bored silly and made an exit strategy one of the first orders of gubernatorial business. Second, the best part of any Crist campaign, for both candidate and voter, is the tease. In that sense, Crist has already peaked. Now come the long months of hard work, any appetite for which Crist has disguised comprehensively. Third, Tallahassee, the Albany of the American South, is an acquired taste, and there are persistent rumors that the new Mrs. Crist has yet to acquire it. Fourth, Scott has spread the word that he's prepared to spend $50 million of his own money in an air war that could muss anybody's hair. (Threats of this sort, empty in most cases, are credible coming from Scott.) Why, then, the tease? Why would Charlie Crist *appear* to be running for governor?

Here's my surmise, based, I confess, not on exclusive revelation but on multiple seasons of bemused Crist-watching: What would be highly attractive to him, not to mention to the missus, would be a high-visibility, low-responsibility appointed position. Lots of ink, lots of tube time, short office hours—that sort of thing. Not in Tallahassee, most likely, but in Washington or even in the world beyond.

Well, then, why not just ask his pal the president for a job, rather than head-faking toward a 2014 campaign? Charlie Crist doesn't ask for favors. He accepts them. He may have reckoned that his endorsement of Obama, punctuated by the abject groveling at the Democratic convention in Charlotte, would excite a big-time offer from a gratefully reelected administration. No such luck, it appears. So Crist is making his own luck. By galvanizing Rich, Sink, and other high-powered Floridians who delivered the state for Obama and who now want Crist removed from the gubernatorial race, he has assembled a formidable lobbying organization for . . . Charlie Crist. A big-time offer just might materialize.

That's my position, anyway, and in the spirit of Charlie Crist, I'm sticking with it until something better comes along.

National Review
June 13, 2012

ANGUS KING STROLLS TO THE SENATE

He's not that independent.

—Augusta, Maine

Well, at least he'll have an opponent.

The two major parties nominated their candidates last night for Maine's open U.S. Senate seat. For the GOP, it will be Charlie Summers, who, as a longtime aide to the retiring Olympia Snowe, is both well-connected and well-liked inside the party. An old-school plugger, he might make a race of it come November. For the Democrats, it will be Cynthia Dill, an underfunded state senator from the shrill Left. Her chances are currently calibrated at somewhere between Not Much and No Way. In polls to be released over the next few days, both Summers and Dill will doubtless trail independent Angus King by hefty, double-digit margins.

King is popular to a degree almost unknown in the flip-cam era, in which private indiscretions are recorded and drudged before the sweat dries. A recent poll measured King's "favorables" at a remarkable 62–24, which puts him in a regional league with David Ortiz of the Red Sox and Tom Brady of the Patriots, not to mention Elizabeth Warren of the Indians. King is widely regarded as the prohibitive favorite for election to the seat being vacated by the nominally Republican Snowe, whose patience for partisan politics seemed to expire just as her constituents' appetite for ideological clarity sharpened. King will run as an independent, beyond party entanglement and petty concern, so to say, parlaying his image as a frugal Yankee businessman. And you might as well commit that last phrase to memory. The Media Caucus, in solemn conclave assembled, seems to have passed a resolution mandating its inclusion in all stories about King.

While you wouldn't know it to meet him now, King was born and raised in Virginia and graduated from the University of Virginia's law school in Charlottesville. There is no trace of that King in this King. These days, he is dressed exclusively by the House of Bean: On public occasions, the former governor can almost always be found redundantly fleeced and sensibly mud-booted. You half-expect to see an L. L. Bean patch emblazoned on his barn jacket, in the manner of a professional golfer professing allegiance to an insurance company. When King salts his speeches with aphorisms from Aroostook County, it must be admitted even by the skeptics that King's conversion from southern lawyer to Yankee businessman has been comprehensively realized.

About the frugal part, there's more dispute. In 1994, running as an independent in a three-way race, King was elected governor. He served for two terms and, happily for all concerned, his tenure happened to coincide not only with a national boom but with a rare burst of Maine prosperity. During the King years, business was good, tax revenues flowed, and budget surpluses grew—to almost $400 million at one point. Best of all, the economy produced more than 75,000 new jobs, which, in a poor state with a population of only 1.3 million, amounted to a historic gusher. And yes, as he proudly asserts, Angus King governed in a nonpartisan style. He funded special-interest projects from the Left, from the middle, from the Right, and, when the buzz began to wear off, from supplicants not all that eager to identify themselves.

King's penchant for the grandiose was for the most part well-contained. His signature program to equip seventh and eighth graders with laptop computers, he proclaimed, would "transform education." Needless to say, it didn't, but the hype was a rare crack in King's new Yankee reserve. The facts, however, spoke loudly enough for themselves. During his eight years in Augusta, King ran up state spending by 90 percent and burned through the rainy-day fund. While not even the hard Left could come up with a plausible reason to do so during the boom years, yes, it remains true that King did not raise the (already confiscatory) marginal tax rates.

In early 2003, Angus King walked out of the statehouse, waved to the crowd and resumed his career in the quasi-private sector. His successor, Democrat John Baldacci, joined in the hearty applause before settling into his new office. There he found in a desk drawer a bill for the King years. The incoming governor was facing what soon revealed itself, after deconstruction of convoluted accounting schemes, as a billion-dollar hole in the state budget. Baldacci spent the next eight years digging out: For him, there would be no transforming programs, only morning-after clean-up chores. With each rejection of a new funding request, inevitably, Baldacci lost a few fair-weather political friends. It was thus no small irony that when Snowe announced her plans to step down, the "popular" King quickly brushed aside the "unpopular" Baldacci in the line of succession.

As for his professional career, Angus King is a businessman in the Al Gore sense of the word. As a promising newcomer to the Maine political scene, King was promoted endlessly by the state's public-broadcasting network, which gave him his own talk show for more than a decade. (That's a larger deal than it sounds: The public network has repeater stations across the state, while much of the state's audience for commercial broadcasting is served by Boston stations that cover Maine as a distant and only occasionally relevant province.)

Established as an affable celebrity by the state network, King then made a financial score, possibly two. The first was a consulting firm, grandly named Northeast Energy Management, that advised clients on how to trim their electric bills. It wasn't rocket science; King once claimed credit for persuading Bowdoin College to turn off its exhaust fans when unneeded. Launched in 1989, Northeast Energy was purchased in early 1994 by Central Maine Power (CMP), the state's dominant provider of electric power. King has said that he personally took $8 million out of the deal. To some observers, it was a curious transaction: Why would a giant power company buy a small consultancy that showed CMP customers how to use less of its product? Theories abound, some of them catnip to the conspiracy-minded. What was not in question was the political reality: A heavily regulated utility handed a large check to an ambitious politician just nine months before he was elected governor. King himself has acknowledged that it was the CMP payout that enabled him to skip an unwinnable Democratic primary and self-fund his independent campaign.

King's second score, possibly, was at another start-up named Independence Wind. I say "possibly," because King sold his shares to a private investor just weeks ago and the terms have not been disclosed. The objective of Independence Wind was to saw off the tops of Maine mountains to accommodate serried ranks of wind turbines; the premise was that the output of the turbines would provide energy resources alternative to the old-line, non-renewable fuels. The key to the Independence Wind deal, as it is to most green-energy deals from solar panels to Solyndra, was a federal loan guarantee. What the guarantee means in practice is that if the venture succeeds, the private owner wins; if the venture fails, the taxpayer loses. Call this business model "public equity" or crony capitalism or whatever you wish, it is a dance with moral hazard. The guarantee brings with it both the privatization of profit and the socialization of risk. As a business model, it is—to use the fashionable word—unsustainable.

And a note about that adjective "independent," insofar as it is routinely applied to Angus King. Does it—should it—suggest that King is equipoised somewhere midway between conservative Republican and liberal Democrat? Well, take a moment to thumb through his political résumé. King grew up in a home he has described as "Roosevelt Democrat;" his earliest political activism was in the civil-rights movement; he then served as an assistant on labor matters to a Democratic U.S. senator; he came to Maine as an attorney for a left-leaning public-interest law firm; he supports the full pro-choice, same-sex-marriage, subsidized-contraception social agenda; his political career has been financed lavishly by the Media-Enviro-Industrial Complex; in his only tour in public office he was a promiscuous spender of taxpayer money; he has dismissed the Ryan plan for fiscal sobriety as "a disaster;" and he has endorsed Obama and, more specifically, Obama's overhaul of the nation's health-care system. This is not the itinerary of a restless mind searching for elusive truth. This is the pilgrimage of an ideologue walking the stations of the liberal cross. And it prompts this question: From what, exactly, is Angus King "independent?" Clearly, he's not independent from the governing dogmas of the Democratic party.

ROAD
ADVENTURES

National Review
August 15, 1994

SCHOOL'S OUT

I t never rains in California, as the beach poet says, so I thought to bring along my umbrella. Call it New England conservative meets postmodernist Los Angeles.

My daughter the actress has just graduated from the University of Southern California. Now the word "University" is not one I usually slide in there right next to "Southern California." Where I come from a university is at least 200 hundred years old, covered with mortar-fed ivy, and dominated by a sociology department from Hell. It's a place of high learning and higher pretension, a place where action is no substitute for words, a place where a boy feels no unseemly pressure to grow to be a man. A proper university, Eastern and effete, is a wondrous thing: Dodgers of drafts can become leaders of men, they tell me.

The folks here at USC, in the heart of the country's second largest city, call for different strokes. The graduates, more than 7,000 strong, are led onto the lawn by the Trojan Marching Band, a precision, marching, tune-carrying band. (Those adjectives are meant to convey a sense of awe. Where I come from, the college band appears to be re-enacting Washington's withdrawal from Valley Forge.) And the mascot! While my people settle for a neutered puppy who urinates on the players' shoes, USC boasts the Man of Troy—breastplate shining, tunic fluttering, bareback astride a splendid white steed. Play that Trojan fight song again and I'll take on those sumbitches from UCLA.

But these differences are merely biological, as the young William Buckley once said of the differences between Beame and Lindsay. The real difference is in the academic ceremony. Back home, our custom is to award honorary degrees to shrinks who have unlocked troves of repressed memory, minority writers who have shifted paradigms, and recently retired pols, exhausted from shoveling grants to the politically well represented. Out here, at the epicenter of earthquakes and entertainment factories, they cut right to the chase. The first honorary degree goes to Ella Fitzgerald, the second to George Lucas, the third to Steven Spielberg. And that's it. No Pontiac dealers, no lieutenant governors, no pigeons from Japan. Just world-class artists who have earned our affection and our gratitude. Seems like the way to do it.

My daughter the actress steps forward to receive her degree, and pandemonium strikes Row 27, Section C. Yes, our family is out in force, for this is our last child and we are doing it right. Spago for dinner, overnight at Checkers, private tour of the Nixon Library, a spritz of Hollywood hobnobbing. We are celebrating not one, but two great events this day. My daughter is, manifestly, the best and brightest of her sparkling class (but, I suppose it should be noted, only marginally more gorgeous than the 3,419 other blondes on campus).

But there's another rite of passage here as well. My daughter's parents are ratcheting up one demographic notch, from the group marked "bill paying" to those marked "bill paid." We are graduating, too. And the sense of possibility is all around us.

Back a generation, in the '60s, I sat down with a financial planner. My purpose was to find out what I would need to provide for my growing family. He studied the figures, punched away at his calculator, and said with memorable simplicity: "It's going to take all you're going to have." He was about right. For the next 20 years, those words served as an organizing principle in our lives.

But he was wrong about something else. He predicted with the force of experience that once we were past 50 our thoughts would turn inexorably to leisure activities, slowing down, planning for retirement. Most clichés are overpoweringly true. (I fought for years before yielding to the Big One: When you have lots of small children, you should buy a house in the suburbs and get a station wagon and a dog.) I can report to you on the basis of firsthand survey research that there is no truth whatsoever to this middle-age factoid. What I find is quite the opposite. Most of my coevals are beginning to reconnect, to look for ways to leverage their skills and their assets. They are growing more tolerant of risk, more inclined to build than to earn. They are a dangerous band, these men with their bills paid. School's out.

National Review
September 4, 1981

A Letter From Camp

Dog Days, August

Dear Bill:
 You may find this hard to believe, but some readers, more'n a few, weren't all that happy with my last letter from camp. Seems they didn't understand what a story on football was doing in these august pages. One guy wrote that he loves football and he loves *NR*, but like champagne and pickles, he prefers 'em one at a time. Well, you know me. I'm no quitter. I'm going to keep doin' this piece 'til I get it right.

First of all, you might ask, why am I talkin' funny like this? Here I am a New Englander born and bred and I'm drawlin' all over this page till it's sticky to the touch. Just practicin', that's all. I've been interviewing the coaches this week and you've got to keep your geocultural guard up. Football, see, is your basic redneck sport, even when it's played in your basic frostbelt stadia. I first learned that fact the hard way, when I asked the old Jet quarterback Joe Namath, the pride of the Pennsylvania mining country, where he picked up his Southern accent. He gave me those laser-beam eyes for the long count and oozed out: "I picked it up playin' baaal." Judgin' from the jivin' that proceeded to commence in the locker room, I had just been dealt one jumbo ready-to-go *bon mot*. Playin' baaal is a one-way ticket south punched by Messrs. Mason and Dixon.

Yesterday I went lookin' for the head coach. (He's the senior field executive, not a psychiatric aide.) You can always pick him out because he's the one wearing shorts tailored tight across the tush. Everybody else wears uniforms or jeans. And he's always on the sunny side of the field, squinting into the sun. The coach never wears sunglasses, so when he comes in out of the sun and relaxes his facial muscles, he has these little streaks of bleached skin fanning out from the corners of his eyes—sort of a cross between the Marlboro man and KISS.

Anyway, he is, as we say at camp, a piece of work. He is gnawing

279

a good hunk of Red Man and watching the players hit the numbers. *Spraat.* To look at him you might think he was concentrating deeply on Xs and Os, but he's really looking for an opening to fire off a round of brown juice at your shoe. *Spraat.* The coach gets in the habit of breaking in the players, see, and he can't seem to stop himself from trying to break in the writers. *Spraat.* He's got a sweet rhythm that betrays him, though, and the good move is to wait for the pre-launch nod of the head before shuckin' briskly a step and a half to windward. When he launches the spume—*spraat*—it slides by nice as you please. Then he's ready to talk.

Some people have trouble talking to football coaches because they never say what they mean. It's not exactly that they lie. It's that they prefer to proceed with caution, poking snake sticks into the grass ahead of them. For instance, when a coach says of one of his players, *That boy really comes to play*, your casual listener may pick up nothing but the background noise of red-dirt clichés. To the trained ear, however, comes the message: "This player's competitive attitude, pharmaceutically honed, has settled into that fine groove between the merely savage and the starkly maniacal. Which is good." Or take these other examples culled from the echoes of a day at camp:

He's in the best shape of his career. His liver doctor scared him real good.

Our fans can expect an exciting team this year. Fumbles will kill us.

He lacks quickness. He's white.

He's got great peripheral vision. Look at those eyes. He's sick with fear.

He's had some difficulty picking up our system. The guy has the IQ of a mushroom.

He's surprisingly'quick for a big man. Absolutely meaningless. It is said of every pro player who weighs in excess of 300 pounds, of which every team has one. Not two. One.

He has great hands. He's slow.

He's got a great attitude. The kid's insane. He'll hit anything that moves, from an opponent to a laundry truck.

He hears footsteps. He's experiencing a gonadal deficiency.

We could go all the way this year if we get settled down early. I'm hoping to renegotiate my contract before the first game.

He's got great moves. He could teach St. Vitus how to dance, but we need guys who can block and tackle.

He's a leader off the field as well as on. The guy's bimbo book is encyclopedic.

We're an improving ballclub. We don't have a chance.

He's our big-play man. The laziest sumbitch on the team.

The guys really look up to him. That's why they elected him union rep. They hate him.

There's really nothing to it, once you get the dang thing down.

See y'all,
NBF

The American Spectator
September 29, 2010

LET SLIP THE DOGS OF (TAX) WAR

A speech to Maine Heritage Policy Center.

L   ike everybody else in his right mind, I love Maine, and I fear for her future. In my case, the roots of love run deep. My grandmother came from Old York, just as, the family Bible records, did her grandfather, and his grandfather. My sister still lives in the family house built in 1690.

I confess to being a serial entrepreneur, which is to say that I come from no place in particular. I have started four businesses—one each in Virginia; Washington, D.C.; Florida; and, most recently, British Columbia. On each of those occasions, because I love Maine, I looked for a rationale to start my new venture here. On each of those occasions, I was unable to make the business case.

Why was that? For two reasons, one obvious, the other perhaps less so. The first reason is that Maine has a famously high-tax, high-regulation legal construct. Some of my colleagues describe Maine's attitude as anti-business. I don't see it that way. In my own experience, Maine seems to be agnostic on the question. The established wisdom—be it from the dominant unions or the academy or the loudest voices in the political conversation—seems to be that business exists for one reason only: to pay taxes. And that, derivatively, business hires employees so that they can pay taxes, too. If the fissiparous character of business creation is left unexamined—if no thought is given to its macroeconomic value or its social utility—then business can make only the weakest of claims on public support. In the world of politics, inevitably, business thus gives way to other, ostensibly more high-minded claims on public support.

The second reason not to launch a venture in Maine is more cultural than financial. All Mainers take pride in our vibrant public-service culture. We have long contributed disproportionately to the political life of the nation. From Margaret Chase Smith and Ed Muskie to George Mitchell and Olympia Snowe, we have produced abundant political talent from a state with only one-third of 1 percent of the nation's population. By contrast, however, a roster of great Maine entrepreneurs might take its place on the shelf of the world's thinnest books, just a tad thicker than such volumes as *Great British Chefs* and *Famous Italian War Heroes*. Indeed, what is striking about Maine—given its well-educated and self-reliant workforce—is the barren nature of the business culture. What we know from the history of economic development is that sustained prosperity depends on *thick* networks of product and service designers, marketers, venture funders, managers, and—most importantly for small business—angel investors and former entrepreneurs. From Route 128 and Silicon Valley, to Phoenix and Jacksonville, to Bangalore and Guangdong province, economic prosperity requires a *culture* of job creation, an environment in which business conversation is conducted idiomatically on the basis of shared assumption and common goal. It's often said of *Fortune* 500 CEOs that "it's lonely at the top." For the Maine entrepreneur, I can assure you, it's lonely at the bottom. He or she has little in the way of a support system and Maine has made no systematic effort to nurture one.

These two factors—the high-tax regime and the absence of a business culture—have in part caused, and in part been aggravated by, Maine's unique demographic problem. That problem, in a word, is that we're *old*. Maine's median age is almost 41. That makes us the oldest state in the nation. If we were a separate country, it would make us one of the oldest in the world. The median age of France, in the heart of Old Europe, is 39. China's is 34, India's 25, Iraq's 20, Afghanistan's 18. What our aging population means, of course, is that Maine will get to the future first—a future now being reconfigured in its basic fiscal and monetary dimensions by the Obama administration. If the polls are to be believed, fewer and fewer Americans are optimistic about that future. Nobody seems to want to get there first.

So what can be done about Maine's demographic problem? Let's look first to its cause, and then for a solution. I'm no demographer, but even I can identify at least three major factors at work here. First is immigration. The person moving to Maine today is more likely to be a 58-year-old ex-cop from Worcester than a 16-year-old lettuce picker from Guadalajara. More old white guys than young brown guys. The second factor is emigration. The person moving out of Maine today is more likely to be a 22-year-old recently minted Colby graduate than a 46-year-old civil servant from Bangor. More young whizzes brain-draining away than mid career employees moving up and out. And finally, there is the birthrate of 1.8 per Maine woman, one of the lowest rates in the world. That's as low as Russia's, which has already seen its population shrink to one-half the size of the U.S. population, well on its way to one-fourth by the middle of this century. With a 1.8 birthrate, which is far below replacement level, Russia's population, within one generation, will be smaller than Mexico's.

These three factors, in my sense of the problem, suggest very different responses. First, for the young college graduates barreling down I-95 in search of their future elsewhere? I think that we can ignore them for now. They're flexible. As soon as we offer a value proposition—as soon as our young people believe they can realize their dreams right here in Maine—they'll make a 180-turn at the Vince Lombardi stop on the Jersey Turnpike and be on their way back. If you've spent four years at Colby College, after all, you know exactly the way life should be.

As for the Maine women who've stopped having babies? We will have to forget them for now, too. They are immovable. Young mothers are the most conservative force in any society and they're unlikely to change *their* ways until we can demonstrate that we've changed *our* ways—until, that is, we can offer their kids a shot at a good life.

No, I would suggest that our focus should be on immigration and, more specifically, on the *kinds* of new residents we might be able to attract. By an accident of geography, Maine has a great advantage in this tender area of public policy. Mainers are not preconditioned—as is much of the rest of the country—to see immigration as a threat. We have no boat people coming ashore at Cape Elizabeth. We have no migrant workers wading across at Kittery. There are no refugees streaming over the bridge at Calais. Mainers are well positioned to see immigration for what it really is—a neutral phenomenon which, if perceived clearly, can present rare opportunity.

As it happens, political circumstance has just presented Maine with such an opportunity.

For perspective, let me take you back a few years to one of the signal moments in immigration history—the 1997 handover of Hong Kong to the mainland Chinese. One of the perks of owning a television production company, as I did at the time, is that you get to make the crew assignments. Over loud intramural objections, I assigned myself to cover the handover. We set ourselves up in Kowloon's Peninsula Hotel overlooking Victoria Harbour—at the time, the finest hotel in the world, a magical combination of colonial elegance and Chinese efficiency—and we proceeded to watch history unfold. Our attention was concentrated by a huge digital clock installed on the shoreline— perhaps 25 feet wide—that counted down the days, hours, and minutes to the handover. Anxiety ran high. Would the British and the other developed nations come to the defense of Hong Kong, a citadel of Western capitalism? Would the colonial lease be revised, or extended? Or would Hong Kong's fledgling democracy movement be snuffed out? Would private wealth be confiscated? Would the Chinese army, reported to be massed at the border, roll in with tank battalions? Into this vacuum of reliable information rumors rushed, and then mutated. Each day, anxiety ran higher, as that clock we all came to hate continued to tick down.

Ten days before H Day, I had some business in Singapore and I took the morning flight over. We entrepreneurs always ride in the back of the plane, but on this occasion a client had given me a first-class ticket, so I boarded first and sat up front. As the economy passengers moved down the aisle and filled up the plane, I noticed something strange. Hong Kong is notable for its fast-paced pedestrian traffic. Hong Kongers march to their own up-tempo, free-market drummer. But my fellow passengers were shuffling and stumbling down the aisle, as if they had just been released from the tubercular ward of the Royal Hospital. I asked my seatmate to explain and, wordlessly, he reached into his pocket and extracted a fistful of gold coins. My fellow passengers, it seems, were on their way to their new second homes—many of them located in safe-deposit boxes—and they were taking with them everything they could carry: rubies, diamonds, works of gold and platinum, coins, and jewelry. Some of the women carried shoulder bags jammed with 30 or 40 pounds' worth of ingots. On the plane back the next afternoon, I saw many of these same people, all of them lighter on their feet and moving once again at Hong Kong-speed. It's fair to say that Singapore was re-capitalized that day by what I couldn't resist describing as "flight capital."

Returning to Hong Kong, and newly sensitized to the high stakes of the historical moment, I began to look more closely at the options open to Hong Kongers seeking to escape their fearful Communist future. What I found, of course, was mostly ad hocery born of panic. Crazy stuff. But here and there was real innovation. The single most focused and aggressive initiative was undertaken by (of all people) the Canadians. Yes, by those mild-mannered, self-effacing, incrementalist Canadians. The Mainers of the family of nations. What Canada did was to frame the handover as a kind of NFL draft day—an occasion to restock its team with world-class economic players. But unlike the New England Patriots, who might be looking on draft day for, say, a tight end in one round and a cover corner in the next, Canada was looking to draft every player in every round. Canada wanted to upgrade its team at every position, all at once. And they took a strikingly unsentimental approach. Canada did not say, as might have been expected, "Give me your tired, your poor, your huddled masses yearning to breathe free." No, it said, quite distinctly, "Give me your successful capitalists, your proven performers, your players with critical skills and liquid assets." Canada had admitted to itself, uncharacteristically, that it wanted to compete in the global economy and that it wanted to win. And so it made an offer that Hong Kong's capitalist all-stars couldn't refuse. Taxes? "We'll cut them to the bone." Red tape? "We'll rip right through it." Family problems? "We'll assign a concierge until you're comfortably settled."

How did that little recruiting trip work out? Well, those of us who watched the winter Olympics several months ago saw a dynamic and prosperous host city, the first Chinese city on the North American continent. For Canadians from coast to coast, Vancouver has become not only an engine of economic growth but a source of glowing national pride.

My question is this: Can at least some elements of the Canadian experience be adapted to the current situation in Maine? I think they can be. First, consider the existential threat. For the prosperous American in the Age of Obama, the digital clock has begun to tick. The administration is delivering on its implausible campaign promise to shift the government's bills from the society at large to the prosperous Americans at the top—to the 5 percent of taxpayers earning more than $250,000 per year. Already fixed by law—as a result of health care reform and the expiration of the Bush tax cuts—are future increases in marginal tax rates of 24 percent on interest income, 59 percent on capital gains income, and 189 percent on dividend income. The administration has acknowledged—and CBO projections will demand—that new and larger taxes will be imposed in due political course, which is to say, after the next election. To the prosperous American, it appears that a class war has just been declared—and that he has somehow become an enemy of the state.

On the flip side of that existential threat, of course, lies opportunity. An opportunity for the polity with the wit and resolve to realize it.

Consider: those prosperous Americans have been startled by a frontal assault by this administration; they have been shaken from their comfort zones and opened to new possibility. They have begun looking for political shelter, places that will respect their accomplishment and recognize their contribution. They are in a high-anxiety zone and they will be susceptible, at least some of them, to an aggressive recruiting pitch.

And thus, the rare opportunity. Not as dramatic as Hong Kong's, to be sure, but arriving at a moment critical to the Maine economy. What I am suggesting is that Maine reposition itself so as to be hospitable to prosperous newcomers. What I am suggesting is, for those seeking refuge from Mr. Obama's class war, that Maine provide a kind of safe harbor.

What might such a recruiting campaign look like? As a conversation-starter, let me propose the following. Suppose that we invited out-of-staters earning more than $250,000 to move to Maine and, in return, we agreed to exempt them from state income tax? Not for the rest of time, but for long enough to shock the system—10 years, perhaps. I can assure you that such a proposal would be of interest to Maine expatriates. I have myself on several occasions met former Mainers—in Jacksonville, in Naples, in Scottsdale, and elsewhere—who left Maine shortly after state income taxes became their largest single discretionary expense. They love Maine, but they're not willing to pay an extra 50 or 100,000 dollars a year for the privilege of being here in February. I suspect this invitation would be tempting, as well, to Maine's neighbors in punitively high-tax areas such as Boston, Providence, and Hartford.

Maine enjoys, as we all know, a rich tradition of hospitality to the traveling public. We can roll out the red carpet with the best of them. But in the current economic environment, that's not going to be enough. We're going to have to compete aggressively for the scarce resources of talent and capital. While it won't come naturally to most of us, we're going to have to think selfishly, as chauvinistic Mainers. We're going to have to focus on what Maine could receive *in return* for its tax exemption.

First, as the marketers say, we could qualify the prospect. By establishing an age floor of 50, for instance, we would attract new residents who don't send their kids to public schools or wind up on Medicaid rolls or in other ways ratchet up state spending. Second, we would attract affluent homeowners who would winterize seasonal homes, or buy new ones, thus propping up the high-end real estate market even as they generate new property-tax revenues and, ultimately, new estate-tax revenues. Third, these new residents would bring with them their spending habits: We would attract upscale consumers who, beyond their numbers, would patronize restaurants, gift shops, and other retail outlets, thus boosting town economies and generating new sales-tax revenues. Finally—and this is by a wide margin the most important factor—we would attract the successful executives, investors, and entrepreneurs needed to form our own business culture, the scaffolding for a new business structure here in Maine. To extend the Canadian analogy: By opening, say, a two-year window for the new tax exemption, we could put ourselves in position to draft Maine's missing generation of mentors, advisors, and angel investors. We could put ourselves in position, that is, to upgrade our economic team from one end of the roster to the other.

There is one characteristic common to all successful business people. They are recidivists. They can't help themselves. They just keep doing it, again and again. And when they can no longer do it themselves, they advise and inspire and invest in younger protégés. These successful business people—our former neighbors in Maine and our current neighbors in New England—are *precisely* the people we need to power the economic recovery. They have the skills, the contacts, the seed capital, the ability to discern business opportunity and the instinct to seize it. My message is that we should not just be willing—we should be eager—to compete for their allegiance. They can help us. They are up for grabs. There's a deal to be made here. Let's make it.

National Review
December 14, 1992

POST-ELECTION FIGHT

—Las Vegas, Nevada

R ichard Nixon used to tell his associates, exhausted after a long campaign, not to take vacations right away. Work for a while, he'd say, taper off for a week, and then go to the beach for a long sun-soak. My own counsel is different. I recommend, especially after a campaign like this, a politically incorrect weekend in Las Vegas, complete with professional prizefight.

The restorative process begins as your plane skids to a stop at McCarran Airport. Yes, it's named after former Democratic Senator Pat McCarran, who, for those of you who are too young to remember the Great War, was known in the phrase of the day as a dedicated anti-Communist. Fact is, on his good days he made Tail Gunner Joe look like a wimp. Fact also is, though, that McCarran was only small potatoes in these parts. The city father was none other than Bugsy Siegel, who said he'd build the place and then they'd better come. He did and they did. A civic leader of broad vision, Siegel supported entrepreneurial capitalism, empowerment, and school choice. He was a consistent critic of prosecutorial zeal.

Your white stretch limo awaits you. Don't get too excited. Stretch limos await everybody. Indeed, Las Vegas has become a cashless society, with everybody drinking, gambling, and carrying on as a "guest" of somebody else. I'm not quite sure how this comes out black at the bottom line, but I think it has to do with the speed with which the pea moves around under the shell. Or, if you're given to political metaphors, think of it this way: We're in for a weekend during which the rich will get richer, the middle class will get the shaft, and the bill will be presented to our children's children. At any rate, it should be fun.

Now it's on to the Mirage for the big fight. This place is worth going about ten miles out of your way to see. Every so often a mechanical volcano erupts in the front yard, shooting real flames into the night sky and scaring the hell out of pedestrians plodding between one casino and another. Old Carville missed a bet here. This volcano could have become a fixture in Clinton spots. Whatever the opposite of infrastructure is, this just might be it.

Inside, there are acres of felt tables, slots, hookers, costume-party cowboys and (most amazing of all to these D.C. eyes) men in tuxedoes that fit. It's showbiz and everybody is starring in his own movie, wearing sunglasses indoors, snapping fingers at cocktail girls, tossing away the rent money with more flair than they do back home. The fight crowd moves a little quicker than the rest, getting a buzz in time for the undercard.

The fight, featuring champion Evander "Real Deal" Holyfield against Riddick "Big Daddy" Bowe, will be held on the campus, as they say, of the University of Nevada at Las Vegas. (This move itself scores pretty well on the Political Incorrectness meter. While most universities were primping this fall to attract a presidential debate, the Runnin' Rebels of UNLV had their eyes on the prizefight.) The Thomas and Mack Center, where the college team plays hoops, has the look of a big-time urban arena, replete with neon signage for competing beer companies. And here in the $800 seats, I find what we were looking for the past six months—a solid GOP precinct. Orange County may be gone, but Row 6 is holding. And the celeb watching is primo.

Best Hair: Andre Agassi, sporting a shoulder-length tri-color tangle.

Best Entrance: Magic Johnson. The crowd surges forward to touch him, for some reason.

Worst Entrance: Jack Nicholson. Great actor, though. He is believable tonight as a small, creepy, Goodwill-clothes kind of guy.

Best Voice: Michael Buffer. Invisible-hand-wise, this guy may be the last piece of the puzzle. He makes six figures for intoning, "Let's get ready to rumble" before big fights.

Best Jacket: Mr. T. He edges out Melvin Laird (of whom my streetwise seat-neighbor says, "Hey, there goes Dean Rusk").

Best Height Spread: Kareem Abdul Jabbar and his 5'2" blonde friend.

All of Hollywood's tough guys are here—Sylvester Stallone, Mel Gibson, Kevin Costner, Bruce Willis. They are here to see two really tough guys—Holyfield and Bowe—beat each other within an inch of their lives. (Have you noticed? Nobody ever complains about fighters being overpaid.) And of course they are here without their wives. There are no women in Las Vegas. Only broads.

Michael Buffer enters the ring to hype his way through the introductions. He assures us that this bout is sanctioned by the Nevada State Ath-a-letic Commission. (Pause. Imagine, if the handle is nine figures, a human activity that would be left unsanctioned by the Nevada State Ath-a-letic Commission. Pause. I give up.) He brings on the sculpted, 205-pound Holyfield and the towering, 235-pound Bowe. The bell is struck and the fighters begin to move, stick, cross, and combo. For 12 rounds they batter each other, shoving, grabbing, sucking for breath. At the end, Holyfield, with one eye puffed closed and the other glazed with blood and sweat, mounts a final furious attack. It is not enough and the championship goes to the better man. The crowd stands and applauds long into the night.

National Review
April 3, 1981

TALES FROM THE BUREAUCRACY

We recently drew some short-term duty at a federal agency, helping to run the place until the president could get his man confirmed. What started out as a two-week hitch turned and twisted and backslid into two months, which is to say that the entire process was accelerated to accommodate our quirky desire to return to the private sector. It was a learning experience, combining approximately equal parts frustration, ennui, and exhilaration. Herewith a few excerpts from the memory file:

• The financial disclosure laws, reflecting as they do both the bureaucratic accretions of a generation and the extraordinary "reforms" catalyzed by Watergate, are draconian. To accept federal employment is to invite a stranger into the most private recesses of your financial affairs. Personnel officers are required to know what you make, what you own, indeed what you did with what you used to own. The forms are lengthy, detailed, and in many places ambiguous. Calculatedly ambiguous, we suspect. One is encouraged to err on the side of too much detail rather than too little: The candidate is set to serious form-filling only after being photographed and fingerprinted. (You are permitted to retain your belt, shoelaces, and sharp objects.)

The redeeming aspect of the transaction is that all information is held in the strictest confidence. It says so right on the forms themselves. Only authorized personnel officers have access to your files and then only for the purpose of ensuring compliance. As we put it to our examiner: "You would withhold this information even from Ronald Reagan?" Came the reply: "Unless he were duly authorized to receive it, yes."

• Two days after we signed on, we chaired a senior staff meeting on the subject of personnel. As we moved the name-cards about on the cork-board organization chart, it became apparent that we had no qualified candidate for a particularly sensitive line position. We stared at the gap in our rapidly developing organization. Bureaucrat Number One broke the silence by looking at us and saying cheerily, "You would be perfect for that job." We nodded graciously. Bureaucrat Number Two then chimed in quickly with, "But of course you wouldn't want to take a pay cut of —," mentioning a figure that exactly covered the difference between what the federal job paid and our private salary.

Nobody here but us duly authorized personnel.

• The mightiest weapon in the arsenal of bureaucracy is the meeting. It can be used both offensively and defensively. In the former case, meetings can be used to define the agenda and thus the business of the agency; or to reshape the organization by excluding bureaucratic opponents; or to provide a captive audience for a dominant personality. In this last connection, the most highly prized professional attribute is something called "presentation skills." We have seen presenters who are the stuff of legend, and we recognize—even if we cannot fully explain—why they are so highly regarded. Part of it is the charts (color overlays mark the superior presentation), part of it is the obsequious goo spread over those who have participated in the development of this remarkable program / budget / conference / whatever (the presenter must acknowledge by name more than half the people in the room), but by far the largest part is the *manner* of the presenter.

We don't pretend to have penetrated to the ultimate secrets, but the superficially identifiable characteristics are these: First, one must speak softly. This technique not only quiets the end-of-the-table chit-chat, but also draws the listeners closer, the better to hear. Second, one must pause before each important sentence, the better to emphasize the full wisdom to follow. (Pause *after* your major point and you're finished. Someone asks a question or, worse, "seeks clarification," and you might as well toss your pointer away and sit down. It's now their meeting rather than yours.) Finally, one must adopt that peculiar, modulated tone of voice that one hears throughout the bureaucracy. It is a flat, almost monotonal voice that fairly throbs with professional objectivity. Lead singers at the Metropolitan Opera probably spend fewer hours training their voices than do bureaucrats honing their presentation skills.

We mentioned that the meeting can also be used defensively. In every bureaucracy, the newcomer will encounter or incite opposition, people who, in the president's apt phrase, "don't get with the program." The best place for these people to be is in a meeting. Since nothing gets done at a meeting, you can rest assured that they are neither tunneling under your plans nor hatching ill-conceived ideas of their own. Just as obviously, if you're spending all day in meetings, you're not getting on with your own plans. Thus you know you are in the presence of bureaucratic genius when you see A lure his opponent, B, into a long meeting with C, A's subordinate.

During our days in the bureaucracy we found only one foolproof way to end a meeting. The chairman should gather up his papers, slide his chair back from the conference table, and say genially. "Well, I know you all have to get to your other meetings."

• A common mistake in the bureaucracy is to assume the obvious, namely, that a meeting is over when it is adjourned by the chairman. You can spot the inexperienced meeting-goer by watching where he goes after he leaves the conference room. If he proceeds directly to the restroom, he has committed the classic blunder. He will be pursued by an opponent, or more commonly by a sycophantic supporter, and he will find it difficult to disengage. Sharing restroom facilities is a leveling experience. Hierarchical distinctions, carefully cultivated, are likely to be blurred.

The appropriate disengagement technique is to proceed briskly to your own office, where you control the border crossings, or to the office of a bureaucratic peer whose territorial boundaries will not be violated casually by your pursuer.

The American Spectator
November 1, 2008

GOODBYE TO MOST OF THAT

—York, Maine

I've been down this road before. I first made the drive from York to San Francisco back in the proto-conservative era, running political errands along the way for one William F. Buckley Jr. All of us young conservatives, one way or another, were making our way to the Goldwater convention. As the junior member of that yet-to-be-vast conspiracy, I drew the short straw and the long route. Our coalition needed a nip here and a tuck there, and I became the designated nipper-tucker. It was part of Buckley's genius to see among the shards of a broken post-Eisenhower politics the makings of a new conservative majority. With the indispensable help of his *National Review* colleagues Frank Meyer, Brent Bozell, and William Rusher, Buckley had stitched together an assemblage of social, traditional, and national defense conservatives and then grandly pronounced them a "movement."

Such was the force of Buckley's personal charisma and rhetorical thrust that many right-leaning citizens suspended their disbelief and declared themselves our co-conspirators. More sober political observers, including those now known as the mainstream media but then known simply as The Media, were dismissive. To them, serious political personalities on the right were ontologically inconceivable. But even other, less tendentious observers were skeptical as to whether Buckley, as the infamous *NR* office memo put it, could make the "Holy Rollers lie down with the high rollers."

Courtly James Burnham, the oldest and wisest of the Buckleyites, could be heard muttering that a cause depending simultaneously on social conservatives and free-marketeers smacked of an "unprincipled coalition," which in Burnham's lexicon was the least promising form of political life. It was not until the *New York Times* began referring to us as a "movement" that we knew we had arrived.

When I say that the coalition was stitched together, I don't mean that it was tied snugly with rawhide strips. I mean that it was tacked up with a basting stitch. The fusionist movement relied from the outset on the force of moral commitment generated by religious conservatives, while neither of the other coalition partners, foreign policy hard-liners and free-market absolutists, were consistently adherent to traditional values. It was also clear from the earliest days that the traditionalists' moral commitment never ran unreservedly to support of the free market. For them, economic concerns were subordinate to social concerns. And it was equally clear that the foreign policy hard-liners, then as now, were smart and vocal but a bit thin on the ground and never likely to be a player in organizational politics. The coalition was, if not unprincipled, at least fragile and susceptible to fracture. But the tactical imperatives of the day, especially the need to resist Soviet expansionism, prevailed. The Buckley coalition, cemented by the anti-Communist cause, worked as a unified political force until the fall of the Soviet Union and for some years beyond.

Valuable travel tips, unavailable elsewhere at any price. The nicest town in the U.S., hands down, is Elkhart, Indiana. A single vignette, drawn from a stuffed folder in the mental file. The missus and I are enjoying a late supper (that would be 7:45 Elkhart time) in a deserted Applebee's when a second party saunters in—four biker dudes comprehensively pierced and inked, trailed timidly by a 45ish woman. Hmmm, is she a hostage? A combination love slave and short-order cook? Is she, Lord help her, counting on me to rescue her from the four all-beef patties in the dungaree buns? The Applebee's staff crowds in and breaks into song and it becomes clear that Mom is treating Biker Boy and his friends to a gala dinner. At the end of a notably high-carb meal, Biker Boy drifts out to the parking lot, kisses Mom, ties his birthday swag neatly to the back of his hog and chuffs off into the Indiana night.

Looking back over the last eight years, it seems obvious that George W. Bush has been a vastly underrated politician. Not just in one election, but in two, he persuaded the entire conservative movement to stand with him—even as he took a series of Great Leaps Forward. First, he nationalized education, a constitutional stretch by any reckoning and the realization of a liberal dream running back almost half a century. Then he nationalized prescription drugs for senior citizens, which represented a monumental achievement for liberal ideology. (I won't drown you in numbers but consider this: The unfunded liability in the Social Security system, about which we have been perspiring heavily for 30 years, now stands at $13.6 trillion. The unfunded liability of the Bush drug benefit—and that's *after* premiums, co-pays, and all projectable revenues—is already at $17.2 trillion.)

Tooling through Scranton, we scan the sidewalks for the ghost of Joe Biden's dad. Sen. Biden, now celebrated for rising magnificently from his blue-collar roots, once described his dad as the best-dressed sales manager in town. Perhaps that collar was something in a nice Oxford blue with French cuffs.

As I write these words Bush has just nationalized the residential real estate market through the takeover of Fannie Mae and Freddie Mac. (When did it become part of the American Dream to live in government housing?) Forget his "discretionary" war and the incalculable costs, both strategic and economic, it will incur. How did Bush do it? How did he manage to keep all the partners inside the coalition, sullen but not quite mutinous? The answer is brilliant campaigns, textbook brilliant, followed by governance that destroyed the base.

You know that list of the hundred things you must do before you die? Good luck. But on your list of, say, ten things, you must include a Notre Dame football game. As a delegate from WASP nation I have observer status only, but, I tell you, it's a near-spiritual experience. I now understand why head coach Charlie Weis has never returned to the pros. At the pep rally before the home opener against San Diego State, 20,000 fans bow metronomically, forming a "W" with their fingers and thumbs. The fans are worshipping the coach! Where I come from, they threaten the wife and kids. By the time the Fighting Irish band shakes down the thunder from the sky, I'm ready to hit a San Diego doofus myself.

Which leaves you, the reader, in a unique situation: For the first time in your life you have no conservative candidate for whom to vote. John McCain? I got to know him a bit in Washington and he's a guy's guy, full of wit and vinegar. He's fun to be around and his word is good. His only conceit is that he thinks he's a principled politician, which is not quite right. He's an honorable politician, clearly, but he has more attitudes than principles, the difference being that a politician with attitudes can be ideologically scammed. And he has been. I sometimes think that David Brooks cooked up that "national greatness" nonsense with a consumer market of one in mind. Whatever the marketing strategy may have been, though, Brooks made himself one big sale. John McCain seems fully engaged only when going abroad in search of monsters to destroy.

Cleveland won't be trapping many tourists anytime soon, but if you find yourself in the area, check out the Rock & Roll Hall of Fame. It's all there—stuff from Chuck Berry and Jerry Lee Lewis,

Janis Joplin's Porsche, Jimi Hendrix's axe, Mick Jagger's costumes—the full panoply of your misspent youth. One glaring omission: there's no mention of the great late-'50s band, The Zebras. I use "great" here in the sense that it paid enough to buy my first car, an aquamarine, chick-magnet Ford convertible. And if you're wondering about the name of the band, yes, I was the white guy.

Not to belabor the point, but another example of McCain's confusion of attitude with principle is his signature campaign against congressional earmarks. A principled conservatism would oppose the earmark and return the money to the taxpayer. An attitudinal conservatism would oppose the earmark and send the money to the executive branch. The planted axiom in McCain's campaign is that, while Sen. Stevens may waste the money on a bridge to nowhere, a nameless Transportation Department bureaucrat will spend it wisely in the public interest. Experience would not seem to support McCain's confidence on this point, but he labors on, not seeking to limit the scope of government but rather seeking to clarify exactly which government office will allocate the funds. A popular attitude by most evidence, but not a principle.

Ever wonder how far a couple married long enough to have eight grandchildren can stand being cooped up in a small automobile? I speak with authority. We encounter a bit of turbulence just outside Webster City, Iowa. Nothing serious. By the time we reach Clear Lake, that toddlin' town, domestic tranquility has been restored. It was Kingsley Amis who first noted the similarity between women and Russians—"If you did exactly what they wanted all the time you were being realistic and constructive and promoting the cause of peace."

McCain's problem, from the conservative perspective, is that he has no framework, ideological or philosophical, into which he can feed experience and from which he can adduce policy. He is all moral sensibility, without system, without intellectual base. It's useful to remember that

Ronald Reagan, the professional actor, was rarely emotive. As the world now knows from his writings, he was relentlessly analytical.

> *I had never thought of Pennsylvania and Ohio as one end of the Farm Belt, but for the better part of 200 miles it's corn, corn, and more corn. (Who says that ethanol scam isn't working?) South Dakota, where one man's mesa is another man's butte, is the real deal. Big-time grain operations, hour after hour, both sides of the road, with soybeans and sunflowers and other specialty crops mixed in. By the time you hit Wyoming, the farming has turned to ranching, with one* Dances with Wolves *set eliding into the next. Everywhere you see signs of mines reopened, wells uncapped, and the commodities boom in full swing. If a recession can be detected with the naked eye, sorry NBC, but there's not much bad news to report and none at all for the folks who dig things and drill things and grow things.*

John McCain is a voracious if undisciplined reader, and he insists on sharing his literary enthusiasms. For reasons that escape me, he tells everybody who will listen that his favorite fictional character is Robert Jordan from the Hemingway novel *For Whom the Bell Tolls*. For those of you some years removed from high school English, Jordan is the American volunteer in the Spanish Civil War who opts for death in a hopeless and effectively pro-Communist cause. We'll give McCain the benefit of the doubt and presume that he likes the dying part better than the Commie part. Don't cry for McCain. If he wins, he's president. If he doesn't, perhaps he can find satisfaction in having taken a beating for his party.

> *Sorry, but whenever I get anywhere near Chicago I'm reminded of Richard Jeni's explanation of how the city got started: "A bunch of people in New York said, 'Gee, I'm enjoying the crime and the poverty, but it just isn't cold enough. Let's go west.'"*

Carly Fiorina, the senior McCain aide and former Hewlett-Packard executive, blurted out the gaffish truth that John McCain is not fit to be a corporate CEO. She said the same thing, with more accuracy, about Barack Obama. He's never run anything bigger than a law review, and the questions about him, your correspondent can confirm, still swirl across the fruited plain. Even the people who embrace his "message" of hope and change add a "but," such as: But the only old friends we seem to know about are the convict, the terrorist, and that hate-pretzel of a preacher. Or: But when he's untethered from the teleprompter, he seems to float in rhetorical space, a man of no fixed intellectual address. Or: But there seems to be more change here than a Bolshevik could stand today, more hope than a red-mopped urchin could contemplate tomorrow. Or: But about this family thing—what's up with that brother who lives in the hut in exurban Nairobi? These are not the usual concerns lingering in the final weeks of a presidential campaign.

> *Another entry for your must-do list! Spearfish Canyon, located near the old Homestake gold strike in western South Dakota. The word for it is awesome, in the pure, pre-Valley Girl sense. Limestone cliffs, crashing falls, bird- and fish-stuffed wetlands, an area so pristine as to justify the local poet's judgment that it is soul-nourishing to "get out into the silent places." If you've never been a tree hugger, I recommend that you start with the Ponderosa pine. The bark smells like butterscotch. And you don't have to take my word for any of this. A previous visitor, Frank Lloyd Wright, said of Spearfish, "How is it that I've heard so much about the Grand Canyon, when this is even more miraculous."*

Over the past 20 years, Obama has held a series of brief, small-beer jobs, all of them in the nonprofit sector, which is another way of saying that he has made a living out of the economic value created by somebody else. The only real money came when he found the literary subject of a lifetime: himself. At age 46, he has already published two autobiographies, both of them commercially successful. What, you might reasonably ask, would a man who hasn't accomplished anything write about in *two* autobiographies? Feelings. What Barack felt about this, what he felt about that, what he almost felt about this, what he should have felt about that. After 500 pages of this picaresque monologue, the reader is moved to scream at the page, "Barack, we know how you feel. Do something!"

You've heard the marketing motto, "What happens in Vegas, stays in Vegas"? If only, my friends. If only.

It is the universal temptation to divide the human tribe into two neat categories. Some people see the fundamental division as that between men and women. Others see it as between blacks and whites. Or rich and poor, gay and straight, straight and addicted, night people and day people. The late Herman Kahn used to tell me that the critical distinction, the one that really matters in public life, is the one between those who care what the *New York Times* says about them and those who don't. Myself, I've always been an O'Hara man. The novelist John O'Hara saw the world around him separating itself cleanly into two groups—people who do things and people who describe things.

Barack Obama is a describer. He's not running to accomplish great things. He's running to be president, and he'll get a helluva book out of it. The rest of us will get a describer in chief.

There comes that moment in road life when you can either starve or pick a logo from the billboard misleadingly labeled, "Food." Hidden in that list of cholesterol palaces is a gem. Go with Chili's. The Southwestern Cobb is reliably good.

And thus the choice you face on November 4, a choice between Too New and Too Old, a choice between a TR Republican and (I guess) a Kennedy Democrat, an election between two career legislators face to face at last with those "tough choices" they pretend to relish, both of whom seem likely to yield to inflation (and mete out the concomitant punishment to savers and investors) rather than swallowing a stiff dose of fiscal medicine. Maybe Buckley, that master of political theater, knew just when to tap-dance off stage.

No better time than the end of a trip to slip into the apodictic mode. I have seen the future and I'm pretty sure it's not California. Not so long ago, whatever happened in America tended to happen first in California. Now, I strongly suspect, only the bad things will happen there first. The state can no longer afford the politics of social impulse, the politics of ideological whim. Those are the indulgences of youth and wealth and California is past its prime with the bills of boom now coming due. No, I think it's more likely that the future will unfold first, both the good and the bad, in its neighbor to the east, Colorado. With a layered economy, built on the sedimental foundation of successive booms in energy, telecommunications, and finance, with the spirit of the trailblazer and the grit of the cowboy, Colorado has shown early promise in its efforts to balance past and future, city and town, techie and farmer, and the varied interests of the whites and browns and blacks among its citizenry. My advice is to go west, young man, but not all the way.

And then, and then . . . and then along came Sarah Palin. I should disclose that I know her a little and like her a lot. I lobbied persistently for her selection as VP. Whatever I write now will sound like time-capsule stuff by the time you read it, but here was my thinking way back in the summer of 2008. Point One: The suits—Pawlenty, Romney, Lieberman— are all fine fellows but will be unable to help McCain move off 42–45 percent of the vote. Point Two: Sarah will reshuffle the deck by stunning the media, caffeinating the base, arresting (at least momentarily) the migration of Hillary voters, and intriguing that huge swath of the country that doesn't give a damn about politics ten months of the year. Point Three: Should McCain somehow manage to win, Sarah will embolden his best instincts and inspire his inner reformer. She'd be a great vice president. I didn't bother to make Point Four. With all of her upside, Sarah also brings great risk. Everybody has a tough first lap around the national political track. Biden did, pratfalling twice. Bill Clinton did, with that apparently career-killing keynote address to the 1988 convention. Hillary did, losing most of the caucus states (!) this year to a no-name, no-account junior senator. If form holds, Sarah will be stumbling and crumbling by October. Maybe she won't. But even if she does, we have been re-minded—as have the media and the powerbrokers—that there is a latent conservative constituency out there, waiting for the spark of leadership, listening expectantly for the sound of the trumpet.

National Review
February 6, 2012

THE GOP WINS THE SUPER BOWL

The Republican streak reaches XLVI

P erhaps you've already heard: The G-Men beat the Pats, 21–17. Here are my game notes—buffed to high luster, no doubt, by the benefactions of a well-stocked bar situated thoughtfully, let's see, nine steps from my well-appointed seat.

• Americans, especially those of the wagering class, love underdogs, and the Giants go off as lovable three-point underdogs. But with a passion exceeding even their affection for underdogs, Americans hate losers. Good luck on that long trip home, Patriots.

• The NFL, both officially and otherwise, emphatically opposes gambling, and for all of the reasons you inscribed in your childhood book of max-ims—namely, that gambling is "the child of avarice, the brother of iniquity, the father of mischief, the sister of anxiety, and the uncle of stupidity." Okay, I made those last two up. But the first three were coined by no less an authority than the father not of mischief but of our very own country (or, quite possibly, by Alexander Hamilton, who for a modest fee would doubtless have been willing to take the other side of the question). There is no gambling up here in the suites, of course. It would be lily-gilding. Some of these guys have already bet a half-billion or so just to buy a team.

• The game features two high-profile quarterbacks, one great and the other knocking on the door, as we grizzled sports scribes like to say. Tom Brady is brilliant, no question, but he dresses a bit too carefully, fusses continually with his hair, struts camera-ready poses with off-putting regularity. What's up with that? This is football, not polo. When he steps out with his wife, a Brazilian supermodel, they look as if they've been booked in a fashion shoot. I'm an Eli Manning guy. He's still slogging along in the shadow of his big brother. Eli grinds it out, year after year: When he's flushed from the pocket and has to run for his life, you can almost hear him say, *Oy!* In the open field, his gait is decidedly more geezer than gazelle. Eli is also self-effacing, courteous to all, loyal to Ole Miss, loving to his mom, faithful to his college sweetheart. I know a GOP voter when I see one.

• The coaches offer no such contrast. The difference between the Pats' Bill Belichick and the Giants' Tom Coughlin is the difference between old school and older school. They both apprenticed under the legendary coach Bill Parcells whose path-breaking insight was that you can break an opponent's will by hitting him harder than he hits you. There's an undeniable logic there, even if it affronts Eastern sensibilities. Coughlin, at 65, still sets the clocks five minutes early at the Giants' practice facility: To be on time, in other words, you have to arrive early. I'm told that it makes perfect sense once you've taken the one-way trip into the heart of Coughlin World.

• The rule of thumb when attending Super Bowls, Oscar ceremonies, royal weddings, and other large entertainments is that you must consign yourself, body and soul, to the proper Sherpa. There is no lonelier or more un-American place in the world than the holding pen just outside a velvet rope. Avoid it whenever possible. Or lose the one chance in your life to be up close and personal with Michael Douglas, Steven Tyler, Kenneth the Page, and Amani Toomer. (If you don't know Amani Toomer, shame on you.)

• Hmmm. I may have used that "rule of thumb" inappropriately. A medievalist friend of mine insists that the phrase originated in 15th-century

England, where men were enjoined from beating their wives with sticks thicker than their thumbs. A good custom, that. We observe it to this very day in the Freeman household. (Joke alert! Joke alert!)

• The modern NFL smells of money, much of it crispy new. Seventeen hundred private planes clot the tarmac at Indy-area airports. Robert Kraft of the New England Patriots is the prototypical NFL owner. Full of puff and posture. He made a fortune in the paper and packaging business and then bought the Patriots in 1994 for $175 million. *Forbes* magazine recently appraised the value of the team at $1.4 billion. The owner of the Giants, John Mara, is what passes in the NFL for old money. His grandfather, a New York bookmaker, bought the franchise in 1925 for $500. *Forbes* says the Giants are now worth $1.3 billion.

Suck wind, Bain Capital.

• The Giants are hammering the Patriots. We may be witnessing an old-school breaking of wills. Was it Longfellow, the Grantland Rice of his era, who once said, "In this world a man must be either anvil or hammer"? (Or was it Emerson? Orestes Brownson? Nordlinger will know.)

• The Pats are beginning to lose focus. Napoleon Bonaparte, a product of that great 19th-century French program, taught us that we should "never interfere with the enemy when he is in the process of destroying himself." The Giants are interfering, anyway.

• I am hopeful that, due to some massive scheduling snafu, President Obama will make a midfield appearance at halftime. Booing is thoroughly American, don't you agree? No such luck tonight. It's Madonna, sweetly demure as always.

• In the crowd tonight, there's a handful of one-percenters. The rest of us are all one-percenter wannabes—strivers, wagon-pullers, dream believers. Save for a few crony capitalists and ne'er-do-well nephews, there's not an Obama partisan in the house. The real question is whether this crowd is for Romney or non-Romney. I'm calling it 65–35 for Mittens.

• Football is an atavistically binary game. There is, at the end of every contest, a winner and a loser. That's it. No runner-up, no armful of plaques for most improved or best effort or some muffled recognition of process at the expense of result. The winner gets the ink, the endorsements, the bonuses. The loser gets nothing, save for a multimedia opportunity to explain his manifold inadequacies. ("Briefly, please. We're cutting to the winner's locker room in 30 seconds.")

• There's a certain appeal to that hard, old-fashioned word: loser. You don't hear it much in contemporary America, now that the organizer-in-chief has reorganized our community. There's something about him, maybe you've noticed, that simply can't abide a binary choice. Winners? Losers? They don't exist in Obama's America. In his America, we don't even win or lose wars. If he has his way—and Gallup suggests, ominously, that he might—all Americans would finish the race of life in a 300 million-way tie for last. I suppose that we could all then give each other plaques for Most Public Spirited.

• I never attend a Super Bowl without thinking of WFB. His wildly generous hospitality over the years always posed a gnawing problem for his young friends. How could we possibly return his many favors? Could we do so by inviting Bill and Pat to our exurban home teeming with mangy pets and mewling children? I didn't think so. For the urbane Buckleys, that kind of evening would have been less a favor returned than a sentence imposed. My answer—each of us had his own—was to take them to off-track cultural happenings: a concert featuring an exciting newcomer, lunch at a new ethnic restaurant, anything Yale-related. Things balanced out a little bit, I hope. But I always saved a Super Bowl ticket for Bill. And he always declined. He may have been the only conservative in America who didn't like football.

The Weekly Standard
June 30, 1996

ESCHATOLOGY ON ICE

I ce hockey is a Bob Dole kind of sport: It's about hard work; it's about small-town values; experience; whatever. Growing up in the New York exurbs, I became a New York Rangers fan, waiting on them year after year as they fumbled away every chance to repeat their Stanley Cup triumph of 1940. But I hung in there and it was well worth the wait. After 54 grinding years and a bone-tiring seven-game series, the Rangers finally did it. For those who like their gratification deferred, the 1994 season was perfect heaven.

Deferred longing need not be the fan's common state. There's a new paradigm in town and it will be studied in sports-management courses for decades to come. The new paradigm will appeal to all those sports fans who favor immanentizing the eschaton, and, Lord knows, nobody ever went broke overestimating their number. Call it the Colorado Avalanche paradigm, for the Avalanche last week set a record that will never be broken—by winning the Stanley Cup in the team's first season.

I am on the board of the company that owns the team, and here are the lessons of this unparalleled experience:

1. *Buy an existing team, not an expansion team.* Why build a team out of rookies and has-beens when you can buy a team for roughly the same price that already has players, some of them very good? We bought the Quebec Nordiques last summer and shipped them—yes—1,996 miles to Denver.

2. As a corollary, *Buy a Canadian team and import them across the border.* First, by the miracle of currency exchange rates, the players get a raise—which means they get a good first impression of the new owners. Second, because Canadian teams are virtually invisible in American media, you can reposition the franchise and promote the players anew. Just as significant, the players can't hold you up. They have no fan support. When one of the team leaders, Wendel Clark, got crosswise with manage-

ment, he was priority-mailed to the lowly New York Islanders. From the fans, not a peep. Denver didn't know Wendel Clark from Ramsey Clark. In the trade for Clark, we received an East Coast malcontent, Claude Lemieux, who instantly became one of our best and toughest players.

3. *Ride a secular trend.* Hockey in all its forms—rollerblading, street hockey—is in a bull market. The games are fast, intense, and watchable. Both Fox and ESPN are learning how to televise the sport and, over the last two years, have developed the first network stars. ESPN's Gary Thorne and Bill Clement may be the best broadcast team since the early days of the great football duo of Pat Summerall and John Madden, and Barry Melrose may be the best studio analyst ever.

4. *Find a genius as general manager and let him make a deal a week.* GM Pierre Lacroix, a former agent, went out and got Lemieux, Sandis Ozolinsh, Mike Keane, Dave Hannah, and a former client named Patrick Roy—all without stripping the team of young talent. An amazing batting average, considering that his only possible recruits were players other teams were willing to do without. Just as important, Pierre traveled to the Arctic Circle last summer and persuaded Chris Simon, known as "the Chief," to return to the team. Simon, a native Canadian, was out of sorts and preferred to go fishing. Literally.

Just what Pierre said to Simon will remain forever sealed in the igloo, but Simon's contribution to the team turned out to be irreplaceable: Every time an opposing player took a shot at our nifty All-Star center Joe Sakic, the Chief, at 247 pounds, would hit the offender twice as hard. Don't tell me deterrence doesn't work. It's almost as good as retaliation.

So there you have it. Buy a team in July. Get them a name in August. Design some uniforms for the October debut. And skate the Cup in June. I think that may be the way to go.

The Weekly Standard
June 30, 1997

A HONG KONG DIARY

S ATURDAY. I have been coming to Hong Kong for more than 25 years, sometimes to do business, sometimes to prepare for trips to Taipei or Beijing. Other times, I come just to catch a glimpse of what comes next in the global economy. Hong Kong is not so much a country or a colony as a running convention of go-getters, people beating a path to your door with better mousetraps. When Bill Gates talks about the "frictionless economy" in cyberspace, he's really talking about a digital version of Hong Kong. Here there are no barriers to success. Or failure.

After the usual death-defying plunge to the tarmac at Hong Kong's outmoded Kai Tak airport, we taxi to a stop next to a Cathay Pacific jumbo jet. Owned until recently by Swire, one of the great British trading houses, the Cathay Pacific airline is now controlled by Citic, a mainland conglomerate closely associated with the People's Liberation Army. The Cathay stock passed to the PLA at a remarkably low price. As did a chunk of China Light & Power, the big public utility. As did a big piece of Hong Kong Telecom, the world-class telephone system. Sounds like an infrastructure play, like Beijing is making offers that can't be refused.

We check into the Peninsula Hotel, where high tea is preceded immediately by lunch and followed immediately by dinner. What better place to watch the sun rise for the last time on the British empire.

SUNDAY. The *South China Morning Post* has a poll this weekend. It reports that 72 percent of all residents are positive about the future of Hong Kong. Most of the rest think the future will be about as good as the recent past. Even in America, perhaps the only country in the world where change is routinely equated with progress, euphoria has never run this high. What's up? Friends here offer three explanations. First, the poll has been conducted ineptly, and possibly on purpose. Second, those being polled suspect their views may be transmitted to the PLA and thus they have the smiley faces painted on. Third, the colony is filled with cockeyed optimists.

I think it's No. 3. China is the most nubile market in the global economy, and the greed instinct, never well modulated here, is throbbing loudly. Hong Kongers want a piece of that action. A second theme is the palpable fact of ethnic nationalism. Everywhere one sees evidence of Chinese pride, the sense that Beijing is reversing an ugly historical injustice. One sees it even among Western-educated, Chardonnay-sipping upper-crusters.

Hong Kong is not a settled community caught flatfooted by a Red revolution, after all. The locals came here in waves, most of them fleeing terror—the Taiping rebellion more than a century ago, the warlords in the '20s, Japan's invading army in the '30s, Mao in the '40s, and the cultural revolution in the '60s and '70s. In each case, it was a difficult passage, no stroll across the border from Tijuana. Even into the '80s, they dashed past the attack dogs or tried to float past the sharks at Mirs Bay.

In 1984, it was made clear that the game would change—and exactly when. In the so-called Joint Declaration of that year, Margaret Thatcher pledged that the British garrison would sail out of Victoria Harbor on June 30, 1997. Given that kind of lead time, Hong Kong's highly mobile residents mobilized again. By the thousands and then by the tens of thousands they airmailed themselves into exile. By the early '90s, 70,000 Hong Kongers a year were moving abroad, most of them to Canada or Australia, some to the U.K. and the west coast of the United States. It was the greatest migration of wealth and talent in the second half of the century, and cities that recruited effectively—Vancouver, Sydney, and the rest—propelled themselves into the front ranks of the world economy.

And just who was it that packed up and shipped out? Some of the best and brightest, to be sure. And the politically radioactive. They reckoned that their names had been inscribed on special lists in Beijing. Why wait around and take the risk? But even as the exiles left, their places were taken by new arrivals, many of them PRCers looking to beat the post-handover rush. So in raw numbers, the population has remained at approximately 6 million, but it's a different 6 million: Almost everybody wants to be here, wants to be a part of greater China.

There are exceptions, of course. My new friend Lo Fu made a place for himself on one of those lists in Beijing. He had a nasty habit of saying what was on his mind. So the PRC came after him, and he escaped the mainland, making his way to Hong Kong—and now this! Think of a young Jose making his way across the straits from Havana only to read in his *Miami Herald* that Lawton Chiles had just ceded South Florida to Fidel.

MONDAY. You've read about the democracy movement here, Martin Lee and company? You may have read more about them than the average Hong Konger. The democrats are hyperactive, skilled at media relations, and indisputably on the side of the angels. But at one level they are running a theme park for the amusement of Western journalists. They do not appear to be organically connected to the people they represent. When they speak to their constituents, the democrats are shouting into a stiff breeze of confusion laced with indifference. Hong Kongers have been British subjects for 99 years and expect to be Chinese subjects for at least as long. They have little experience with democracy and, truth be told, not much interest in politics. To be sure, a little pressure from the heel of a boot could excite the democratic instinct, but as of now the message just does not resonate.

Then there are the refugees from the Chinese mainland now well settled here. They despised the old PRC enough to risk everything in a mad dash for the border. Now they look forward to the "Special Administrative Region" of the PRC that Hong Kong will soon become. They thus want to give every appearance of believing that Beijing has changed. Indeed, they are rolling out the inevitably red carpet. Parties, concerts, light shows, parades, mass dancing in the parks, a "Reunification Spectacular at Happy Valley"—events are scheduled hour by hour until the moment of the handover. At the tony Regent Hotel, under a Union Jack snapping smartly in the harbor breeze, a countdown clock ticks off the seconds.

TUESDAY. The Hang Seng Index, the equivalent of the Dow Jones Industrial average, continues to outperform even the U.S. market, fueled by fresh money in so-called red-chip stocks—securities in companies with mainland connections. At the current pace, stock-market activity for the first six months of the year will exceed that for all of 1996, which was itself the most active year on record. A friend at First Boston—a mainland-born, U.S.-passport-holding, Mandarin-speaking banker—tells me that real-estate prices are doing even better. A house he bought on Victoria Peak in 1986 has appreciated "eight or nine times." The new real-estate buyers? Mainland businessmen as well as multinational corporations stocking up on executive housing.

Think of June 30 as a giant initial public offering and you've got a sense of the deal. The PRC will be obliged, it is presumed, to "support" the deal in the aftermarket by propping up prices for stocks and real property. But after a decent market-clearing interval—say, a year or two—what's left? To me it looks like a classic bubble market. The really smart money is, as always, carefully hedged. Most of the Hong Kong elite hold foreign passports (500,000 of them at a guesstimate), stuff cash in foreign bank accounts, and position close relatives in London, San Francisco, Sydney, or elsewhere. More than half of the companies listed on the Hang Seng are now domiciled abroad, up from fewer than 10 percent in the mid '80s. For all their booster rallies, these all-star capitalists could be in business in some third country by next week. An item in the paper caught my eye: "Indian socialites are packing their most dazzling jewelry into travel bags and heading for Singapore as the handover approaches."

Interesting conversation with a military attaché from a European country. Why, he wanted to know, is the United States allowing Hong Kong favored status on export controls? Didn't I understand, he pressed, that Hong Kong would instantaneously transship to China any U.S. technology with military application? Didn't I understand that Japan and other sophisticated nations were tightening controls even as we were relaxing them? How could we be so naïve? he harrumphed. I recited the U.S. position as best I could discern it. But his question lingered, reminding me later of the dog that did not bark in the strange case of Hong Kong. In four long days of talk, interview, and harangue, the name Bill Clinton has never come up. A neat trick. How does the leader of the world's only superpower make himself irrelevant to the biggest geopolitical story of the decade? I find it hard to believe that Ronald Reagan would have looked on quietly as the "handover" became the coda to the American century.

WEDNESDAY. At last I meet somebody who is high-tailing it out of here. A boutique dealmaker, he has done fabulously well in Hong Kong but is planning to move to the New York area, to a "place with good schools, probably Greenwich, Connecticut." Why the move? Does he tremble at the prospect of the Big Red Machine rolling down Salisbury Road? Hardly. "What I used to think of as excitement now looks to me like hassle." I may be witness to the birth of a new lifestyle option—moving to New York for the quiet life.

One hears reports of beeper messages intercepted, newspaper columnists self-censored, political conversations hushed. But at the official level, the Chinese government is advancing in small, barely perceptible increments, none of them so discreetly shocking as to cause the frog to jump from the hot water. In odd moments, though, one calibrates the cumulative distance traveled. Tonight at the China Club, where the politically correct gather in retro-chic, faux-Shanghai surroundings to prolong the business day, I have a drink with a local lawyer. He is an American employed by a fancy New York firm, a veteran mid-level appointee of the Reagan administration. He drops a phrase into conversation that comes back to me hours later as I ride the last Star Ferry back to Kowloon. When he speaks of the final takeover of the mainland by Mao Zedong five decades ago, he calls it the "liberation of '49."

ACKNOWLEDGMENTS

O f acknowledgments, I have a surfeit.

To begin with, I chose my parents well. My dad was a paid-up member of the Greatest Generation. He came home from the Big War, raised a family, built a business, ran for the school board, and tended his suburban lawn fanatically. By any definition, and emphatically by mine, he was a good man.

He was also a bit of a hardbottom and was given to apodictic pronouncement. One night at dinner—I must have been 14 or 15—he announced that there were only two colleges in the country worth the price of admission, Harvard and Yale. If I could get into one of them, he would pay my way. It was the kind of conversation that can concentrate the mind. When a few years later I brought home my acceptance letters, he seemed less excited than I was, but he paid the fare. A deal was a deal.

My mom was the perfect complement—gentle, literate, even bookish, loving not only to family and friends but indiscriminately so to animals. She held a special attraction for the lame and the halt and I had to wait until I had a home of my own to get a four-legged dog.

Every school night, as soon as my sister and I got home from school, and Dad got home from work, Mom would serve a sit-down dinner for the four of us. It's true, I swear. An astonished anthropologist might have called us a thermonuclear family.

If I chose my parents well, I chose my early bosses brilliantly. My first real boss was a fellow named William F. Buckley Jr. He was an extraordinary man and in these pages I record an insider's account of some of his more extraordinary feats.

I learned much from Bill Buckley, most importantly that I should make a few demands on life. My WASPy parents had neglected to tell me that I could forgive myself for being ambitious and for pursuing my goals without apology.

Soon after I went to work for Bill in 1963, I came to share his opinion that the world was in need of improvement and that, with everybody else either unable or unwilling to do the necessary, he should take up the assignment himself. Over the next 45 years, I made myself available at almost every invitation to play a supporting role in the Buckley Program for World Improvement. Whatever the Gentile form of *chutzpah* may be, we were both well stocked with it.

It was a big job—changing the world, that is—and it required the full attention even of William F. Buckley Jr., who worked seven long days a week for most of his 82 years. Along the way, I was introduced to some of his uptown tastes—good wine, great music, a home at the shore, ocean sailing and the other accoutrements of a well-upholstered life. When I got married, I followed the advice of my insurance agent and forswore three of life's most actuarially perilous activities: smoking cigarettes, riding motorcycles, and sailing with Bill Buckley. But it's probably fair to say that Bill dazzled me with his neon appeals of money, power, and fame. Over time, I learned that I could do without the fame. Of money and power, though, I asked John Kerry's question about the huntin' and fishin' licenses: Where can I get me some?

It was no secret that Bill craved fame. One of the happiest moments of his life popped its cork when I reported, courtesy of a well-placed source, that he would soon appear on the cover of *Time* magazine. He fairly bounced with pleasure and it was impossible not to enjoy his enjoyment. Later, after he became a television host and the celebrated leader of a burgeoning political movement, there would be many occasions for such enjoyment. But I soon got a glimpse of the cost of fame, too.

In the '70s, Bill published the first of a series of Blackford Oakes spy novels, *Saving the Queen*. He was traveling abroad on publication date and asked me to collect the first batch of reviews. When he called in for a recap, I read him the first seven or eight, every one of which reviewed the author in fine detail while virtually ignoring the book itself. How remarkable it was, they all said in one formulation or another, to see a right-wing polemicist writing a novel! How clever! How cute!

Bill was crestfallen. He had poured his considerable energies into the book, hoping to pull off a literary coup on the order of a John le Carre, or at least a Constantine Fitzgibbon. Instead, he was in the eyes of the critics no more than a dog walking on its hind legs. Bill had been trapped by a fame from which he would never really escape. Ever the tactician, he plowed ahead with the Oakes books for some years, writing them for diversion and money but with hopes abandoned for literary acclaim.

My second boss taught me other things. William Randolph Hearst, Jr. was the oldest of five sons of "The Chief," William Randolph Hearst Sr., who had been to the 20th century what Rupert Murdoch, multiplied to the fifth power, is to the 21st. The Hearst Corporation published magazines, books and newspapers, operated radio and television stations, produced television and motion picture programming, and owned huge tracts of real estate, one of them a stretch of 100 uninterrupted miles of California coastline. (And that was all before an investment in a little television property called ESPN.) When I was there, the Hearst Corporation was one of the largest privately held companies in the world and there were few cities of consequence that did not host at least one Hearst outpost—a headquarters building, a penthouse apartment, a downtown office, even, here and there, a castle. The Chief had a thing for castles.

Bill Hearst Jr. traveled in imperial style and touched down only rarely on non-Hearst-occupied territory. And he was wondrously well-connected. Running into each other one day in the lobby of a Buenos Aires hotel, we found that we would both be speaking at the same conference that afternoon. Bluff and gregarious, Bill pulled me aside and said, "Come up to the suite about seven. I'll find some interesting people and we'll make a dinner of it." That evening I found myself seated between the foreign minister and the publisher of the country's largest newspaper, and directly across the table from an actress billed not implausibly as "the Elizabeth Taylor of Argentina."

Bill Hearst taught me most of what I know about how the world works. He allowed me to see up close how doors could be opened and relationships could be built and deals could be cut. With his encouragement, his associates taught me the basics of business development—deal structure, the pace and sequence of negotiation and the salience of that mother of all investment tools, capital allocation.

About fame, I learned two things from Bill. First, that it was cheap and, second, that it was expensive. The Hearst publicity machine, with its global reach and in-house media power, was a thing of marvel. Over the years Bill and I minted celebrities by the dozen—household names that I will gallantly omit for the reason that we promoted all of them well beyond their abilities. (If we'd known what to do with them afterward, we'd have created our own passel of Kardashians.) As a young man still shaping his career in soft clay, I saw both how easy it was to become famous and how hard it was to reclaim obscurity.

Bill Hearst himself was Example A. He was a bright, innovative executive and a fearless, story-chasing journalist. He won his Pulitzer, basically, by barging into Nikita Khrushchev's office in the Kremlin at a key moment during the Cold War. There may have been three other reporters in the world, tops, who could have pulled that off. If Bill's name had been William Randolph, he would likely have carved out a lustrous and satisfying career for himself. But lugging around that megatonic surname was a burden, and it wore him down.

I am deeply indebted to both Bills, Buckley and Hearst. Without them I never would have been able to assemble the resources or find the nerve to chase my own entrepreneurial dreams.

Then there were the publishers of my favorite, blue-bordered magazine, the first five of whom became cherished friends. Michael Mooney may never have carried the title of *NR* publisher, but he carried most of the responsibilities, the most onerous of which was advertising sales. Selling a right-wing magazine to epicene Madison Avenue-types was always—and I'm sure it remains so to this day—a hand-over-hand climb up the sheer face of a wintry mountain. Mike plugged along doggedly, cheerfully and, now and again, successfully. Then came William A. Rusher, who may not have known much about publishing but knew everything there was to know about politics and most of what was worth knowing about life itself. Bill became one of my closest friends and I hope the portrait included in this book captures his Rusherian essence.

Wick Allison then served briefly but brilliantly, importing a badly needed sense of professionalism to our scruffy cast of publishing irregulars. Wick was followed by the legendary Edward Capano. Eddie started early—about the same time I did—and stayed for a lifetime, devoting his entire career to the magazine and the cause it serves. Then came Jack Fowler, who has earned affection from the *NR* family of writers and editors by demonstrating a generous respect for the people who built the institution. I look forward to working with Garrett Bewkes, named earlier this year as the next man up.

Together, these men have performed an act of prestidigitation. For more than 60 years, they have levitated a journal of opinion. Talk about an extraordinary feat.

I am indebted, as well, to the three editors of *National Review*, who over the last 54 years have spared me embarrassment, ridicule, physical assault, legal retribution, and public shaming. But nobody's perfect. Despite their best efforts, I managed to muddy myself in multiple skirmishes.

For writers, talking about your editors is like talking about your old girlfriends. They all had their strong points and they all knew your weak points. Bill Buckley, who had been my editor when I was a kid editorial writer and then a Washington correspondent, hired me in three different decades to write a column for *NR* (the first time as Cato, the next two under my own name). Each time, I left to do something that seemed more important at the time. Each time, Bill said I was making a mistake; each time, dammit, he was right. I regained some of that lost ground when, years later, I became the editor of his syndicated newspaper column. I will confess that morning coffee never tasted better than when I would catch him misstating a fact or misquoting a source. That was a nice feeling. And on those rare occasions when the famously sesquipedalian columnist would ask me the meaning of an unfamiliar word? That was an even nicer feeling. I think they call it a *frisson*.

Every single time I or anybody else published a piece in *NR*, Bill Buckley would send a handwritten thank-you note. An editorial, a column, a feature article, even a book review would elicit a few words of appreciation inscribed on a blue notecard. What an exquisitely gracious gesture! Bill knew what all writers know, namely, that whenever you express your thoughts in a public forum, you're taking a risk. You're exposed. You're vulnerable. Those little blue missives were Bill's way of saying that he had your back and by making those gestures he emboldened three generations of tentative scribblers. (I know writers who saved every one of those notecards, as if they were classic collectibles autographed by Honus Wagner or Stan Musial.)

John O'Sullivan had the difficult job of following Buckley and the impossible job of becoming the leading voice of American conservatism while speaking in an unmistakably foreign accent. With wit and wisdom and a bit of British pluck, John pulled it off. As his plummy accent fell more and more gently on the ear, we began to think of him as thoroughly American, hailing perhaps from an Anglophiliac enclave somewhere in the upper Midwest.

John's editorial style differed from Bill's by approximately 180 degrees. While Bill edited heavily on a line-by-line basis—leaving the occasional writer smoldering over what he deemed to be a "rewriting"—John would involve himself deeply in discussion of the story and then leave point-to-point navigation almost entirely to the writer.

John discontinued the blue notecards, but once or twice a year he would send an elegant letter, suitable for framing, expressing his gratitude for hard work and valued product. All writers need that balm. The letters would arrive just in time and the honest if unspoken response was frequently, "Thanks, I needed that."

NR's third editor, only 48 years old today but thoroughly blooded in the ideological wars, is Rich Lowry. A child of the digital era, Rich probably works no harder than Bill or John, but he clearly works faster. His style is terse and telegraphic and he tends to force the pace of his analog-bound colleagues. Such as, to pick a random example, me.

Happily for *NR* and for those who depend on it for ideological sustenance, Rich is tanned, rested and ready for the challenge ahead. While Bill Buckley helped to design and build the conservative movement and John O'Sullivan helped to maintain it, it now falls to Rich Lowry to re-assemble and redirect it following the electoral pile-up of 2016.

It was also my good luck to know and befriend most of the "founding fathers" of post-war conservativism. Not just Buckley and Rusher, but Willmoore Kendall, Frank Meyer, Russell Kirk, John Chamberlain, James Burnham and Brent Bozell. These were the men who made a movement and I am grateful for the privilege of having worked beside them. Here and there in this book, I particularize my gratitude to some of these men. In hindsight, I see that I should have written about all of them. My only excuse is that, at the time, they seemed to be friends and colleagues more than historical figures.

I also wish to salute the "second generation" of conservative leaders, the men and women who came along behind the founding fathers and signed on to our cause with scant prospect of personal gain; indeed, many of them scrambled aboard our rickety ship just about the time it became wholly uninsurable. Here are a few of the people I met and admired, either aboard the good ship *NR* or at one of her customary ports of call. Linda Bridges. Randy Richardson. John Coyne (who, though a helluva speech-writer, wisely saved the best stuff for himself). Chris Symonds. Les Lenkowsky. Al Regnery. Roger Moore (who should have been chairman of every board, not just *NR*'s). Geoff Kelly. Keith Mano (who even in WFB's company stood out as a dazzling writer). Lawry Chickering. Gerry Ohrstrom. Daniel Oliver. Evan Galbraith (I was always torn. Was Van the nicest man in the world? Or was it Jim Buckley? I attempt an adjudication below.) Carol Dawson. William Rickenbacker (whose picture appears in most standard dictionaries next to the word, "polymath"). Tom Pauken. Aram Bakshian. Mike Uhlmann. Stanley Goldstein (who, in moments of character-testing, never blinked). George Gilder. Frances Bronson. Neil McCaffrey. Joe Donner (who was on the *NR* board when I arrived and was still there when I departed 38 years later—our own Cal Ripken). Arlene Croce. Dusty Rhodes. Mike Thompson. Marvin Liebman. Rose Flynn (who paid the bills, some of them on time). John Von Kannon. Tom Winter. David Jones (one of our more indefatigable plot-hatchers). Jeff Bell. Peter Lawson-Johnston. Jim Piereson. Tony Dolan. Pat Korten (who made my films sound better than they were). Paul Gigot. Emmy Lewis. Christopher Buckley (who could write a little bit himself). Dick Allen. Allan Ryskind. Ross Mackenzie. Dan Peters. Rich Vigilante (who, it was conceded, had the best right-wing byline of all time). Larry Kudlow. Lee Edwards. Dino Pionzio (who was the spy who loved us). Dan Mahoney. John Ryan. Mona Charen. Stan Evans (whose death left an almost WFB-sized hole in our ranks). Morton Blackwell. Irving Kristol (who became my foxhole buddy in the public broadcasting wars). Jay Parker. Rick Brookhiser (who was, and is, a humongous talent). Agatha Schmidt. Craig Shirley. Diana Bannister. Jim Roberts. Ed Feulner (who made a habit of leaving large footprints). Fred Barnes. Mike Hodin. Jim McFadden (who discovered in the U.S. Constitution a right to live. Who knew?). Ron Docksai. Rob Sennott (who could sell space heaters to Costa Ricans). Don Lambro. Richard Viguerie (who became my most faithful correspondent). Bob Tyrrell. Brent Bozell (who, when he turns 87, will still be "young Brent" to me). Jameson Campaigne. Joe Sobran (who, like Frank, did it his way). Phil Terzian. Priscilla Buckley (who, like Ronnie, kept the peace through strength). Wlady Pleszczynski. Ed Meese (who was the only man to whom I gave a proxy with no time stamp). And Patsy Buckley, the one and only Mrs. WFB (who was inducted into the Freeman Hall of Fame after saying loudly of Dr. Kissinger's postprandial remarks at an *NR* dinner, "Henry, you're making no sense at all. Thank God we've got Neal here to straighten this out.")

I append to that last paragraph a blanket apology. I have no doubt whatsoever that, the day after this page sees print, I will think of a dozen other must-have names, slap my forehead, and, fumbling for a pertinent Buckley apercu, blurt out instead, "How could I be so [deleted] stupid?" Sorry.

I also acknowledge here the editors of three of my favorite publications—*The Weekly Standard*, *The American Spectator* and *The Wall Street Journal*—for granting permission to reprint material originally published in their pages. I am grateful, as well, to Roger Ream and The Fund for American Studies, co-founded 50 years ago by WFB, for their support.

Penultimately, and *con brio*, I wish to thank my three sources of on-